SOUTH KOREA
INDIA
THAILAND
VIETNAM

PASSPORT TO FLAVOR

100 GLOBAL DISHES YOU CAN MAKE ANYWHERE

ABBY CHESHIRE

Dedicated to three generations of cooks:

GiGi, my great-grandmother, who lived fearlessly until the age of one hundred and who taught me to be resourceful.

Nana, my grandmother, who laughed so heartily that she sometimes snorted and who taught me to be innovative.

Mom and Dad, my parents, who are so in love with each other and with life that we, their family and friends, gather around them as often as possible. Thank you for modeling what a rich life looks like when you open up your heart and let people in.

Passport to Flavor

Published by Harper Celebrate, an imprint of HarperCollins Focus LLC, 501 Nelson Place, Nashville, TN 37214, USA.

HarperCollins Publishers, Macken House, 39/40 Mayor Street Upper, Dublin 1, D01 C9W8, Ireland (https://www.harpercollins.com)

Cover design by Sabryna Lugge
Interior design by Kathy Mitchell, Emily Ghattas, and Lori Lynch
Cover and food photography by Kris D'Amico Photography
Recipe and food creation by Chef Abby Cheshire
Yachts and marina by HMY Yachts
Photography on pages xxiv, 3, 63, 107, 112, 144, 147, 195, 234, and 237 by Shutterstock; pages 22, 25, 56, 59, 74, 77, 90, 93, 108, 111, 153, 175, 180, and 183 by istockphoto; pages 40, 43, 124, 127, 162, 165, 198, 201, 216, and 219 by Adobestock

ISBN 978-1-4002-5168-1 (HC)
ISBN 978-1-4002-5169-8 (epub)

Printed in Malaysia

25 26 27 28 29 VIV 5 4 3 2 1

CONTENTS

HAWAII
ITALY
IRELAND
MEXICO
JELL-O

FRANCE ★ FRANCE
GERMANY ★
GREECE ★ GREECE

INTRODUCTION

Welcome to my galley!

Have you ever dreamed of traveling the world and sampling the distinctive flavors, the history-rich cuisine, and the regionally fresh entrées other lands have to offer? Or maybe you've wanted to take a cruise to a tropical island or a boat ride to an international city to experience a new culture?

As a private yacht chef, I've had the unique honor of tasting my way across the globe. My galley is small but mighty, and I'm able to make the tastiest foods with limited equipment and rationed supplies. And because there's only so much space and storage on the boat, I rely on fresh ingredients and local produce when I arrive at a port—a perfect way to make friends with a new place and its charming culture. The yacht is my temporary home while at sea, but the port is where I really get to experience a place, meet its people, and bring its colorful flavors to my guests and crew on board.

Whether you travel regularly or want to taste global cuisine right in your home—no deck shoes required—let me share my galley and my adventures with you!

GOT YOUR PASSPORT?

Hop on board our luxury yacht in these pages as we circumnavigate the globe. We'll "port crawl" to fourteen international harbors that are unique in their diverse landscapes and local flavors. As different as each country and its cuisine may be, they all speak in a universal love language everyone understands: *great food*!

This is a journey we can take together, without even leaving home. Easy-to-find ingredients become world-class meals when prepared from my no-nonsense recipes. You'll cook up global-scale tastes that burst out of your kitchen with far-reaching flavors.

Are you on board, Little Chef?

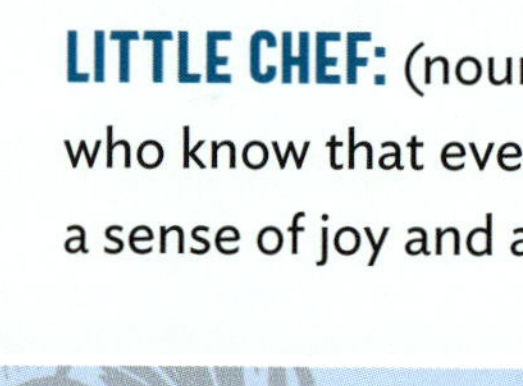

LITTLE CHEF: (noun) a term of endearment used to describe those who know that every recipe is within reach when approached with a sense of joy and adventure.

THE WORLD IS MY HOME

Even before I started working as a yacht chef, I had a deep love for exploring different cultures and, of course, their delicious foods and flavors. My parents raised me to think of the world as my home. Even though we traveled light for our overseas adventures, each with a simple backpack and budget, my exposure to international foods began early and left a big impact on me. I could leave our Florida home behind and taste the exciting, scrumptious world beyond.

With an extra croissant and boiled egg from the breakfast bar, we would start off on our hikes. On the way out of town, Mom would stumble upon a local market to stock up on fresh bread, cheese, nuts, and salami for the journey ahead. Dad would find a regional wine to add to the post-hike picnic that would situate us somewhere as mouthwatering as the food—at the top of a glorious mountain, along the edge of a majestic river, or beside an engineering wonder of the world. Thanks to our adventurous parents, my brother, sister, and I felt like royalty with our feast of local cuisine without the fancy price tag. On foot, by train, on two wheels, or with a loaner car from a friend, we would make our way through Alpine villages, Mediterranean towns, desert outposts, remote rain forests, glacial valleys, seaports, and even neon cities. Everywhere we went, the food and its people made a lasting impression.

Life can be sweet no matter where you are.

I especially remember how my parents would make friends with the butcher and the baker (and even the candlestick maker) when we traveled. Why miss an opportunity to listen to tasty tales from hardworking merchants who cultivate beautiful food for us to eat? Why pass on an invitation to meet up at the neighborhood *trattoria* (a cozy, informal Italian restaurant, often family run), where the *cuoca* (Italian for "chef") looks like your own grandmother, with marinara sauce on her apron, and sits down with you to ask in Italian if you like her homemade ravioli? *Can I be her, please?* My hope is to be as lucky as this woman when I am eighty, with friends old and new gathered around my table.

Beach time with Dad, Bro, and Mom

With this adventurous upbringing, it's no wonder I became a yacht chef. Every summer, I cater to the most discerning palates and travel to the most luxurious locations imaginable. My career path is unique yet quite perfect for someone who loves to travel, cook, share, eat, and repeat daily.

To showcase my cool yacht experiences with family and friends back in the States, I made short, entertaining videos of my life on board when I first began my yacht travels in my mid-twenties. This way they could see what I was up to and follow along on the ride. Little did I realize, in posting my culinary adventures on the high seas to my social media accounts, I would gather around my table *millions* of people—from all parts of the world—who wanted to share in this journey with me. Now I post regularly since I love celebrating food and making it accessible to everyone, whether in a yacht galley, a standard kitchen, or a decked-out gourmet cookery.

Sharing knowledge is important to me, and when I'm not on the boat, I use my culinary skills to teach high school students how to be service-industry ready and prepared for top-notch jobs with esteemed national certifications and competitions under their belts (actually, their aprons). I love empowering others as they masterfully execute a recipe with joy and skill (and even a sense of humor)—something I hope for you too, Little Chef! If you watch my videos online, you'll see that we are all Little Chefs together, and we can step into the kitchen to make gourmet food with confidence.

A DAY IN THE LIFE OF A YACHT CHEF

What is it like to be a yacht chef? If you don't follow me online (@abbyinthegalley), let me give you a little preview. Not only am I responsible for all the meals on board, but I'm also a pro at provisioning. It's my job to know what we need, how much we'll need, how long it will last, and how to organize it all. There's no grocery delivery in the middle of the ocean, so it's crucial to get this right.

Accounting for each guest's food preferences, I stock the 100-foot yacht for our ten-week journey. Initially, that means 300 pounds of fresh produce (prepared within a week), 250 pounds of beef (that's half a cow), 250 pounds of chicken, 100 pounds of lamb, 100 pounds of fish (plus what we catch on our own), 50 pounds of shellfish (again, more to be caught on our voyage), 50 pounds of pork, 20 pounds of duck, 40 pounds of rice, 20 pounds of butter, 6 pounds of salt, and more. At every port, I provision locally sourced foods to remain fully stocked.

Luring in dinner at an early age

These provisions are distributed among ten freezers and refrigerators on board, plus twenty storage containers located in various places around the yacht. You might find loaves of bread hiding under a crew cabin bed, cans of beans buried under the main salon couch, or bags of potatoes stowed away under the sky lounge game table. This hide-and-seek provisioning game keeps my mind as well as my muscles agile!

Still reeling 'em in on the yacht

I prepare seven recipes a day for the guests and crew, who have a myriad of food preferences. To meet each person's needs, I individualize and personalize every meal. With an average of eight to twenty-four guests a day, you would expect that I generate a lot of dishes to clean, right? I don't.

Kayaking back to the yacht with provisions

Instead, I reduce my load with strategic preparation and effective recipe design. Averaging seventy-five plates a day, I need to run only three loads of dishes. I have learned to be highly efficient. And I always make sure to have time on deck to savor the sunset as the dolphins dance in our wake (and as Thurston, our yacht dog mascot, begs for a good belly rub) after I provision for tomorrow's produce with a quick kayak ride to the farmers' market near the marina.

You might not be cooking for crowds like this every day, but I guarantee that what I do on the yacht can be replicated at home, for however many you are feeding. The process and the product can be successful in every kitchen with some help from me, your fellow Little Chef.

And because yacht cooking is even *more* limited and *more* constrained in comparison to conditions at home, you are at an advantage! On the yacht, I don't have every gadget at my disposal, nor the space or time to use multiple bowls for measuring everything. I turn up my jam music as I prep, listening through my earbuds, and since I make multiple trips to and from the hold at the ship's bottom to gather ingredients (quite a workout), I don't need to spend time formally working out. Once, when making pork ribs and beef brisket for twenty-four guests on board, I logged twenty thousand steps according to my smartwatch, simply transporting ingredients to the galley.

Celebrate the simplicity of your own kitchen. I truly want to hug my simple refrigerator at home whenever I have that luxury!

TIE YOUR APRON AND PREPARE

First things first: Before I prep a single dish or chop a vegetable, I make sure I'm prepared with the most essential "ingredients" that play out in every culinary creation:

Humility: Don't take yourself too seriously. The kitchen is open to everyone, beginner or pro, landlubber or water warrior.

Laughter: This isn't a physics final but rather an international port crawl! Laughter and a sense of adventure are a must.

Creativity: Bring your free-spirited, quirky ideas so you can have fun in the process and embrace who you are. Your family and friends will cherish this authenticity too.

Passion: Food is our love language on this journey. Honor the place in your soul that desires to celebrate life fully and to share your passion with others. Make the kitchen the heart of your home.

Once you have these core ingredients in your heart and the actual recipe ingredients in the galley, I recommend approaching food prep with *mise en place,* which is French for "everything in its place." Whether this means you measure things out in separate containers, organize your ingredients by recipe order, or prep your ingredients before starting the instructions, this important step is critical and will serve you well, my fellow Little Chef. Here's my preparation process:

Read the recipe fully to make friends with the ingredients, cookware, and time needed. Don't forget to read the notes following each recipe for any substitutions or tips.

Prepare ingredients on a clean counter to dice, chop, peel, grate, mash, mince, and more.

Arrange ingredients with logically positioned and appropriately sized bowls, no more than required in the recipe.

Maintain workstation efficiency by setting the oven temperature, cleaning along the way, and using spare time proactively.

Organize tools, with all cookware and equipment within reach and without extra clutter (a constant challenge in my yacht galley with its limited space).

Even the grandest of kitchens will seem chaotic if not paying homage to the mighty *mise en place*. It's the key to saving time and space. My recipes spell out details succinctly so you can prepare, arrange, maintain, and organize your dishes with efficiency.

STEP INTO MY GALLEY

A Yacht Chef's Itinerary

6:00 a.m. Wake up to the sound of the seagulls greeting the fishermen heading out to sea.

6:15 a.m. Panic because four more guests fly in later today and you forgot to thaw the extra rack of lamb.

6:30 a.m. Brush your teeth, and stop panicking because you can bike from the port to the fresh market that opens soon.

7:00 a.m. Secure provisions from the market, and add fresh pineapple to the menu since it speaks to you.

8:00 a.m. Prepare breakfast for eight guests who love to watch the blue herons and other feathered friends from the deck before heading out to the beach.

10:00 a.m. Watch the diving pelicans yourself as you design a game plan for a beachside lunch.

11:00 a.m. Dice, chop, peel, grate, mash, and mince.

12:30 p.m. Finish the picnic basket and send it with the deckhand on a tender to the beach.

1:00 p.m. Dice, chop, peel, grate, mash, and mince.

2:00 p.m. Play the ukulele on the back of the boat while the lamb marinates and the new guests arrive.

4:30 p.m. Serve cocktails and appetizers on the boat's bow, where a shade canopy casts shadows on the lounging guests.

6:30 p.m. Grill the lamb, zucchini, and onions on deck, making all the other yacht chefs anchored around you second-guess what they are cooking for dinner.

7:00 p.m. Run up and down the steps (15x) to the upper deck to serve the three-course meal.

9:00 p.m. Clean up, down, and everywhere.

10:00 p.m. FaceTime with your family and friends before drifting off to sleep.

STOCKING THE GALLEY

Before we leave the marina, we must make sure we have all the equipment, pantry goods, and starting-point ingredients we'll need at sea. Of course, we'll be stopping at port towns to get fresh food, which is listed alphabetically for you in the index.

Let's start with the equipment. Every kitchen, small or otherwise, needs essentials in the cabinets to make preparation possible. Here are my suggestions to provision your own galley for greatness, with three levels based on your kitchen setup and space. And don't worry if your galley is small since even the "must-haves" can handle food preparation for up to eight people. The "add-ons" and "supplements" just make it more efficient when there are lots of mouths to feed.

SMALL-GALLEY MUST-HAVES

Pots and Pans

Casserole dish (9-by-13-inch, ceramic or glass)

Medium pot with lid (5 to 6 quart)

Medium sauté pan with lid (10 inch)

Baking Equipment

2 large-rimmed sheet trays (13-by-18-inch)

Glass liquid measuring cup (1 quart)

Large colander (5 quart)

Loaf pan (9-by-5-inch)

Measuring cups

Measuring spoons

Utensils

Bottle opener

Box grater

Can opener

Chef's knife (8 inch)

Corkscrew

Kitchen shears

Ladle

Large metal spoon

Large metal tongs

Large slotted metal spoon

Metal spatula

Paring knife (4.5 inch)

Pepper grinder (freshly ground pepper is always preferred)

Rubber spatula (silicone preferred, heat safe)

Serrated/bread knife (8 inch)

Whisk

Wooden spoon

Y peeler

Appliances

Coffee maker (I love my moka pot and French press)

Digital thermometer

Immersion blender

General Supplies

Aluminum foil

Medium mixing bowl (3 quart, heat safe)

Medium wooden cutting board

Parchment paper

Plastic food-storage bags

Plastic wrap

STANDARD-KITCHEN ADD-ONS

Pots and Pans

Small pot with lid (2.5 quart)

Small sauté pan with lid (8 inch)

Baking Equipment

Cooling rack

Muffin tin (12 cup)

Roasting rack

Square cake pan (9-by-9-inch)

Springform pan (9 inch)

Appliances

Blender

Hand mixer

General Supplies

Bamboo sushi mat

Cheesecloth

Cocktail shaker

Fine-mesh strainer (5 inch)

Kitchen twine

Meat hammer

Set of 4 ramekins

Small mixing bowl (1 quart, heat safe)

Small wooden cutting board

DECKED-OUT SUPPLEMENTS

Pots and Pans

Large pot with lid (8 to 10 quart)

Large skillet with lid (6 quart, oven safe)

Large sauté pan with lid (12 inch)

Baking Equipment

Bundt pan (10 inch)

Large roasting pan with lid (11-by-15-inch)

Round cake pan (9 inch)

Utensils

Julienne Y peeler

Lemon/lime squeezer

Microplane

Pastry brush

Potato masher

Rolling pin

Appliances

Food processor

Rice cooker

Stand mixer

General Supplies

Large mixing bowl (5 quart, heat safe)

Large wooden cutting board

A streamlined galley containing only the necessary kitchen items frees you up to move around more easily. But even though the items in the second and third lists are not essential in a small galley such as the one I have on the yacht, they are of great value in my kitchen at home.

PRE-VOYAGE SETUP

Of course, we'll stock the pantry, refrigerator, and freezer with the freshest provisions possible when we arrive in port, and all are listed in the index so you can secure them at that very point when your recipe is selected and you are ready to create it. Use seasonal and regional availability as a driving force in your selections. To help with this, I have included "Provision Pointers" at the back of the book to help you select, store, and use your perishables wisely. This means you can use pristine produce and protein as your starting point for any of my recipes and then bring them to their fullest flavor profile using the lists below. All of these initial pantry, refrigerator, and freezer items belong in your kitchen, even in a small-galley setup.

BASIC NEEDS

All-purpose flour

Baking powder

Baking soda

Black peppercorns (freshly cracked ground pepper, yes!)

Cocoa powder

Cornstarch

Honey

Kosher salt (simply the best)

Oil (canola, olive)

Sugar (granulated, brown)

Vanilla

Vinegar (balsamic)

OTHER PANTRY ESSENTIALS

Beans and legumes (black beans, cannellini beans, chickpeas, kidney beans, lentils)

Canned tomatoes (crushed, diced, paste)

Condiments (Dijon mustard, hot sauce, mayonnaise, soy sauce, Worcestershire sauce)

Dried fruits, nuts, and seeds (all types)

Grains (pasta, rice)

Stocks (chicken, beef, seafood, vegetable)

REFRIGERATOR REGULARS

Butter (salted)

Cheese (cheddar, feta, Gorgonzola, mozzarella, Parmesan)

Cream cheese

Eggs

Heavy whipping cream

Milk (whole)

Sour cream

Yogurt (Greek)

FREEZER FUNDAMENTALS

Breads (individual slices are perfect for quick and portioned defrosting)

Fruits (berries and mangoes freeze beautifully)

Vegetables (corn, peas, and spinach maintain great flavor and integrity)

A CELEBRATION OF HERBS, AROMATICS, AND SPICES

Food would not reach its full potential without herbs, aromatics, and spices. To follow are two lists—one of fresh herbs (on my windowsill and counter) and the other of dried herbs (in my pantry). No kitchen should be without these small but mighty game changers.

FRESH HERBS AND AROMATICS

Basil

Chives

Cilantro

Dill

Garlic

Ginger

Green onions (scallions)

Mint

Oregano

Parsley (Italian flat-leaf)

Rosemary

Tarragon

Thyme

DRIED HERBS AND SPICES

Allspice (ground, cloves)
Basil leaves
Bay leaves
Caraway seeds
Cardamom
Cayenne pepper
Celery seeds
Chili powder
Chives
Cinnamon (ground, sticks)
Cloves (ground, whole)
Coriander (ground, seeds)
Cumin (ground, seeds)
Curry powder
Dill weed
Fennel seeds
Garam masala
Garlic (granulated)
Ginger (ground)
Herbes de Provence
Mexican dried peppers (ancho, chile de árbol, guajillo)
Mint leaves
Mustard (ground, seeds)
Nutmeg (ground)
Onion powder
Oregano
Paprika (smoked, sweet)
Parsley leaves
Poppy seeds
Red pepper flakes
Rosemary
Saffron
Sesame seeds
Tarragon
Thyme
Turmeric

NAVIGATION KNOW-HOW

With your kitchen stocked and this cookbook in your hands, Little Chef, you are ready to travel with me to experience the best cuisine the world has to offer. Imagine we are on a luxury yacht, circumnavigating the globe.

Together, we will travel more than 20,000 nautical miles (1 nautical mile equals 1.15 miles or 1.85 kilometers). We will be at sea for more than 100 days at a comfortable speed of 15 knots (about 17 miles per hour). It's fun to imagine, right?

We'll start our journey in the Bahamas, travel up through North America, head east to Europe, then cruise into Asia, and finally end in Mexico to bring us back home.

Each country has meal options for you. Whether you want to pick and choose the recipes that sound the most enticing or you want to entertain your guests for a full day in the country of your choice is up to you. But just like on the yacht, I am offering seven recipes for each day: breakfast, lunch, cocktail hour with an appetizer and cocktail, and dinner, which includes a soup or salad and, of course, a scrumptious dessert.

Our meals will look like a million bucks and taste even better, but let's keep the recipes simple, okay? I'm not a fussy person, nor a fancy chef. Let's focus on the freshness of the ingredients and the miraculous ways the different flavors complement each other. We will honor classic flavor profiles and then elevate them.

You can be the captain of your galley, Little Chef!

Here's how:

Demystify it—without forgetting the historical context.
Simplify it—without skimping on traditional techniques.
Reconstruct it—without overlooking textural trends.

Essentially, we are mixing the old and the new. History, tradition, and trends become friends in these recipes that are designed for all of us, Little Chef. Luxurious gourmet dishes are not reserved for a select few. They can be enjoyed by everyone!

HOW TO READ THE RECIPES

Each recipe includes the full amount of time to prepare the dish, which I call the **Total Trip**. If there is a mix of active and inactive time, I break it down for you. I call active preparation the **Cruising Time** since it calls for all hands on deck. The inactive minutes are deemed **Idle Time** as the dish marinates, cooks, rests, and the like. You can go up on deck or outside and enjoy the sunshine during these moments of downtime.

Ingredients will be detailed in all their simple glory as we find safe harbor in each port. Called **Provisions**, these ingredients are easy to obtain in most American grocery stores. No need to travel to exotic lands to shop when you can capture the flavor stateside!

Finally, in some recipes, you'll find unique hints that I wish to share with you—tips I rely on to prepare fine meals wherever I go (which is just about everywhere!):

Throttle Control (recipe adjustment) empowers you to play with various amounts of ingredients in the recipe to suit your own fancy. For example: Love a spicier spicy tuna roll? "Throttle up" and adjust the heat level of the sriracha. Want less sweetness in your sweet tea? "Throttle down" and reduce your "sugar speed" without altering the consistency. The takeaway is this: Consider your taste preferences. Adjust where indicated with my advice. Enjoy!

Navigating an **Alternate Course** (ingredient substitution) is also an option for many recipes. Your journey can be different but reliable each time you prepare the dish. Recipes are just a guide, so use your own personal touch alongside my written instructions. We've all been there, where listed ingredients aren't an exact match for what you need, want, or have. Maybe you live where fresh mangoes grow (lucky you). Use them instead of the peaches I prescribe. Or perhaps you can't eat chocolate without wishing you hadn't (unlucky you, but no worries). Take a different route using carob.

But watch out for a **Rogue Wave** (recipe warning), which signals where my past failed attempts have led me to a solution for you. I want to spare you from toughening your tuna steak from too much heat. I want to release you from the frustration of unevenly roasting your vegetables because you forgot to cut even slices.

And now, Little Chef, you're ready to journey with me and dine around the world. Our yacht is provisioned and prepared for the open seas. We are on our way. *Bon voyage!*

THE BAHAMAS

Great Exuma, Bahamas

Are you ready for island life, Little Chef?

Let's soak up the beauty of the Bahamas, our first port. Everything seems brighter here. The waters, clear and cool, reflect the sunshine on every surface on and around the yacht. I regularly don my best sunglasses and flip-flops to provision fresh seafood and produce from town or, more often, from locals who meet me at the marina.

The Bahamian people are super friendly and super chill. Here, everyone is on island time, so no one needs to worry about daunting decisions or deadlines. There's no rush. You can learn the ease of living at a slower pace from cool islanders who work and play together in harmony on their laid-back shores.

A friend from the marina who knows I am in the market to buy his fresh conch, limes, and avocados usually shows up. That means I can serve the guests ceviche when they return from the beach on Great Exuma, along with a *switcha* drink. Like lemonade, this Bahamian favorite takes limes to the next level with a perfect blend of tart and sweet. What a refreshing thirst quencher after a day in the sun.

As I wait for the guests to return, I prepare local favorites on the deck. I often grill chicken with fresh pineapple and use the idle time to bask in the sun with a favorite travel companion, my ukulele, resting on my tanned legs. Four easy chords create a soothing Caribbean sound. Other than my light strumming, it is so quiet that I can hear the sizzle when the fat hits the flame.

Can you smell it, Little Chef? Warm spices and fresh citrus brighten up the chicken, sending zesty, tangy scents across the deck.

A sea turtle glides by effortlessly, followed by a colorful swarm of tropical fish glinting in the sun. This is an escape to a place of timeless leisure. Try this menu and feel it for yourself.

Pig Beach, Staniel Cay. These fatties love my leftovers so much that they stalk me down the beach.

Compass Cay. The nurse sharks are so docile that you can swim with them without fearing for your life (that is, until a tiger shark shows up).

Great Exuma, Bahamas

BREAKFAST

Bahamian Johnny Cake

with Coconut-Lime Butter and Mango Jam

LUNCH

Barbecue Chicken Platter

with Peas and Rice, Coleslaw, Macaroni Pie, and Fried Plantains

COCKTAIL HOUR

Goombay Smash

Calypso Cracked Lobster

DINNER

Island Fish Salad

Seared Scallops with Corn and Sweet Potato Chowder

Rum Cake

Great Exuma, Bahamas

BAHAMIAN JOHNNY CAKE WITH COCONUT-LIME BUTTER AND MANGO JAM

Historically known as a "journey cake" because it travels well, this baked loaf is a Bahamian staple. Make extra of this carb-boosting treasure to take on a beach outing. Slather it with coconut-lime compound butter and mango jam, which keeps in the refrigerator for months, ready for future uses. Making jam will preserve fruit that would otherwise be wasted, so grab your mason jars and get jammin'!

TOTAL TRIP: 1 hour, 15 minutes

CRUISING TIME: 45 minutes

IDLE TIME: 30 minutes

SERVES: 8

PROVISIONS FOR THE CAKE

3 cups all-purpose flour

1/3 cup granulated sugar

3 tablespoons baking powder

1/2 teaspoon kosher salt

1/4 cup salted butter (1/2 stick), softened, cut into 4 pieces

1 cup evaporated milk

1/2 cup water

2 eggs, beaten

1/2 cup salted butter (1 stick), melted, divided

PROVISIONS FOR THE COMPOUND BUTTER

1/2 cup salted butter (1 stick), softened

1/3 cup sweetened shredded coconut

2 teaspoons fresh lime zest (1 medium lime)

PROVISIONS FOR THE JAM

2 cups fresh mangoes (2 small), medium diced

1/2 cup water

1/2 cup granulated sugar

1 tablespoon fresh lime juice (1/2 medium lime)

DIRECTIONS FOR THE CAKE

1. Preheat the oven to 350°F. Grease a 9-by-5-inch loaf pan.
2. In a medium mixing bowl, whisk together the flour, sugar, baking powder, and salt.
3. Add the softened butter. Use your fingers to work the butter into the dry mixture until it is equally distributed into a coarse meal consistency.
4. Add the evaporated milk, water, and eggs and 1/4 cup of the melted butter, reserving the rest. Using a rubber spatula, mix the batter until just combined.
5. Pour the batter into the greased loaf pan and bake for 30 minutes.
6. After 30 minutes, remove the loaf from the oven and brush the top with the remaining 1/4 cup of the melted butter.
7. Return the loaf to the oven for approximately 15 minutes, until the top is golden brown.
8. Once done, remove the johnny cake to cool for 15 minutes.

DIRECTIONS FOR THE COMPOUND BUTTER

1. While the cake bakes, in a small mixing bowl, combine the butter, coconut, and lime zest.
2. Using a fork, mash all of the ingredients until combined.
3. Spoon the mixture onto a 12-inch square of plastic wrap.
4. Roll the mixture into a cigar shape and chill in the refrigerator for 30 minutes before serving with the johnny cake.

DIRECTIONS FOR THE JAM

1. While the cake bakes, in a small pot, combine the mangoes, water, sugar, and lime juice.
2. Bring the mixture to a boil over medium-high heat, and boil for 5 to 8 minutes or until the mangoes start to break down.
3. As the mangoes become tender, mash them using a potato masher or fork until thickened into a jam consistency.
4. Allow to cool and serve on top of the johnny cake.

Throttle Control: For the compound butter and jam, adjust the amounts of lime (tangy), coconut, and mango (both sweet) based on taste preferences.

Alternate Course: For the johnny cake, milk or buttermilk can be substituted for the evaporated milk. To make a buttermilk substitute, combine 1 cup of milk with 1 tablespoon of white vinegar. For the compound butter, any fruit (freeze-dried or in small fresh pieces) can be used in place of the coconut for variety. For the jam, instead of the mango, use any tropical fruit available. And if you can't get fresh fruit for the jam, use frozen, as it maintains great flavor.

Rogue Wave: For the compound butter, be sure not to melt the butter, as this changes the chemical structure. Only soften the butter at room temperature.

Throttle Control: Adjust the amounts of cinnamon, ginger, allspice, and nutmeg (all are warming spices) based on taste preferences.

Alternate Course: If without a grill, bake in the oven at 400°F for 35 minutes or until an internal temperature of 165°F is reached.

Great Exuma, Bahamas

BARBECUE CHICKEN PLATTER

The beauty of grilling is best understood by our taste buds. High heat and direct contact with the food allow the outside to crisp up and the inside to stay moist. Firing up the grill will make any day a special occasion. Our guests, returning from a midmorning beach outing, usually can't wait to dig in once on board. We serve this platter of chicken with peas and rice, macaroni pie, coleslaw, and fried plantains.

TOTAL TRIP: 1 hour, 30 minutes (up to 12 hours)

CRUISING TIME: 30 minutes

IDLE TIME: 1 hour (or more, to marinate)

SERVES: 4

PROVISIONS

4½ pounds chicken quarters, bone-in, skin-on

2 tablespoons canola oil

2 teaspoons garlic powder

2 teaspoons onion powder

½ teaspoon cayenne pepper

1½ teaspoons freshly ground black pepper

1½ tablespoons kosher salt

2 teaspoons fresh thyme leaves (or 1 teaspoon dried)

½ teaspoon ground cinnamon

½ teaspoon ground ginger

⅛ teaspoon ground allspice

⅛ teaspoon ground nutmeg

2 tablespoons fresh lime juice (1 medium lime)

1 cup honey barbecue sauce

DIRECTIONS

1. In a large mixing bowl, add the chicken quarters, oil, garlic powder, onion powder, cayenne pepper, black pepper, salt, thyme, cinnamon, ginger, allspice, and nutmeg.
2. Using your hands, mix the herbs with the chicken until evenly seasoned.
3. Add in the lime juice and barbecue sauce. Mix with your hands until evenly distributed.
4. Cover the bowl of seasoned chicken with plastic wrap and place in the refrigerator for at least 1 hour or overnight to marinate.
5. While the chicken is marinating, work on preparing the side dishes to be added to your lunch platter.
6. Once the chicken is done marinating, preheat the grill to 450°F.
7. When ready to barbecue, use tongs to place the chicken skin side down on the hot grill and close the lid. After 6 minutes, when the skin is caramelized, flip the chicken and cook for another 6 minutes.
8. Move the chicken to the upper rack to cook for another 15 to 20 minutes or until done using indirect heat. Check the internal temperature of the chicken to ensure it reaches 165°F.
9. Once done, transfer the chicken to a serving dish with side dishes. Or place the chicken on a large sheet tray and keep it warm in the oven on the lowest setting (170°F) while preparing the rest of the platter.

Great Exuma, Bahamas

PEAS AND RICE

Bahamians use the small but mighty pigeon pea in this regional dish. Technically beans, pigeon peas are round, like our black-eyed peas in the United States. A little sweet, a little earthy, a little nutty—this Bahamian side dish makes a perfect addition to our barbecue chicken lunch platter.

TOTAL TRIP: 1 hour

CRUISING TIME: 40 minutes

IDLE TIME: 20 minutes

SERVES: 4

PROVISIONS

1/4 cup canola oil

1 cup yellow onion (1/2 medium), small diced

3/4 cup green bell pepper (1/2 large), small diced

1/4 cup celery (1 small stalk), small diced

1 tablespoon garlic (4 cloves), minced

2 teaspoons kosher salt

1/2 cup Roma tomato (1 medium), small diced

2 teaspoons fresh thyme leaves (or 1 teaspoon dried)

1/2 teaspoon garlic powder

1/2 teaspoon red pepper flakes

1 tablespoon tomato paste

1 tablespoon browning sauce

1 cup pigeon peas, canned, drained and rinsed

2 cups white long-grain rice, rinsed 3 to 4 times

2 1/2 cups water

DIRECTIONS

1. Heat a large sauté pan over medium-high heat.
2. Once hot, add in the oil, onion, bell pepper, celery, garlic, and salt. Sauté while stirring occasionally with a wooden spoon until the onion is translucent, approximately 5 minutes.
3. Add in the tomato, thyme, garlic powder, red pepper flakes, tomato paste, browning sauce, and pigeon peas, and stir to cook for 2 minutes.
4. Add in the rice and water.
5. Bring to a boil and cook for 1 minute.
6. Reduce the temperature to low. Stir to ensure that the rice is not sticking to the bottom, then cover and let cook for 15 to 20 minutes (17 is the magic number for me) with no stirring.
7. While the peas and rice are cooking, work on preparing the rest of the platter.
8. When the peas and rice are ready, fluff with a fork and serve as part of the platter.

Throttle Control: Adjust the amount of red pepper flakes (heat) based on taste preferences.

Alternate Course: Instead of the pigeon peas, black-eyed peas can be used. Instead of the browning sauce, a beef bouillon cube can be substituted, but true authenticity will be lost.

Great Exuma, Bahamas

COLESLAW

Originating in the Netherlands in the eighteenth century, coleslaw comes from the Dutch word *koolsla,* meaning "cabbage salad." In this version, fresh Bahamian lime adds a splash of tanginess, making this dish another great addition to the barbecue chicken lunch platter.

TOTAL TRIP: 10 minutes

SERVES: 4

PROVISIONS

2/3 cup mayonnaise

2 tablespoons granulated sugar

1 1/2 teaspoons kosher salt

2 tablespoons fresh lime juice (1 medium lime)

4 cups green cabbage (1/2 head), pre-shredded "angel hair" thinness

1 cup red bell pepper (1 small), thinly sliced

1 cup carrots (2 medium), pre-shredded

Throttle Control: Adjust the amount of lime juice (tangy) based on taste preferences.

DIRECTIONS

1. In a large mixing bowl, combine the mayonnaise, sugar, salt, and lime juice.
2. Once combined, add in the cabbage, bell pepper, and carrots.
3. Using tongs, mix until combined.
4. Keep the coleslaw in the refrigerator while preparing the rest of the platter.

MACARONI PIE

Who doesn't love the combination of pasta and cheese in a casserole dish? In this version, jalapeños and evaporated milk create a distinctly Caribbean comfort food that guests will enjoy on its own or as part of the barbecue chicken lunch platter.

TOTAL TRIP: 1 hour, 30 minutes

CRUISING TIME: 30 minutes

IDLE TIME: 1 hour

SERVES: 4

PROVISIONS

1 pound ziti pasta

1/2 cup salted butter (1 stick)

1/2 cup yellow onion (1/4 medium), small diced

1/3 cup green bell pepper (1/3 small), small diced

1/3 cup red bell pepper (1/3 small), small diced

1/4 cup jalapeño pepper (1 large), finely diced

1/3 cup celery (1 medium stalk), small diced

2 teaspoons kosher salt

1 1/2 cups evaporated milk

3 eggs, beaten

4 cups cheddar cheese, shredded, reserving 1 cup for topping

DIRECTIONS

1. Preheat the oven to 350°F. Grease a deep 9-by-13-inch casserole dish.
2. In a large pot, cook the pasta in boiling salted water until al dente, according to the directions on the package. Drain in a colander and set aside.
3. While the pasta cooks, heat a medium sauté pan over medium-high heat.
4. Once hot, add in the butter, onion, bell pepper, jalapeño, celery, and salt. Sauté while stirring occasionally with a wooden spoon until the onion is translucent, approximately 5 minutes.
5. Transfer the vegetables to a large mixing bowl and allow to cool, approximately 10 minutes.
6. When the vegetables are cooled, add the evaporated milk and eggs and 3 cups of the cheese to the bowl and mix together.
7. Once combined, fold in the cooked pasta.
8. Transfer to the greased casserole dish and top with the remaining cup of the cheese.
9. Bake for 45 minutes, until bubbling and the top is golden brown.
10. While the macaroni pie is baking, work on preparing the rest of the platter.

Throttle Control: Adjust the amount of jalapeño (heat) based on taste preferences.

Alternate Course: Instead of the evaporated milk, use heavy whipping cream for extra creaminess.

Rogue Wave: Jalapeños can be spicy! To tame the heat of the pepper, remove the seeds, veins, and pith when preparing.

FRIED PLANTAINS

With a lower glycemic index than a banana, plantains offer loads of vitamins A and C, as well as iron. Let the skin turn black and the inside soften before frying, which may take several days, so plan accordingly. I set mine on the galley window that gets indirect sunshine reflecting off the water. The plantains add the finishing touch to the barbecue chicken lunch platter.

TOTAL TRIP: 15 minutes

SERVES: 4

PROVISIONS

2 cups canola oil, for frying

2 plantains, peeled and cut on a bias to 1½ inches thick

DIRECTIONS

1. In a large pot, preheat the oil to 375°F over medium heat.
2. Once the oil is 350°F, use a slotted spoon to gently add in the plantains. Deep-fry until a deep golden brown, 3 to 5 minutes, using the spoon to ensure the plantains do not stick together or to the bottom of the pot.
3. Using the slotted spoon, remove the plantains to drain on a plate lined with paper towels.
4. Keep the plantains in a warm oven while preparing the rest of the platter.

Rogue Wave: Avoid frying in oil that is too hot, as the plantains will burn on the outside and remain undercooked on the inside. And if the oil is not hot enough, the plantains will be soggy.

Great Exuma, Bahamas

GOOMBAY SMASH

Wanna know the secret to why this drink is so special? Bitters. Bitters are a botanical tincture of herbs, spices, fruits, roots, and bark that give cocktails their wow factor. For this tropical drink, I use orange bitters, which include orange peel, anise, cardamom, caraway, coriander, and cinnamon. Wow is right.

TOTAL TRIP: 5 minutes

SERVES: 4

PROVISIONS

1 cup dark rum

1 cup coconut rum

1/2 cup triple sec

1 cup pineapple juice

1/4 cup fresh orange juice (1 small orange)

1/4 cup fresh lime juice (2 medium limes)

8 dashes of orange bitters

4 fresh orange slices (1/4 orange), for garnish

4 maraschino cherries, for garnish

4 pineapple leaves, for garnish

DIRECTIONS

1. Into the pitcher, add the rums, triple sec, juices, and bitters and stir with a large spoon to combine.
2. Serve in fun individual cocktail glasses with ice, and garnish each glass with an orange slice and a cherry. For extra tropical vibes, garnish each glass with a pineapple leaf, and find your favorite beach chair to escape to the tropics.

Throttle Control: Adjust the amounts of coconut rum (sweet) and dark rum (intense) based on taste preferences.

Alternate Course: Instead of the triple sec, use passion fruit or apricot liqueur for an equally wonderful tropical flavor.

Rogue Wave: Don't forget that the pineapple, orange, and lime juices in this libation are a welcome boost of vitamin C for us scurvy-sidestepping sailors, matey!

Great Exuma, Bahamas

CALYPSO CRACKED LOBSTER

Most of us are familiar with the cold-water lobster of Maine, but in the Bahamas, we are treated to a warm-water crustacean called the Caribbean spiny lobster. While smaller and without enlarged front claws, this local native measures up for our special vacation-in-place cocktail hour. Remember Calypso, the mythological nymph that tempted Odysseus with her beauty? With our Calypso dipping sauce, prepare to be lured in and enchanted.

TOTAL TRIP: 30 minutes

SERVES: 4

PROVISIONS FOR THE CALYPSO SAUCE

1/4 cup mayonnaise

4 teaspoons ketchup

2 teaspoons fresh lime juice (1/2 small lime)

1 teaspoon Tabasco hot sauce

PROVISIONS FOR THE LOBSTER

2 eggs

1/2 cup whole milk

4 lobster tails, any kind

4 cups canola oil, for frying

2 cups all-purpose flour

1 1/2 teaspoons kosher salt

1/2 teaspoon freshly ground black pepper

1/2 teaspoon finishing salt, for sprinkling

Lime wedges, for garnish

DIRECTIONS FOR THE CALYPSO SAUCE

1. In a mixing bowl, add the mayonnaise, ketchup, lime juice, and hot sauce and stir together with a spoon.
2. Set aside and prepare the cracked lobster.

DIRECTIONS FOR THE CRACKED LOBSTER

1. In a large mixing bowl, combine the eggs and milk. Whisk until combined.
2. On a cutting board, extract the lobster meat from the tails and cut it into 1-by-1/2-inch strips. Add to the bowl with the eggs and milk.
3. In a medium pot, preheat the oil to 375°F over medium heat.
4. Meanwhile, in a medium mixing bowl, combine the flour, salt, and pepper to create the dry dredge.
5. Drain and transfer the lobster from the wet mix to the dry dredge, coating each piece of lobster evenly.
6. Once the oil is at 375°F, use your hands (or a slotted spoon) to add the lobster gently into the oil and fry until golden brown, approximately 3 minutes. Use a slotted spoon to move the pieces around to ensure the strips do not stick together or to the bottom of the pot.
7. Drain on a large sheet tray lined with paper towels and sprinkle with the finishing salt while hot. Serve with the Calypso sauce and the lime wedges.

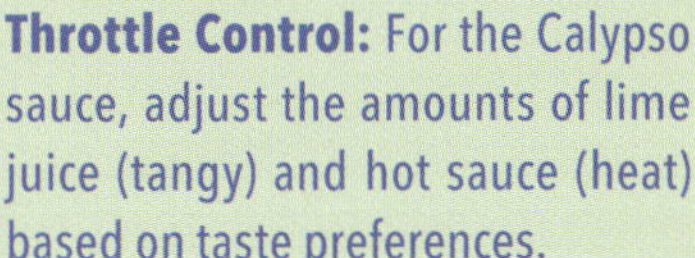

Throttle Control: For the Calypso sauce, adjust the amounts of lime juice (tangy) and hot sauce (heat) based on taste preferences.

Alternate Course: If you aren't in the Bahamas, use a Florida spiny lobster (it's the same species) or a cold-water Maine lobster. Or, as a substitute for the lobster, use fish, shrimp, or the most authentic of all seafood specialties in the Bahamas, conch.

Rogue Wave: Avoid frying in oil that is too hot, as the breading will burn on the outside, and the seafood will remain undercooked on the inside. And if the oil is not hot enough, the breading will be soggy and fall off.

Great Exuma, Bahamas

ISLAND FISH SALAD

Start dinner off right with this fresh seafood starter. Better known as ceviche, fish salad employs salt and citrus juice to marinate raw fish. Both lime and orange juice play a starring role in this Bahamian favorite.

TOTAL TRIP: 45 minutes (up to 1 hour, 15 minutes)

CRUISING TIME: 15 minutes

IDLE TIME: 30 minutes (up to 1 hour, to marinate)

SERVES: 4

PROVISIONS

1-pound Caribbean grouper fillet, cubed in 1/2-inch pieces

1/2 cup Roma tomato (1 medium), small diced

1/4 cup green bell pepper (1/4 small), small diced

1/4 cup red bell pepper (1/4 small), small diced

1/3 cup sweet onion (1/6 medium), small diced

2 tablespoons jalapeño pepper (1/2 large), finely diced

1/3 cup fresh lime juice (2 large limes)

3 tablespoons fresh orange juice (1/2 large orange)

2 teaspoons kosher salt

DIRECTIONS

1. Place the fish, tomato, bell peppers, onion, and jalapeño in a gallon-size plastic food-storage bag.
2. Add the lime juice, orange juice, and salt to the bag. Before sealing, remove any extra air to ensure that the juice is covering each piece of fish.
3. Place the sealed bag in the refrigerator for 30 minutes to 1 hour to "cook" the fish in the marinade.
4. After no more than an hour, pour all of the ingredients from the bag, including the liquid marinade, into a serving bowl to enjoy like a cold salad.

Throttle Control: Adjust the amounts of lime juice (acidic), jalapeño (heat), and vegetables (flavors) based on taste preferences.

Alternate Course: Instead of the grouper, use any semifirm whitefish such as red snapper. Or, if raw seafood is to be avoided, use cooked shrimp. Follow the same instructions.

Rogue Wave: Please note that this fish is not "cooked" with heat, so there could be pathogens that should be avoided by some folks. Yes, the citric juice "denatures" the protein for the fish to undergo a change similar to cooking it, but it is not the same. And remember that jalapeños can be spicy! To tame the heat of the pepper, remove the seeds, veins, and pith when preparing.

Great Exuma, Bahamas

SEARED SCALLOPS WITH CORN AND SWEET POTATO CHOWDER

Sunsets and seafood—is there any better way to end your Bahamian day than with buttery, sweet scallops floating in a warm bath of yumminess? This pairing with sweet potatoes will take your guests on an instant vacation.

TOTAL TRIP: 45 minutes

CRUISING TIME: 30 minutes

IDLE TIME: 15 minutes

SERVES: 4

PROVISIONS FOR THE CHOWDER

2 tablespoons extra virgin olive oil

2 tablespoons garlic (8 cloves), roughly chopped

1 cup yellow onion (1/2 medium), medium diced

1/2 cup carrot (1 medium), medium diced

1/2 cup celery (1 large stalk), medium diced

1 cup red bell pepper (1 small), medium diced

3 cups sweet potatoes (2 medium), peeled, small diced

1/4 cup jalapeño pepper (1 large), small diced

1 tablespoon fresh thyme leaves (or 1 1/2 teaspoons dried)

1 cup frozen corn

2 teaspoons kosher salt

1 teaspoon freshly ground black pepper

1 3/4 cups unsweetened coconut milk (13.5-ounce can)

2 cups vegetable stock

2 ears fresh corn on the cob, sliced into 1/2-inch portions

PROVISIONS FOR THE SCALLOPS

1 1/2 pounds sea scallops (20 large)

1 tablespoon kosher salt

4 tablespoons salted butter (1/2 stick)

1/4 cup each of radishes, thinly sliced, red bell pepper, small diced, corn kernels, and cilantro leaves, chopped, for garnish

DIRECTIONS FOR THE CHOWDER

1. Heat a large pot over medium-high heat.
2. Once hot, add in the olive oil, garlic, onion, carrot, celery, bell pepper, sweet potatoes, jalapeño, thyme, frozen corn, salt, and pepper. Sauté while stirring occasionally with a wooden spoon until the onion is translucent, approximately 5 minutes.
3. Add in the coconut milk and vegetable stock. Simmer, uncovered, until the sweet potatoes are tender, approximately 8 minutes. Meanwhile, prepare the scallops.
4. When the sweet potatoes are tender, transfer 3/4 of the simmered stock and vegetables into a blender (or a tall container to use an immersion blender) to puree into a soup consistency, reserving 1/4 in the pot to remain chunky. Return the pureed soup to the pot.

5. Add in the fresh corn portions and simmer for 2 minutes.
6. Turn off the heat. Transfer to bowls when the scallops are ready to serve.

DIRECTIONS FOR THE SCALLOPS

1. While the chowder is simmering to cook the corn, heat up a large sauté pan over high heat.
2. Dry the scallops with paper towels and evenly coat with salt on both sides.
3. Once the sauté pan has reached high heat (and not before), add in the butter to melt.
4. Sear the scallops in 2 batches, making sure not to overcrowd the pan.
5. Cook the scallops for 1 minute, and then use tongs to flip and cook for another minute. The scallops should have a hard sear on both sides.
6. Place the scallops on top of the corn and sweet potato chowder.
7. Garnish with the radishes, red bell pepper, corn kernels, and cilantro.

Throttle Control: Adjust the amount of sweet potato for a thicker or thinner chowder texture based on preferences.

Alternate Course: Instead of the scallops, use any fish or shellfish. However, be sure to adjust the cooking time based on the size of the protein.

Rogue Wave: Avoid overcooking the scallops, as they can become rubbery. And remember that jalapeños can be spicy! To tame the heat of the pepper, remove the seeds, veins, and pith when preparing.

Great Exuma, Bahamas

RUM CAKE

We can't leave the Caribbean without rum, matey! Instead of a drink, though, here the sweet and toasty liquor is a stowaway inside the cake. So feel free to plunder away without too many regrets. Consider it an homage to history since the hot and humid climate of the Bahamas might have warranted the use of sugar and alcohol to preserve the food for a long voyage in the briny deep. Yo, ho, ho, rumrunner!

TOTAL TRIP: 1 hour, 45 minutes

CRUISING TIME: 30 minutes

IDLE TIME: 1 hour, 15 minutes

SERVES: 8

PROVISIONS FOR THE CAKE

2½ cups cake flour

1¼ teaspoons baking powder

¼ teaspoon baking soda

½ teaspoon kosher salt

1 cup granulated sugar

¾ cup light brown sugar

¾ cup salted butter (1½ sticks)

½ cup evaporated milk

½ cup dark rum

2 teaspoons vanilla extract

1 teaspoon almond extract

6 egg yolks

4 egg whites

PROVISIONS FOR THE GLAZE

½ cup salted butter (1 stick)

¼ cup water

1 cup granulated sugar

½ cup dark rum

DIRECTIONS FOR THE CAKE

1. Preheat the oven to 350°F. Grease a 10-inch Bundt pan.
2. In a large mixing bowl, combine the cake flour, baking powder, baking soda, salt, sugar, and brown sugar and whisk together. Set aside the dry ingredients.
3. In a medium microwave-safe mixing bowl, melt the butter in 10-second intervals in the microwave, until completely melted.
4. Add the evaporated milk, rum, vanilla extract, almond extract, and egg yolks to the bowl. Whisk until combined, then slowly add the mixture to the dry ingredients.
5. Using a rubber spatula, fold the ingredients together.
6. In a separate medium mixing bowl, whisk the egg whites with a hand mixer on high until stiff peaks are formed, approximately 4 minutes.
7. Gently fold the egg whites into the batter with a spatula until just combined.
8. Pour the batter into the greased Bundt pan. Bake for 45 to 55 minutes or until a toothpick inserted comes out clean.
9. Meanwhile, prepare the rum glaze when the cake is almost done so that it is ready when you remove the cake from the oven.
10. Immediately poke approximately 50 holes into the cake with a skewer (or the tip of a meat thermometer) ¾ of the depth of the cake while still in the pan. Pour the glaze on the hot cake right out of the oven.

DIRECTIONS FOR THE GLAZE

1. In a medium pot, add the butter, water, and sugar and bring to a boil for 5 minutes. With a wooden spoon, stir constantly until the mixture is similar to the viscosity of honey.
2. Turn off the heat and remove the pot to add the rum. Stir to combine.
3. Allow to cool for 5 minutes.
4. After 5 minutes, reserve ½ cup of the rum glaze in a small mixing bowl. Pour the remaining rum glaze on the cake, allowing it to seep into the holes for 30 minutes.
5. Flip the cake out of the pan onto a serving platter and use the remaining ½ cup of the glaze to drizzle on top.

Alternate Course: Instead of the evaporated milk, use regular whole milk, but expect less richness.

Rogue Wave: Using cake flour (rather than all-purpose flour) is important since it makes the cake lighter and fluffier.

SOUTH CAROLINA

Charleston, SC, United States

In the South, the pineapple symbolizes hospitality. How yummy a welcome!

Charleston beckons me—and seemingly everyone else from around the world—to soak in its Southern history and charm.

To get downtown, I hop on my bike (kept on the yacht) for the ten-minute trek to historic Charleston. My favorite downtown destination is the Charleston Farmers Market at Marion Square on Meeting Street, where I can find okra, sweet potatoes, Southern peas, sweet peppers, cabbage, collards, and root vegetables.

Foodies go wild in Charleston. Fresh local produce and fish make for the most ideal ingredients. I especially love a traditional low-country boil and fried okra. Real crowd-pleasers.

And if you've never tried the whole crispy flounder in Charleston, get on your bike, your boat, or whatever means of transportation you can find to sample this traditional treasure! The top of the flounder is scored, making it easy to pick up perfect squares of buttery goodness in every bite. Each time my family and I return to Charleston, we hit our favorite restaurant for this classic.

Little Chef, there are so many fresh catches in Charleston that are calling out your name: flounder (my favorite), grouper (the bomb when blackened on the stovetop in a cast-iron pan), tilapia (try it whole and fried), amberjack (like swordfish; I favor it grilled), barrelfish (kind of tastes like crab), triggerfish (again, like crab; great when baked in lemon butter), porgy (similar to snapper; best when broiled), rudderfish (like tuna; I enjoy it pan seared), tilefish (like lobster; try it steamed), and wreckfish (like grouper; I fancy it grilled).

After dinner, stroll up and down the cobblestone streets to savor the "Holy City." With live oak trees and gaslit lanterns to guide you, Charleston's streets display a host of architectural styles: colonial, Georgian, Federal, Classic Revival, Gothic Revival, Italianate, Victorian, and art deco. It's a feast for the eyes.

This showcase of Southern hospitality is something you need to experience for yourself if you can. Or simply pour yourself a glass of planter's punch to sip while feasting on some of these history-making dishes. You and your guests will slip into the Southern style with ease.

Charleston, SC, United States

BREAKFAST

Crab Cake Eggs Benedict

LUNCH

Shrimp and Grits

COCKTAIL HOUR

Planter's Punch

Fried Green Tomatoes

DINNER

She-Crab Soup

Fried Chicken Platter with Collards and Cornbread

Bourbon Bread Pudding with Pecans

Charleston, SC, United States

CRAB CAKE EGGS BENEDICT

This breakfast is perfect for a lazy day on the boat or for a brunch with friends. Succulent crabmeat and buttery hollandaise sauce elevate these poached eggs to perfection.

TOTAL TRIP: 1 hour

SERVES: 4

PROVISIONS FOR THE CRAB CAKES

1/4 cup yellow bell pepper (1/4 small), small diced

1/4 cup red bell pepper (1/4 small), small diced

1/2 cup yellow onion (1/4 medium), small diced

5 tablespoons green onions (2 stalks), sliced

1 cup panko bread crumbs

1/2 cup fresh flat-leaf parsley, chopped

1 teaspoon seafood seasoning

1 egg

1/2 cup mayonnaise

1 tablespoon Dijon mustard

1 tablespoon fresh lemon juice (1/2 medium lemon)

1 tablespoon plus 1 teaspoon Worcestershire sauce

1 teaspoon garlic powder

1/4 teaspoon kosher salt

Pinch of freshly ground black pepper

2 cups lump crabmeat, fully cooked, shredded

3 tablespoons salted butter (3/8 stick), for frying

1 cup baby arugula

PROVISIONS FOR THE POACHED EGGS

Water, for poaching

3 tablespoons white vinegar

8 eggs

PROVISIONS FOR THE HOLLANDAISE SAUCE

2 egg yolks

1 tablespoon fresh lemon juice (1/2 medium lemon)

Water, for double boiler

1/2 cup salted butter (1 stick), melted

Pinch of cayenne pepper

Pinch of kosher salt

DIRECTIONS FOR THE CRAB CAKES

1. In a medium mixing bowl, add the bell peppers, onion, green onions, panko, parsley, seafood seasoning, egg, mayonnaise, mustard, lemon juice, Worcestershire, garlic powder, salt, pepper, and crab. Gently mix with your hands to combine.
2. Form the mixture into 8 patties, each about 3 inches in diameter. Place the butter in a large sauté pan over medium-high heat, and then pan-fry the patties. Using a metal spatula, flip the patties after 2 1/2 minutes on each side, or until golden brown, then place on a large sheet tray.
3. When all of the crab cakes are done, keep them warm in the oven on the lowest setting (170°F) while preparing the poached eggs.

DIRECTIONS FOR THE POACHED EGGS

1. Using a large skillet, bring 3 to 4 inches of water (enough to cover the eggs) to a gentle simmer (not boiling) and then add in vinegar.
2. Crack one egg at a time into a mug and slowly pour the egg into the gently simmering water to poach. Repeat for the remaining eggs.

3. After 3 to 5 minutes, when the whites are cooked but the yolk is still runny, retrieve the poached eggs using a slotted spoon. Drain on a sheet tray lined with paper towels.

DIRECTIONS FOR THE HOLLANDAISE SAUCE

1. In a small heat-safe mixing bowl, whisk the egg yolks and lemon juice together until the color turns pale yellow as air is whipped into it.
2. Meanwhile, in a small pot, bring 2 inches of water to a boil.
3. Once the pot of water is boiling, place the mixing bowl with the egg mixture on top to create a double boiler, making sure the bottom of the bowl is not touching the water. Slowly stream in the melted butter while whisking.
4. Heat and whisk constantly until the hollandaise has thickened, 3 to 5 minutes. Control the temperature by taking the mixing bowl on and off the boiling water pot.
5. Once thickened, remove from the heat. Add in the cayenne pepper and salt.
6. To plate and garnish, begin with the crab cakes, followed by a bed of arugula, a poached egg, and a spoonful of the hollandaise sauce.

Throttle Control: Adjust the amounts of lemon (acid) and cayenne (heat) in the hollandaise sauce based on taste preferences.

Alternate Course: Instead of the crab cakes, use toasted English muffins for traditional eggs Benedict.

Charleston, SC, United States

SHRIMP AND GRITS

Now this is quintessential Southern comfort! Spicy sausage and saucy shrimp jump in the pool with our workhorse starch, Miss Grits. She is a corn grain that can handle this pool party of flavor.

TOTAL TRIP: 40 minutes

SERVES: 4

PROVISIONS FOR THE GRITS

- 6 cups water
- 1 1/2 teaspoons kosher salt
- 1 1/2 cups old-fashioned grits
- 1/2 cup heavy whipping cream
- 2 cups cheddar cheese, shredded
- 1/4 cup salted butter (1/2 stick)
- 1/2 teaspoon freshly ground black pepper

PROVISIONS FOR THE SHRIMP

- 5 strips uncooked bacon, chopped
- 1 pound andouille sausage, cooked, 1/2-inch slices
- 2 cups yellow onion (1 medium), medium diced
- 1 cup red bell pepper (1/2 large), medium diced
- 1 cup green bell pepper (1/2 large), medium diced
- 1 cup yellow bell pepper (1/2 large), medium diced
- 1 tablespoon garlic (4 cloves), minced
- 2 tablespoons salted butter (1/4 stick)
- 1/4 cup all-purpose flour
- 2 cups chicken stock
- 1 tablespoon Worcestershire sauce
- Pinch of cayenne pepper
- 2 pounds jumbo shrimp, peeled, deveined, tail on
- 1/4 cup fresh flat-leaf parsley, chopped, for garnish

DIRECTIONS FOR THE GRITS

1. In a medium pot, boil the water with the salt. Once boiling, add the grits and cook according to the directions on the package.
2. Once the grits are tender, remove from the heat and add the cream, cheese, butter, and pepper. Stir with a wooden spoon until well combined.

DIRECTIONS FOR THE SHRIMP

1. While the grits cook, in an unheated large skillet, add the chopped bacon. Then turn to medium heat to render the bacon, stirring occasionally, approximately 8 minutes.
2. Once the bacon is cooked, add in the sliced sausage and brown over medium-high heat, approximately 5 minutes, since it is already cooked.
3. Once browned, add in the onion, bell peppers, and garlic. Cook for approximately 5 minutes, until the onion is tender.
4. Add in the butter. Once melted, add in the flour and then mix for 1 minute.
5. Slowly add in the chicken stock, Worcestershire, and cayenne pepper while whisking. Increase the heat to high to bring the sauce to a boil for approximately 3 minutes or until slightly thickened.
6. Once slightly thickened, stir in the shrimp and cook over high heat for 2 to 3 minutes.
7. Plate the shrimp with the sauce on top of the grits. Garnish with the parsley. Perfection!

Throttle Control: Adjust the amounts of cheese and butter (richness) in the grits based on taste preferences.

Rogue Wave: Be sure to avoid overcooking the shrimp so it doesn't become rubbery.

Charleston, SC, United States

PLANTER'S PUNCH

Many origin stories for this recipe have floated around since every town in the world wants to claim this winner. In Charleston, it's said that planter's punch took root when royalty served this refreshing libation under a plantation shade tree.

TOTAL TRIP: 5 minutes

SERVES: 4

PROVISIONS

1⅓ cups dark rum

2⅔ cups pineapple juice

1⅓ cups fresh orange juice (4 medium oranges)

½ cup fresh lime juice (4 medium limes)

2 tablespoons grenadine

4 sprigs fresh mint, for garnish, as desired

DIRECTIONS

1. In a large pitcher filled with ice, combine the rum, juices, and grenadine.
2. Pour into mason jars filled with ice.
3. Garnish each jar with a sprig of the mint and enjoy under a shade tree.

Charleston, SC, United States

FRIED GREEN TOMATOES

I am told that in the nineties, when I was born, fried green tomatoes became a "thing" with the release of a movie by the same name. Whatever brought them to where I live, thank you. I think you will find these to be the perfect appetizer for our charming cocktail party on the deck.

TOTAL TRIP: 20 minutes

SERVES: 4

PROVISIONS FOR THE SAUCE

¼ cup mayonnaise

1 teaspoon Tabasco hot sauce

1 teaspoon prepared horseradish

½ teaspoon freshly ground black pepper

Pinch of cayenne pepper

¼ teaspoon kosher salt

PROVISIONS FOR THE TOMATOES

4 cups canola oil, for frying

1 cup all-purpose flour

2 teaspoons kosher salt

1 teaspoon freshly ground black pepper

½ teaspoon cayenne pepper

1 teaspoon garlic powder

4 large green tomatoes, ½-inch slices

2 cups baby arugula, as bedding for the tomatoes

DIRECTIONS FOR THE SAUCE

1. In a small mixing bowl, combine the mayonnaise, hot sauce, horseradish, black pepper, cayenne pepper, and salt to create a sauce.

DIRECTIONS FOR THE TOMATOES

1. In a large skillet, preheat the oil to 350°F over medium heat.
2. In a medium mixing bowl, whisk the flour, salt, black pepper, cayenne pepper, and garlic powder to create a seasoned flour.
3. Coat the sliced tomatoes in the seasoned flour.
4. Once the oil is at 350°F, fry the tomatoes in 2 batches, for 1 to 2 minutes on each side, using tongs to flip. Once golden brown, drain the fried tomatoes on a plate lined with paper towels.
5. To plate, alternate layers of the arugula (½ cup per plate) and fried tomato slices on each serving plate. Use a long toothpick to hold the stack if needed.
6. Drizzle the sauce on top.

Throttle Control: Adjust the amount of horseradish (heat) based on taste preferences.

Rogue Wave: Be sure to use firm green tomatoes, as regular ripe red ones will disintegrate in the hot oil. Avoid frying in oil that is too hot, as the tomatoes will burn on the outside and remain undercooked on the inside. And if the oil is not hot enough, the tomatoes will be soggy.

SHE-CRAB SOUP

This luxurious soup owes its unique briny flavor to the female blue crab with her roe (bless her heart), but we can enjoy this soup with any type of lump crabmeat. It is truly a delicacy.

TOTAL TRIP: 40 minutes

CRUISING TIME: 20 minutes

IDLE TIME: 20 minutes

SERVES: 4

PROVISIONS

6 tablespoons salted butter (3/4 stick)

2/3 cup shallots (4 small), medium diced

1 1/3 cups carrots (2 large), medium diced

1 1/3 cups celery (3 medium stalks), medium diced

2/3 cup dry white wine

2/3 cup long-grain white rice, unrinsed

1 tablespoon plus 1 teaspoon tomato paste

1 tablespoon seafood seasoning

2 teaspoons kosher salt

2 teaspoons Worcestershire sauce

1/4 teaspoon ground nutmeg

2 cups clam juice

6 cups seafood stock

3 cups lump crabmeat, fully cooked

3 cups heavy whipping cream

2/3 cup sherry

1/4 cup fresh flat-leaf parsley, chopped, for garnish

1/2 teaspoon sweet paprika, for garnish

DIRECTIONS

1. In a large pot, melt the butter over medium heat. Add the shallots, carrots, and celery. Sauté while stirring occasionally with a wooden spoon until tender, approximately 5 minutes.
2. Once tender, add the white wine, rice, tomato paste, seafood seasoning, salt, Worcestershire, and nutmeg. Stirring constantly, cook for 2 minutes.
3. Add in the clam juice and seafood stock. Increase to medium-high heat and simmer, uncovered, for 20 minutes, stirring occasionally.
4. After 20 minutes, use an immersion blender (or a regular blender, returning the soup to the pot on the stove afterward) to puree the soup until smooth.
5. Over medium-low heat, add in the crab, cream, and sherry. Cook for another 2 minutes while stirring.
6. Ladle into serving bowls and garnish with the parsley and paprika.

Throttle Control: Adjust the amounts of rice (thickening) and cream (richness) based on taste preferences.

Alternate Course: Instead of the seafood stock, which can be hard to find, use additional clam juice for a similar flavor.

Charleston, SC, United States

FRIED CHICKEN PLATTER

Frying is part of the American way here in Charleston, and you can't get enough of this Southern classic. The fried chicken is the star of the show, but adding collards and cornbread as the sides make this an unforgettable dinner platter. Use the time while the chicken marinates to prepare the collards and cornbread for the full Southern culinary experience.

TOTAL TRIP: 1 hour, 45 minutes (up to 12 hours)

CRUISING TIME: 45 minutes

IDLE TIME: 1 hour (or more, to marinate)

SERVES: 4

PROVISIONS FOR THE MARINADE AND CHICKEN

3 cups buttermilk

1 tablespoon Tabasco hot sauce

3 tablespoons seasoned salt

4½ pounds chicken thighs and drumsticks (or quarters, cut), bone-in, skin-on

PROVISIONS FOR THE SEASONING AND FRYING

8 cups peanut oil, for frying

2 cups all-purpose flour

1 cup cornstarch

1 tablespoon seasoned salt

DIRECTIONS FOR THE MARINADE

1. In a large mixing bowl, mix the buttermilk, hot sauce, and seasoned salt. Using your hands, coat the chicken with the marinade. Cover with plastic wrap and place in the refrigerator to allow the chicken to marinate for 1 hour or more (even overnight).
2. Meanwhile, work on the preparation of the side dishes.

DIRECTIONS FOR THE SEASONING AND FRYING

1. After the chicken has marinated, in a large skillet, preheat the oil to 350°F over medium-high heat.
2. In a medium mixing bowl, blend the flour, cornstarch, and seasoned salt.
3. Remove the marinated chicken from the buttermilk mixture. Place the chicken in the bowl to coat with the seasoned flour.
4. Fry the chicken in several single-layer batches until golden brown, using tongs to occasionally rotate and check for even frying, 15 to 20 minutes for each batch.
5. Drain the chicken on a large sheet tray lined with paper towels, checking for an internal temperature of 165°F by using a meat thermometer.
6. To keep the fried chicken hot while frying the subsequent batches (and to time it to match with the completion of the side dishes), keep the fried chicken in the oven on the lowest setting (170°F).
7. Once ready, plate the fried chicken along with the collards and cornbread. Enjoy this satisfyingly Southern dinner platter as you socialize with your favorite people.

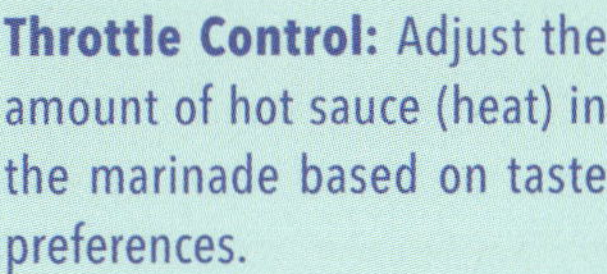

Throttle Control: Adjust the amount of hot sauce (heat) in the marinade based on taste preferences.

Alternate Course: If without the buttermilk, use a ratio of 1 cup of milk to 1 tablespoon of white vinegar to equal 1 cup of buttermilk in a recipe.

Rogue Wave: Avoid frying in oil that is too hot, as the chicken will burn on the outside and remain undercooked on the inside. And if the oil is not hot enough, the chicken will be soggy.

Charleston, SC, United States

COLLARDS

Collards are the perfect complement to our fried chicken platter. Wide and flat, the collard leaf (or "green") provides a healthy supply of vitamins A, B-9, C, and K as well as calcium. Serve this nutritious dish on a platter with fried chicken and cornbread for the ultimate Southern dinner.

TOTAL TRIP: 1 hour

CRUISING TIME: 30 minutes

IDLE TIME: 30 minutes

SERVES: 4

PROVISIONS

3 strips uncooked bacon, sliced

1½ cups yellow onion (¾ large), medium diced

1 tablespoon garlic (4 cloves), minced

9 cups collard greens (1 large bunch), chopped

2 cups chicken stock

2 teaspoons apple cider vinegar

1 teaspoon garlic powder

2 teaspoons granulated sugar

1 teaspoon Worcestershire sauce

½ teaspoon red pepper flakes

2 teaspoons sweet paprika

1 teaspoon kosher salt

1 smoked ham hock

DIRECTIONS

1. In an unheated large pot, add the sliced bacon. Turn the heat to medium to render the bacon, stirring occasionally with a wooden spoon, approximately 8 minutes.
2. Once the bacon is crispy, add in the onion and garlic. Cook until tender, stirring occasionally, approximately 5 minutes.
3. Once tender, add in the collards, chicken stock, vinegar, garlic powder, sugar, Worcestershire, red pepper flakes, paprika, salt, and ham hock. Stir to mix.
4. Cover and cook for 30 minutes over medium-low heat. Stir occasionally.
5. While the collards cook, work on preparing the cornbread and fried chicken for your dinner platter.

Alternate Course: Instead of the collards, use kale, which is less bitter.

CORNBREAD

Cornbread is a must in the South. When in Charleston, I make sure to use a local cornmeal mix from the market. Pair this regional favorite with our fried chicken and collards for the perfect dinner platter. There should be extra for later!

TOTAL TRIP: 45 minutes

CRUISING TIME: 15 minutes

IDLE TIME: 30 minutes

SERVES: 8

PROVISIONS

1½ cups all-purpose flour

1½ cups self-rising cornmeal mix

1 cup granulated sugar

2½ teaspoons kosher salt

1 tablespoon baking powder

4 eggs

1½ cups whole milk

¼ cup sour cream

¼ cup salted butter (½ stick), melted

DIRECTIONS

1. Preheat the oven to 375°F. Grease a 9-by-13-inch casserole dish.
2. In a large mixing bowl, combine the flour, cornmeal mix, sugar, salt, and baking powder. Set aside the dry ingredients.
3. In a medium mixing bowl, combine the eggs, milk, sour cream, and melted butter. Whisk until the wet ingredients are combined.
4. Add the wet ingredients into the dry ingredients, using a rubber spatula to gently mix until just combined.
5. Pour into the greased casserole dish and bake for 25 minutes or until golden brown and a toothpick comes out clean.
6. While the cornbread bakes, work on preparing the collards and fried chicken for your dinner platter.
7. When the cornbread is done, slice and serve warm.

Throttle Control: Adjust the amount of sugar (sweet) based on taste preferences. Since I am partial to a sweeter rather than savory cornbread, modify this sweet recipe accordingly.

Charleston, SC, United States

BOURBON BREAD PUDDING WITH PECANS

Bread pudding's humble European origin as "poor man's pudding" no longer applies to this version with bourbon, caramel, and pecans on the scene. Stale bread works even better than fresh since it is thirsty for moisture. Bonus for less waste!

TOTAL TRIP: 1 hour

CRUISING TIME: 20 minutes

IDLE TIME: 40 minutes

SERVES: 8

PROVISIONS FOR THE BREAD PUDDING

8 cups day-old French bread (1 loaf)

1/2 cup heavy whipping cream

3 cups whole milk

1/4 cup salted butter (1/2 stick), melted

3 eggs

1 cup granulated sugar

1/2 teaspoon ground cinnamon

1 teaspoon vanilla extract

PROVISIONS FOR THE SAUCE

1/2 cup salted butter (1 stick)

1 cup granulated sugar

1/4 cup water

1/4 teaspoon kosher salt

1/4 cup heavy whipping cream

1/4 cup bourbon

2/3 cup pecans, chopped, for garnish

DIRECTIONS FOR THE BREAD PUDDING

1. Preheat the oven to 350°F. Grease a 9-by-13-inch casserole dish.
2. Cube the bread into 1 1/2-inch squares.
3. In a large mixing bowl, add the cream, milk, melted butter, eggs, sugar, cinnamon, and vanilla. Use a whisk to combine the wet ingredients.
4. Add the cubes of bread into the greased casserole dish, and carefully pour the wet ingredients over them. Use a large spoon to press the bread into the liquid.
5. Bake the bread pudding for 40 minutes or until set.

DIRECTIONS FOR THE SAUCE

1. While the bread pudding bakes, in a small pot over medium-high heat, add the butter, sugar, water, and salt and warm. Bring to a boil, stirring constantly with a wooden spoon.
2. Boil and stir for 5 minutes, until the color turns caramel. Then remove from the stove and immediately add the cream and bourbon.
3. Stir in the cream and bourbon until fully incorporated. Set aside and cover to keep warm for when the bread pudding is done baking.
4. When the bread pudding is done, remove from the oven and drizzle the bourbon sauce on top. Garnish with the chopped pecans and serve.

Throttle Control: Adjust the amount of bourbon (intense) based on taste preferences.

Alternate Course: Instead of the French bread, use glazed doughnuts for an extra-sweet treat. True Little Chef move!

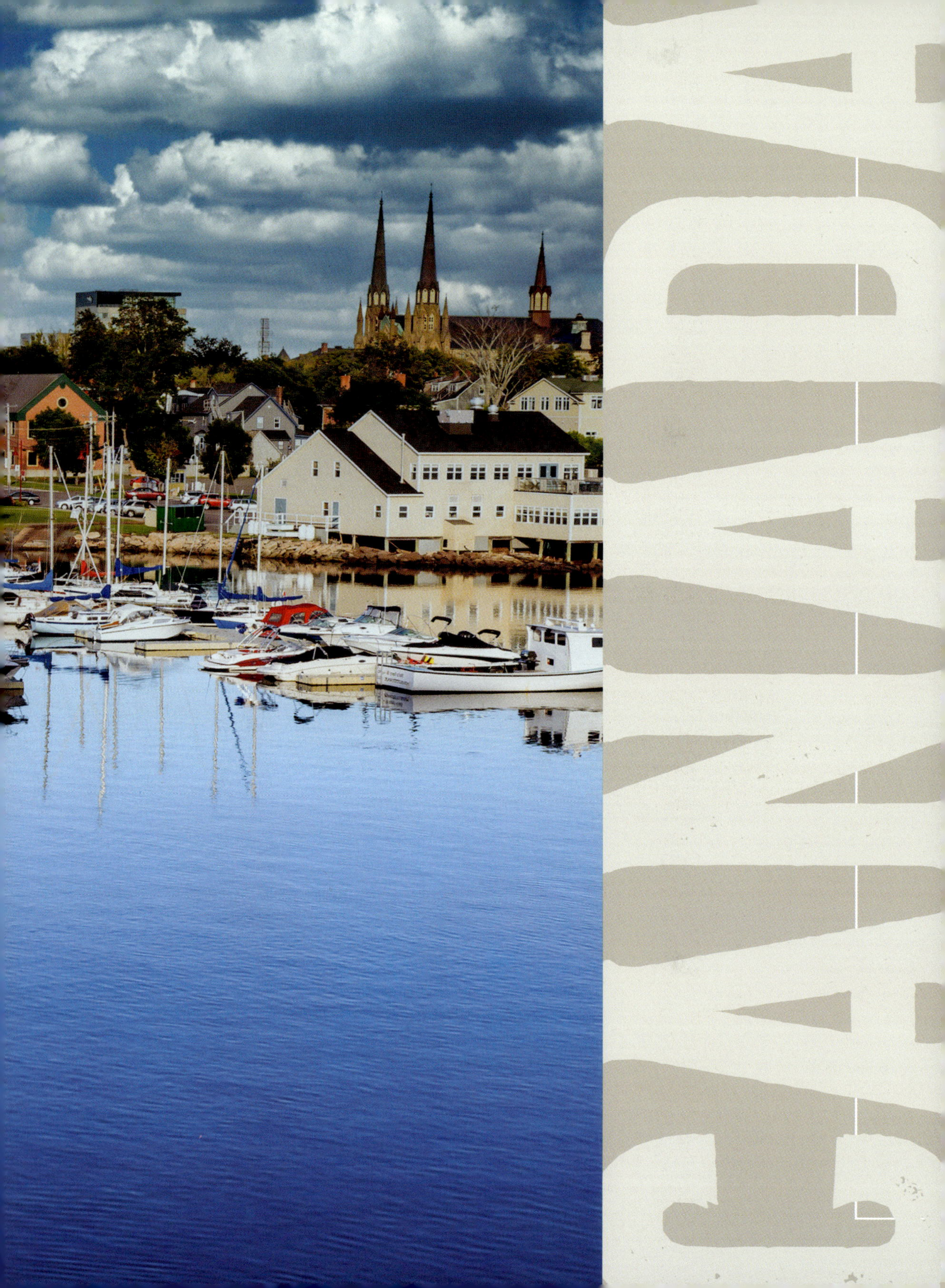
CANADA

Prince Edward Island, Canada

Oh, Canada! We're coming for your crisp, abundant waters!

I love seeing Canada from the vantage point of a yacht as we approach the port at Prince Edward Island. This is nature's playground. PEI conjures up fond memories of local lobster, mussels, oysters, and scallops sourced near the marina. The waters are teeming with life, and I partake of its bounty every time I visit.

The landscape is idyllic. As you look inland from the picturesque coastline, miles of meadows stretch as far as the eye can see. Quaint villages dot this bucolic landscape like a perfectly portrayed oil painting. Far from reality, I imagine myself frolicking in a lace-trimmed, puffy-sleeved dress similar to that worn by Anne in *Anne of Green Gables*, enjoying the wildflowers and the whimsy. The author of the books in this series, Lucy Maud Montgomery, based them on her own childhood in PEI, where she lived in a white farmhouse with green gables.

I would live on Prince Edward Island in a similar farmhouse if summer were eternal, but I would don jeans and farming boots instead of a dress, thank you very much. Summertime conditions are perfect for growing barley, oats, wheat, corn, potatoes, beans, carrots, cabbage, cauliflower, onions, tomatoes, and cucumbers. How ideal is that, Little Chef, to grow beautiful produce right on your own land?

The potatoes from PEI make me giddy. Yes, the potatoes. In fact, historically Prince Edward Island was known as Canada's "Potato Capital" due to its warm summers, cold winters, frequent rain, and iron-rich soil, and only recently (and barely) had its crown snatched by Alberta. Perhaps it will regain its top spot again, given that more than a hundred varieties of potatoes are grown here, including Russet Burbank, Gold Rush, Eva, Superior, Atlantic, Dakota Pearl, Red Norland, Chieftain, Prospect, Yukon Gold, Dakota Russet, and Satina. Mix several varieties together to create an eye-popping palette of white, red, yellow, and purple.

I often add PEI potatoes into this island's signature dish, "Prince Edward Veggie Blend," which consists of yellow beans, green beans, and carrots. Mr. Potato has always had a crush on Miss Carrot, so I do my part in letting them play together in my serving bowl. They are happy; I am happy; the guests are happy. What a win-win-win side dish. Add it to my dinner menu of Dijon Pork Tenderloin with Roasted Apples and Acorn Squash, and you will be happy too.

Grab your beets and everything fresh, Little Chef!

Prince Edward Island, Canada

BREAKFAST

Baked Apple Oatmeal

LUNCH

Mussels and Leeks with White Wine

COCKTAIL HOUR

Hail Caesar

Oysters with Mignonette Sauce

DINNER

Beet and Goat Cheese Salad

Maple-Dijon Pork Tenderloin with Roasted Apples and Acorn Squash

Sticky Toffee Pudding

Prince Edward Island, Canada

BAKED APPLE OATMEAL

As the top producer of maple syrup in the world, Canada capitalizes on this sugary sap for many of its signature sweets. Tap some for your coffee too as we pack this delicious breakfast treat for a forest hike where sugar maple trees thrive. The extra (if there is any!) can be saved for the next hike.

TOTAL TRIP: 1 hour

CRUISING TIME: 15 minutes

IDLE TIME: 45 minutes

SERVES: 8

PROVISIONS FOR THE OATMEAL

2 cups old-fashioned oats

1/2 cup applesauce, unsweetened

1 teaspoon baking powder

2 teaspoons ground cinnamon

1/4 teaspoon ground nutmeg

1/3 cup maple syrup

1/3 cup whole milk

1 egg, beaten

2 tablespoons canola oil

1 cup Granny Smith apple (1 large), peeled, 1/2-inch cubes

PROVISIONS FOR THE CINNAMON GLAZE

1/2 cup powdered sugar

2 teaspoons whole milk

1/4 teaspoon ground cinnamon

Pinch of kosher salt

DIRECTIONS FOR THE OATMEAL

1. Preheat the oven to 350°F. Grease a 9-by-9-inch square cake pan.
2. In a medium mixing bowl, combine the oats, applesauce, baking powder, cinnamon, nutmeg, syrup, milk, egg, oil, and apple. Mix until combined.
3. Bake in the greased cake pan for 35 to 45 minutes or until set.
4. Remove from the oven to cool for 10 minutes.
5. Cut into squares. Serve one square per plate with a drizzle of the cinnamon glaze.

DIRECTIONS FOR THE CINNAMON GLAZE

1. In a small mixing bowl, combine the sugar, milk, cinnamon, and salt.
2. Whisk until the glaze is smooth.
3. Drizzle on the cooled oatmeal squares. Enjoy the coziness!

MUSSELS AND LEEKS WITH WHITE WINE

When I am in port on Prince Edward Island, I head straight to the market, where fresh mussels abound. Sweet and tender, these beautiful bivalves capture my attention every visit—and can capture yours too since PEI mussels are exported and readily available.

TOTAL TRIP: 15 minutes

SERVES: 4

PROVISIONS

2 tablespoons extra virgin olive oil

6 tablespoons salted butter (3/4 stick)

2 tablespoons garlic (8 cloves), thinly sliced

1 cup shallots (4 medium), thinly sliced

5 cups leeks (5 medium stalks), halved, thinly sliced, thoroughly cleaned, discarding dark-green tops

2 teaspoons kosher salt

1/2 teaspoon freshly ground black pepper

2 teaspoons fresh thyme leaves (or 1 teaspoon dried)

1 cup dry white wine

2 pounds mussels, frozen or fresh, thoroughly cleaned

1/4 cup fresh flat-leaf parsley, chopped, for garnish

1 baguette, sliced, toasted

DIRECTIONS

1. Heat a large skillet over medium-high heat. Once hot, add in the olive oil and butter to melt.
2. Once melted, add in the garlic, shallots, leeks, salt, and pepper. Sauté while stirring occasionally with a wooden spoon until the shallots are translucent, approximately 5 minutes.
3. Add in the thyme, wine, and mussels. Cover and steam until the mussels open, 2 to 4 minutes.
4. Garnish with the fresh parsley and serve with the toasted bread.

Alternate Course: Instead of the baguette, use a fresh sourdough loaf. I keep a sourdough starter alive to make bread every week. I named my starter "Olivia Gluten John" since she was a legend. Fresh sourdough is legendary too, so if you can find a sourdough starter friend to love, I suggest you do it.

Rogue Wave: Clean the mussels thoroughly to avoid sandiness. Ensure that the meat remains tender by not overcooking them. And be sure to have a serious conversation with each bivalve before and after cooking: Toss any that are open *before* cooking, as well as those that don't open *after* cooking.

Prince Edward Island, Canada

HAIL CAESAR

Hail to this tomato-based cocktail that is powerful on its own or as a spicy, tangy sidekick to the oyster appetizer recipe that follows.

TOTAL TRIP: 5 minutes

SERVES: 4

PROVISIONS FOR THE COCKTAIL

4 cups Clamato

1⅓ cups vodka

2 teaspoons Worcestershire sauce

1 teaspoon prepared horseradish

1 teaspoon Tabasco hot sauce

1 tablespoon fresh lime juice (½ medium lime)

PROVISIONS FOR THE RIM AND GARNISH

1 lime, cut into 4 wedges

2 tablespoons celery salt

1 small pickling cucumber, cut into spears

4 celery stalks, with leaves

DIRECTIONS

1. In a pitcher, combine the Clamato, vodka, Worcestershire, horseradish, hot sauce, and lime juice.
2. Using a long spoon, stir to combine.
3. Prepare 4 highball glasses by rimming them with the lime wedges and then the celery salt.
4. Add ice. Garnish each glass with one of the lime wedges, cucumber spears, and celery stalks. *Hail yeah, that's good!*

Throttle Control: Adjust the amounts of horseradish (heat in your sinuses) and hot sauce (heat on your tongue) based on taste preferences.

Prince Edward Island, Canada

OYSTERS WITH MIGNONETTE SAUCE

Oh là là! Given the deep-rooted French heritage in Canada, it's no surprise to see the French inspiration behind cuisine such as the mignonette sauce. *Mignonette* in French means "dainty," but here the term refers to a small sachet of black pepper mixed with spices to season a dish. This seasoned classic dipping sauce brings out the best in oysters for a *très luxueux* (very luxurious) appetizer.

TOTAL TRIP: 15 minutes

SERVES: 4

PROVISIONS FOR THE SAUCE

1/3 cup red wine vinegar

1 tablespoon shallot (1/2 small), finely diced

Pinch of freshly ground black pepper

1/2 teaspoon kosher salt

1/4 teaspoon granulated sugar

PROVISIONS FOR THE OYSTERS

24 oysters, raw, shucked on the half shell

2 cups rock salt, for presentation

Lemon wheels, for garnish

DIRECTIONS

1. In a small mixing bowl, add the vinegar, shallot, pepper, salt, and sugar. Mix with a spoon until the sugar and salt dissolve.
2. Plate the oysters on the rock salt, along with the sauce.
3. Garnish with lemon wheels and enjoy.

Alternate Course: Instead of the rock salt, use ice to stabilize each oyster shell. Instead of preshucked oysters, use an oyster knife. This labor of love adds 15 minutes to your prep time. (Or you could use a butter knife and add 3 hours of shucking fun, as I have experienced firsthand when I was stuck in the middle of the ocean ill prepared!)

Rogue Wave: Don't lose the oyster liquor! It's the ocean-salt bomb of flavor you do *not* want to lose if a precious oyster topples over. Remember, though, to be careful when eating raw oysters since there is an increased risk of foodborne illness.

Prince Edward Island, Canada

BEET AND GOAT CHEESE SALAD

Wouldn't you love to go beet picking together this summer on Prince Edward Island, Little Chef? We could fill our baskets with these gorgeous root vegetables. Their earthy flavor is no surprise; they are plucked right out of the dirt with bare hands. Thankfully, you can find fresh ones in your grocery store without having to get your hands dirty!

TOTAL TRIP: 1 hour

CRUISING TIME: 30 minutes

IDLE TIME: 30 minutes

SERVES: 4

PROVISIONS FOR THE BEETS AND BACON

2 whole medium beets, cleaned, skin-on

4 strips uncooked bacon

PROVISIONS FOR THE CANDIED PECANS

4 teaspoons granulated sugar

2 teaspoons water

2/3 cup pecans, roughly chopped

PROVISIONS FOR THE BALSAMIC VINAIGRETTE

1/4 cup extra virgin olive oil

4 teaspoons balsamic vinegar

2 teaspoons Dijon mustard

2 teaspoons maple syrup

1/2 teaspoon kosher salt

PROVISIONS FOR THE SALAD ASSEMBLY

6 cups baby arugula, washed, dried

2/3 cup Granny Smith apple (2/3 large), skin-on, matchstick cuts

2 tablespoons shallot (1 small), thinly sliced

1/2 cup goat cheese, crumbled

DIRECTIONS FOR THE BEETS AND BACON

1. Preheat the oven to 350°F.
2. Wrap the beets in aluminum foil, making sure to seal the edges so steam cannot escape.
3. Place the wrapped beets on a large sheet tray and bake in the oven for 1 hour or until tender.
4. On another large sheet tray, place the bacon strips in a single layer and bake for approximately 15 minutes, until crispy.
5. Meanwhile, prepare the candied pecans and balsamic vinaigrette.
6. Remove the bacon from the oven and remove excess grease by placing on a large sheet tray lined with paper towels. Cool, then crumble.
7. Remove the beets from the oven when tender. Allow to cool and then remove the skins. Slice into 1/4-inch half circles.

DIRECTIONS FOR THE CANDIED PECANS

1. In a small sauté pan, add the sugar and water. Cook over medium heat until the sugar dissolves, approximately 2 minutes.
2. Add in the pecans and continue to cook until the sugar crystalizes onto the pecans, approximately 3 minutes. Remove from heat.

DIRECTIONS FOR THE BALSAMIC VINAIGRETTE AND SALAD ASSEMBLY

1. In a small mixing bowl, add the the oil, vinegar, mustard, syrup, and salt. Mix with a fork or whisk until the vinaigrette is combined.
2. To assemble the salad, start with a bed of the arugula and top with the sliced beets, apple, shallot, goat cheese, candied pecans, and bacon crumbles.
3. Dress the salad with the vinaigrette and enjoy.

Alternate Course: Instead of the arugula, use any lettuce of your preference.

Rogue Wave: Be sure to watch the cook time of the candied pecans. Too much heat exposure burns the sugar and makes it bitter. And don't even think of using canned beets. Make fresh beets a part of your healthy diet (in moderation). If you have additional roasted beets after preparing the salad, freeze them for your next smoothie to be in the pink of health!

Prince Edward Island, Canada

MAPLE-DIJON PORK TENDERLOIN WITH ROASTED APPLES AND ACORN SQUASH

Wouldn't it be lovely if every day were as comforting as Thanksgiving? Even in the summer, the evenings in Canada are cool, so serving this dish feels like that. I like to warm the guests' bellies and hearts with this centerpiece dish on our deck table while the sun sets on the horizon. For extra ease, I marinate the pork the night before.

TOTAL TRIP: 8 hours, 45 minutes

CRUISING TIME: 45 minutes

IDLE TIME: 8 hours

SERVES: 4

PROVISIONS FOR THE MARINADE AND PORK LOIN

1/4 cup extra virgin olive oil

1/4 cup Dijon mustard

3 tablespoons maple syrup

1/4 cup apple cider

1 tablespoon kosher salt

1 teaspoon freshly ground black pepper

1 1/2 pounds pork tenderloin

PROVISIONS FOR THE APPLES AND ACORN SQUASH

4 cups acorn squash (1 medium), large diced

1 1/2 cups Granny Smith apples (2 small), large diced

1 1/2 cups yellow onion (3/4 large), medium diced

1 cup celery (2 large stalks), medium diced

1/4 cup dried cranberries

1/2 cup pecans, chopped

1 1/2 teaspoons kosher salt

1/2 teaspoon freshly ground black pepper

2 tablespoons extra virgin olive oil

1 tablespoon fresh rosemary (or 1 1/2 teaspoons dried)

1 tablespoon fresh thyme leaves (or 1 1/2 teaspoons dried)

1 tablespoon fresh flat-leaf parsley, chopped, for garnish

4 sprigs fresh rosemary, for garnish

DIRECTIONS FOR THE MARINADE AND PORK LOIN

1. In a small mixing bowl, add the olive oil, mustard, syrup, apple cider, salt, and pepper. Mix with a spoon until combined.
2. In a gallon-size plastic food-storage bag, add the pork tenderloin and pour in the marinade.
3. Let the pork marinate in the refrigerator for at least 8 hours. If prepping the night before, now is the time to go to bed since tomorrow is showtime for this showstopper.

DIRECTIONS FOR THE APPLES AND ACORN SQUASH

1. Once the pork is marinated, preheat the oven to 425°F and begin preparing the apples and acorn squash.
2. In an ungreased 9-by-13-inch casserole dish, add the squash, apples, onion, celery, cranberries, pecans, salt, pepper, olive oil, rosemary, and thyme. Stir until mixed, spreading out in the dish.

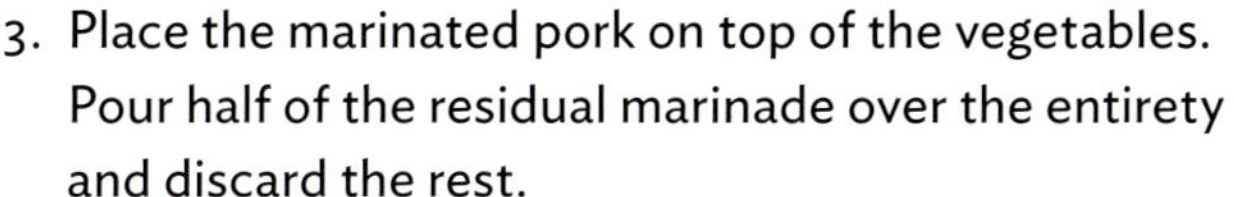

3. Place the marinated pork on top of the vegetables. Pour half of the residual marinade over the entirety and discard the rest.
4. Bake, uncovered, for 30 minutes, then increase the temperature to 475°F and cook for another 10 to 15 minutes or until the pork browns. For food safety, internal meat temperature should be a minimum of 145°F.
5. Remove the pork from the pan and let it rest for 5 to 10 minutes. Slice and plate it on top of the vegetables. Spoon juices from the pan on top of the pork.
6. Garnish with parsley and rosemary.

Alternate Course: Instead of the acorn squash, use butternut squash. Instead of the pecans, use walnuts.

Rogue Wave: Be sure not to overcook the pork, as this dries out the meat and decreases the flavor. Remember that the meat will continue to cook while it's resting. In most high-end restaurants, you'll see a slightly pink center with an internal temperature of 150°F. Check food safety guides and decide accordingly.

Prince Edward Island, Canada

STICKY TOFFEE PUDDING

There are simply no words to adequately describe this dessert. How about you make it and try to find some? Don't be surprised if, after serving this to your guests, you hear only sounds of delight rather than words coming from their lips.

TOTAL TRIP: 30 minutes

SERVES: 8

PROVISIONS FOR THE PUDDING

- 3/4 cup whole milk
- 1 1/2 cups dates, pitted, roughly chopped
- 1/3 cup salted butter (2/3 stick), softened
- 1/2 cup dark brown sugar
- 1 1/2 teaspoons vanilla extract
- 2 eggs
- 1 cup all-purpose flour
- 1 1/2 teaspoons baking powder
- 1 teaspoon baking soda
- 1/4 teaspoon kosher salt

PROVISIONS FOR THE SAUCE

- 1/3 cup heavy whipping cream
- 1/3 cup salted butter (2/3 stick)
- 1/2 cup plus 2 tablespoons dark brown sugar
- 1/4 teaspoon kosher salt
- 1 teaspoon vanilla extract

PROVISIONS FOR THE TOPPINGS

- 1/2 cup heavy whipping cream
- 2 tablespoons powdered sugar
- 1/4 cup pecans, lightly chopped

DIRECTIONS FOR THE PUDDING

1. Preheat the oven to 350°F. Grease 8 (8-ounce) ramekins or an 8-well muffin tin.
2. In a medium microwave-safe mixing bowl, microwave the milk until hot and steamy (but not burnt), approximately 2 minutes. Remove.
3. To the heated milk, add the chopped dates and let sit for 5 minutes.
4. In a large mixing bowl, add the butter and brown sugar. Use a hand mixer to beat until creamy.
5. Add in the vanilla and eggs, one at a time. Beat until combined.
6. Before adding the milk and dates to the mixture, blend with an immersion blender and then pour the milk mixture into the large mixing bowl (or transfer to a blender, blend well, and return to the large mixing bowl). Beat until combined.
7. Add the flour, baking powder, baking soda, and salt. Gently fold in with a rubber spatula.
8. Pour into greased ramekins or greased muffin tins, and bake for 12 to 15 minutes or until the center is slightly set.

DIRECTIONS FOR THE SAUCE

1. While the cake is baking, in a small pot over medium heat, add the cream, butter, brown sugar, and salt. Stirring with a wooden spoon, bring to a boil. Continue stirring for approximately 3 minutes to thicken the sauce.
2. Remove from heat. Stir in the vanilla and allow the sauce to cool slightly.

DIRECTIONS FOR THE TOPPINGS

1. While the cake is baking, prepare the whipped cream topping. In a small mixing bowl, whisk together the cream and powdered sugar. Continue whisking until stiff peaks form, approximately 3 minutes (or 30 seconds with a hand mixer on high).
2. To prepare the roasted pecan topping, place the pecans in a small sauté pan on the stovetop. Using medium heat, roast the pecans until fragrant and lightly toasted, approximately 3 minutes. Remove from heat.
3. Turn out each cake onto a plate and spoon on the toffee sauce.
4. Garnish the cakes with a dollop of the whipped cream and roasted pecans.

Throttle Control: Adjust the amount of salt in the toffee sauce to cut the sweetness based on taste preferences.

Alternate Course: Instead of the milk, use water in the cake preparation.

Rogue Wave: Be sure not to overmix the batter once the flour is added, as this will toughen the cake.

IRELAND

Dingle, Ireland

Do you feel the luck of the Irish yet, Little Chef?

We have arrived in Dingle, Ireland, a quaint and cozy place that makes you feel right at home.

My travels to the Emerald Isle hold a special place in my heart, and this has everything to do with the people. They are so . . . well . . . *Irish*! To me, *Irish* means resilient, down-to-earth, lighthearted, and friendly. That is who I am, or at least who I want to be.

I also love Ireland for the green hills that suddenly end at the water's edge with cliffs that actually scare the leprechaun right out of me. I totally understand why that famous scene in the movie *The Princess Bride* takes place at the Cliffs of Moher. The view is surreal. I remember holding on to Dad's shoulders for the confidence to peer over the edge with Mom. Others flirt with disaster as they dance along the edge, but I am from the flat coast of Florida. I am certain that the grandeur of the cliffs would trump any power of coordination that I have ever had.

In Ireland, there's always a pub nearby. Cozy up, Little Chef, in a pub "snug" (booth), where you can swap stories with newfound Irish friends, dance a jig, and sing folk songs accompanied by uilleann pipes, flutes, fiddles, and bodhráns. Cares of colossal cliffs float away, especially here in coastal Dingle, where you can watch both the ocean waves and grazing sheep outside the leaded glass windows as you order from the bar. How about a boilermaker with Irish whiskey and a pint of a malty red or robust stout side by side? Be sure to pair them with a hearty Irish stew to get warmed up doubly fast.

And don't forget the local bread! Will it be a yeast loaf of wheat or a white pan? A griddle flatbread with boxty or potato? A sweet bread like barmbrack or scone? Whatever the bread, slather it with a thick pat of fresh butter made locally from grass-fed cattle and topped with a touch of sea salt, and find that special place of cozy inside.

As the Irish folk say, "What butter and whiskey won't cure, there is no cure for." *Sláinte* to that!

The Cliffs of Moher scare the leprechaun out of me!

Dingle, Ireland

BREAKFAST

Irish Soda-Bread Scones

LUNCH

Fish and Chips

COCKTAIL HOUR

Irish Sour

Boxty with Smoked Salmon

DINNER

Irish Pub Salad

Guinness Beef Stew

Irish Cream Trifle

Dingle, Ireland

IRISH SODA-BREAD SCONES

Bake with me in true Irish spirit with these delicious breakfast treats. Mark a cross on each scone to let out the fairies or to ward off the evil spirits, the way the locals do. I am all for having some extra superpowers for the day ahead, so bring on the magic!

TOTAL TRIP: *40 minutes*

CRUISING TIME: *20 minutes*

IDLE TIME: *20 minutes*

SERVES: *8*

PROVISIONS

2 cups all-purpose flour

1/3 cup granulated sugar

2 teaspoons baking powder

1/4 teaspoon kosher salt

1/2 cup salted butter (1 stick), cold, 1/4-inch cubes

2/3 cup raisins

1 tablespoon caraway seeds

2/3 cup buttermilk

1 egg

2 tablespoons heavy whipping cream or milk, for brushing

1 teaspoon granulated sugar, for topping

DIRECTIONS

1. Preheat the oven to 375°F.
2. In a large mixing bowl, add the flour, sugar, baking powder, salt, and butter cubes. Combine with your fingers to create pea-size pieces.
3. Add the raisins and caraway seeds to the dough mixture, combining until the raisins are coated.
4. In a medium mixing bowl, whisk the buttermilk and egg.
5. Add the wet ingredients into the dry ingredients, using a rubber spatula to gently mix until just incorporated.
6. Use two spoons to shape the dough into dollops. Drop each of the 8 scones onto a large sheet pan lined with parchment paper.
7. Brush the scones with the cream or milk, and sprinkle the sugar on top. Using a knife, make a cross on top for extra superpowers.
8. Bake for 20 minutes or until golden brown.

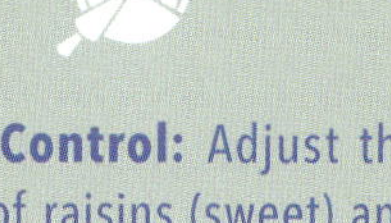

Throttle Control: Adjust the amounts of raisins (sweet) and caraway seeds (licorice flavor) based on taste preferences.

Alternate Course: Instead of dollops dropped on the baking sheet, form the scones in a triangular shape.

Rogue Wave: Be aware that overmixed dough gets chewy and dense, so gently incorporate the ingredients.

Dingle, Ireland

FISH AND CHIPS

When outside of my country, I love to make thick French fries called "chips" that are "chipped" off the potato. Serve your guests this hearty cut to keep true to Irish tradition, my friends. Actually, I should call you *mo chairde* since that is how "my friends" is said in Irish Gaelic. You'll fit right in here.

TOTAL TRIP: 45 minutes

SERVES: 4

PROVISIONS FOR THE POTATOES

4 cups peanut oil, for frying

4 russet potatoes, peeled, cut into ½-by-½-by-3-inch "chips"

8 cups ice water, for soaking potatoes

1 teaspoon kosher salt

PROVISIONS FOR THE FISH

1⅓ cups all-purpose flour, for batter, plus 1 cup more for coating

2 teaspoons baking powder

2 teaspoons garlic powder

4 teaspoons kosher salt

½ teaspoon freshly ground black pepper

2 teaspoons sweet paprika

2 eggs

1½ cups light beer, chilled

1 pound of whitefish fillet (like cod, pollock, or haddock)

1 cup peanut oil, for frying (if needed)

Malt vinegar, optional

Lemon, optional

DIRECTIONS FOR THE POTATOES

1. In a large skillet, preheat the oil to 350°F over medium-high heat.
2. In a large mixing bowl, add the potato "chips" into the ice water to remove the starch before frying. Move the potatoes around with your hands until the water is slightly cloudy. Then allow the potatoes to soak for 5 minutes. Place them to dry on a large sheet tray lined with paper towels.
3. Gently add the dry potatoes to the hot oil to fry for 5 minutes, removing with a slotted spoon before golden brown since a second fry occurs after cooling. Place on another large sheet tray lined with paper towels. Allow the fried potatoes to cool for 5 minutes.
4. Gently return the cooled potatoes back into the hot oil and fry until the chips are golden brown, approximately 5 minutes.
5. Remove the potatoes with the slotted spoon, placing on the same large sheet tray, relined with fresh paper towels. Allow the oil to drain for a hot second.
6. Once drained, remove the paper towels and place the tray of twice-fried potatoes in the oven on the lowest setting (170°F) to keep warm while quickly preparing the fish and until ready to serve.

DIRECTIONS FOR THE FISH

1. In a large mixing bowl, add the flour, baking powder, garlic powder, salt, pepper, paprika, eggs, and beer. Whisk the batter together until smooth and combined.
2. Dry the fish with a paper towel. Coat the fish in the flour that was set aside for breading, and then dip the fish into the batter.
3. In the same hot oil used to fry the potatoes (plus more if needed), gently place the battered fish into the hot oil and fry until golden brown, approximately 5 minutes, based on the thickness of the fillet.
4. Remove the fried fish with a large slotted metal spoon or tongs. Drain on a large sheet tray lined with paper towels.
5. Once drained, remove the paper towels, crank up the Celtic music, and serve the hot fish and chips with optional malt vinegar and lemon.

Alternate Course: Instead of the light beer, use any beer of your choice.

Rogue Wave: Avoid frying in oil that is too hot, as the fish and chips will burn on the outside and remain undercooked on the inside. And if the oil is not hot enough, they will be soggy.

Dingle, Ireland

IRISH SOUR

Irish whiskey dates back to the 1400s, when distillation was used primarily for medicinal purposes, but our version of the Irish Sour is a modern hit that seems to stop time and start the fun. Your guests will want to linger indefinitely while enjoying this drink, so set your cocktail hour accordingly. Here on our yacht deck, it's three o'clock in the afternoon, so we'll enjoy the happiest hour (or two) with a cocktail paired with boxty to add some *craic* (Gaelic for "fun") to our port party.

TOTAL TRIP: 10 minutes

SERVES: 4

PROVISIONS

1 cup Irish whiskey

¼ cup fresh lemon juice (2 medium lemons)

3 tablespoons simple syrup

1 teaspoon Angostura aromatic bitters (8 dashes)

4 pasteurized egg whites

1 fresh lemon, for lemon twist garnish

DIRECTIONS

1. In a large shaker, add the whiskey, lemon juice, simple syrup, bitters, and egg whites.
2. Dry shake with no ice until the egg whites are frothy, approximately 3 minutes.
3. Add a cup of ice into the shaker. Shake until the container is ice cold, approximately 1 minute.
4. Double strain with a fine-mesh strainer (optional but important for extra smoothness).
5. To create the lemon twist garnish, wash the lemon and then gently peel the exterior, trying to avoid the white pith. Use ¼-by-2-inch rinds to make 4 lemon twists (saving the lemon itself for another recipe).
6. Pour the cocktail into chilled coupe glasses. Lift them high and say, *"Sláinte!"*—to your health!

Throttle Control: Adjust the amount of simple syrup (sweet) based on taste preferences.

Rogue Wave: Be aware that the eggs are raw, so make sure to use pasteurized.

Alternate Course: Instead of using two different types of potatoes, use just one.

Dingle, Ireland

BOXTY WITH SMOKED SALMON

Made with grated and mashed potatoes, boxty is a traditional Irish potato pancake. Pan-fry some for guests and bring the sea to your table with smoked salmon on top. To finish off the boxty, add crème fraîche, sour cream's milder cousin. The combination will whisk you away to the Emerald Isle.

TOTAL TRIP: 45 minutes

CRUISING TIME: 30 minutes

IDLE TIME: 15 minutes

SERVES: 4

PROVISIONS FOR THE BOXTY

2 cups Yukon Gold potatoes (2 medium), peeled, medium diced

2 cups russet potatoes (2 medium), peeled, shredded

1/2 cup buttermilk

2 eggs

3/4 cup all-purpose flour

1 teaspoon baking powder

1 teaspoon kosher salt

1/2 teaspoon freshly ground black pepper

2 tablespoons canola oil, divided, for pan-frying

PROVISIONS FOR THE TOPPINGS

8 slices smoked salmon

1/4 cup crème fraîche

4 sprigs fresh dill

1 whole fresh lemon, cut into quarter wedges

DIRECTIONS

1. In a medium pot, add the Yukon Gold potatoes and enough water to cover them by 1 inch. Bring to a boil on high until fork-tender, 10 to 15 minutes.
2. Meanwhile, shred the raw russet potatoes using a box grater (or a food processor with a grater attachment). Spread the shredded potatoes onto a large sheet tray lined with paper towels and dry completely by pressing more paper towels on top.
3. Once the Yukon Gold potatoes are cooked, drain and use a potato masher or a fork to mash them until smooth.
4. In a medium mixing bowl, add the mashed/cooked potatoes, shredded/raw potatoes, buttermilk, and eggs. Use a fork to combine the wet ingredients.
5. In a small mixing bowl, combine the flour, baking powder, salt, and pepper. Use a fork to combine the dry ingredients.
6. Add the dry ingredients to the wet ingredients. Mix gently, just until the dry ingredients are incorporated.
7. Preheat a large skillet with 1 tablespoon of oil on medium heat.
8. Once hot, pan-fry the first of 2 batches by spooning out 4 patties in 3½-inch-diameter disks and cooking for 3 minutes on the first side and 2 minutes on the second side or until golden brown. Remove to dry on a large sheet tray lined with paper towels. Add the remaining tablespoon of the canola oil and repeat for the second batch of 4 patties.
9. Once pan-frying is complete, plate 2 boxty patties on each of the 4 serving plates.
10. Top each boxty with 1 slice of the smoked salmon, a dollop of the crème fraîche, a sprig of the dill, and a wedge of the lemon.

Dingle, Ireland

IRISH PUB SALAD

Pub salads, so colorful and healthy, add perfect lightness before (or alongside) the hearty main course. Try to have pickled beet on hand for your hungry bunch, as they keep in the refrigerator for weeks.

TOTAL TRIP: 1 hour, 30 minutes

CRUISING TIME: 30 minutes

IDLE TIME: 1 hour

SERVES: 4

PROVISIONS FOR THE PICKLED BEETS

1 whole medium beet, cleaned, skin-on

1/2 cup white vinegar

1/2 cup water

2 teaspoons kosher salt

1 tablespoon granulated sugar

PROVISIONS FOR THE SALAD DRESSING

3 tablespoons extra virgin olive oil

1 tablespoon apple cider vinegar

2 teaspoons Dijon mustard

1 teaspoon fresh chives, chopped

1 teaspoon fresh flat-leaf parsley, chopped

1 tablespoon shallot (1/2 small), small diced

1/2 teaspoon kosher salt

Pinch of freshly ground black pepper

Pinch of granulated sugar

PROVISIONS FOR THE SALAD ASSEMBLY

4 eggs

4 cups butter lettuce (1 1/2 heads), chopped

1/2 cup cherry tomatoes, cut in half

1/2 cup Irish sharp cheddar, 1/4-inch cubes

1/2 cup celery (1 large stalk), medium diced

3/4 cup English cucumber (1/2 medium), sliced in semicircles

DIRECTIONS FOR THE PICKLED BEET

1. Preheat the oven to 350°F.
2. Wrap the beet in aluminum foil, making sure to seal the edges so that steam cannot escape.
3. Place the wrapped beet on a sheet tray in the oven for 1 hour or until tender.
4. Once the beet is roasted, remove the skin and cut in 1/4-inch slices.
5. In a medium microwave-safe mixing bowl, add the beet, vinegar, water, salt, and sugar to begin the pickling process. Cook in the microwave for 4 minutes. Set aside to cool.

DIRECTIONS FOR THE SALAD DRESSING

1. While the beet is baking, in a small mixing bowl, add the olive oil, vinegar, mustard, chives, parsley, shallot, salt, pepper, and sugar. Using a fork, mix the dressing and set aside.

DIRECTIONS FOR THE EGGS AND SALAD ASSEMBLY

1. While the beet is baking, fill a small pot with 3 inches of cold water. Place the eggs into the water and bring to a boil. As soon as the water is boiling, remove from the heat.

2. Cover and let the eggs sit in the water for 12 minutes. Transfer the eggs into an ice bath to cool.
3. Once cool, peel and slice the eggs in half vertically.
4. When ready to serve the salad, in a large serving bowl, add the lettuce and drizzle the dressing on top.
5. Top the lettuce with the cherry tomatoes, Irish cheddar, celery, cucumber, boiled eggs, and pickled beet (without any pickling juice). Toss the salad.
6. Serve in individual bowls after tossing.

Throttle Control: Adjust the amount of sugar (sweet) in the pickled beet. Adjust the amounts of tomatoes, cheese, celery, cucumber, and boiled eggs, based on taste preferences. Plus, add any other raw or roasted vegetables and/or seasonings to personalize your salad even more.

Rogue Wave: Be aware that canned beets are not the same as preparing fresh roasted beets. Your time investment of 1 hour of preparation within this recipe is worth it. If you have extra roasted beets that are not pickled, freeze them for your next smoothie, healthy and pink!

Throttle Control: Adjust the amounts of tomato paste (acidic) and garlic/shallots (flavor) based on taste preferences. Adjust the amount of flour to create the desired thickness of the stew.

Alternate Course: Instead of the bacon, use 3 tablespoons of butter or oil.

Rogue Wave: Be aware that "low and slow" is key. If the meat is not tender, stewing must continue until the meat breaks down.

Dingle, Ireland

GUINNESS BEEF STEW

What brewing company makes the highest-fiber beer? Who can make this stew the fastest? Where can we find the biggest tomato? The highest, the fastest, the biggest—competing for the superlative is always fun, especially in an Irish pub. But did you know that Guinness beer is actually connected to *The Guinness Book of Records*? Recording such superlatives became a real thing when heated disputes in Irish pubs needed cooling down.

TOTAL TRIP: 3 hours, 30 minutes

CRUISING TIME: 30 minutes

IDLE TIME: 3 hours

SERVES: 4

PROVISIONS

6 strips uncooked bacon, chopped

2 pounds beef chuck roast, 1-inch cubes

1/3 cup all-purpose flour

1 teaspoon kosher salt, for chuck roast cubes

2 tablespoons salted butter (1/4 stick)

1 tablespoon garlic (4 cloves), minced

1 cup shallots (4 medium), small diced

2 cups celery (4 large stalks), medium diced

2 cups carrots (4 small), medium diced

1/2 teaspoon kosher salt, for vegetables

4 teaspoons tomato paste

4 cups beef stock

2 cups Guinness beer

2 bay leaves

3 russet potatoes, peeled, medium diced

1/4 cup flat-leaf parsley, chopped, for garnish

DIRECTIONS

1. Preheat the oven to 315°F.
2. In an unheated large oven-safe skillet, add the chopped bacon. Turn the burner to medium heat to render the bacon, stirring occasionally with tongs, approximately 8 minutes.
3. Once the bacon is crispy, turn off the heat and use a slotted spoon to transfer the bacon to a medium mixing bowl. Leave the bacon fat in the skillet for a later step.
4. Meanwhile, in a large mixing bowl, add the chuck roast cubes, flour, and salt. Using your hands, evenly coat the meat with the flour and salt.
5. Increase the skillet temperature to medium-high heat. Sear the beef in 2 batches. Use tongs to turn the beef so all sides are browned, for a total of approximately 8 minutes per batch.
6. Remove the cooked meat from the pan. Add it to the mixing bowl with the bacon.
7. In the hot skillet, sauté the butter, garlic, shallots, celery, carrots, and salt, stirring occasionally until the shallots are translucent, approximately 5 minutes.
8. To the skillet, still over medium-high heat, add the tomato paste and stir for 2 minutes.
9. Add in the beef stock, Guinness, and bay leaves. Return the bacon and beef to the skillet to complete the stew mixture. Remove from heat.
10. Cover the skillet with an oven-safe lid or aluminum foil. Bake the stew in the oven for 2 1/2 hours. Then add potatoes and continue baking for another 30 minutes, until the meat and potatoes are tender. Remove from the oven and garnish with the parsley. Serve with bread.

Dingle, Ireland

IRISH CREAM TRIFLE

There's no reason to argue about such "trifles" regarding what method works best to infuse Irish cream into this dessert. I add mine to the cream cheese mixture, but you can stick to tradition and make your trifle by soaking sponge cake or ladyfingers. It all works!

TOTAL TRIP: 30 minutes

SERVES: 4

PROVISIONS FOR THE FILLING

8 ounces cream cheese, softened

1/4 cup powdered sugar

1/4 cup Irish cream liqueur

1 tablespoon cocoa powder

PROVISIONS FOR THE WHIPPED CREAM

1 cup heavy whipping cream

1/4 cup powdered sugar

1/4 cup Irish cream liqueur

PROVISIONS FOR THE TRIFLE ASSEMBLY

16 chocolate sandwich cookies, crushed

DIRECTIONS FOR THE FILLING

1. In a small mixing bowl, add the cream cheese, powdered sugar, Irish cream, and cocoa powder. Whisk until the mixture is combined and set aside.

DIRECTIONS FOR THE WHIPPED CREAM AND TRIFLE ASSEMBLY

1. In a medium mixing bowl, add the cream, powdered sugar, and Irish cream. Whisk with a hand mixer on high until stiff peaks form, approximately 5 minutes.
2. In each of 4 serving glasses, create the trifle, layering with the crushed cookies, then the cheesecake mixture, then the whipped cream. Repeat the layers to fill the glass. Finish with crushed cookies for garnish.

Throttle Control: Adjust the amounts of powdered sugar and liqueur (sweet) based on taste preferences.

GERMANY
Ostseebad Heikendorf
Möltenort

Kiel, Germany

Guten tag! Good day, Little Chef!

We've arrived in one of my favorite places on planet Earth: Germany. What a feast for the eyes—and the belly. I admire how its people care for their pristine land and how they proudly prepare regional foods that satisfy my appetite as well as my soul. I feel alive when I'm here.

My family and I visit some of our dear German friends as often as we can; the experience feeds me. They've welcomed us every summer since I was ten. We backpack through Germany and the surrounding countries on a shoestring budget—but never without the richness of breathtaking vistas and bountiful meals. My favorite? Pork and potatoes . . . with *das Bier* and a hearty *"Prost!"* of course.

Why not continue the tradition? You can start with a port crawl in Kiel, Germany, where clear-water coastlines meet up with the North and Baltic Seas. The sea air, cool and crisp, is therapy for the weary traveler. Grab a bench with the locals in an open-air *biergarten* to order a delicious German meal. I'm always down for pork schnitzel with warm potato salad, along with a massively large pretzel (*Brezel*), crusty on the outside and soft on the inside. Whole-grain mustard, the local dipping sauce here, adds to the experience. I highly recommend that you order a liter of your favorite beer as part of this tradition, Little Chef! Try my culinary ritual: savor, swallow, then swig. Food has a way of tasting even better when followed by a swig of its national brew.

This chef is in sausage heaven here.

Try some bratwurst and sundry sausages (along with sauerkraut, I suggest) to conjure up your own Oktoberfest in your galley tonight. Fill your stein! Maybe you'll even make your own *Brezel* and create new knot shapes that celebrate the nautical "ties" to this robust land. I dare you to try some pretzel knots like these.

Kiel, Germany

BREAKFAST

Muesli Breakfast Bars

LUNCH

Cabbage Rolls

COCKTAIL HOUR

Radler

Schnitzel Sliders

DINNER

Cucumber and Dill Salad

Crispy Pork Knuckles with Braised Red Cabbage

Apple Marzipan Cake

Kiel, Germany

MUESLI BREAKFAST BARS

Get up and go! This take-off-the-boat breakfast comes in super handy when guests are up early to sightsee. Muesli is the perfect blend of oats, seeds, nuts, and dried fruits, all bound together in bar form thanks to nut butter and honey. This recipe makes many bars, so freeze some for the next outing.

TOTAL TRIP: 1 hour, 15 minutes

CRUISING TIME: 15 minutes

IDLE TIME: 1 hour

SERVES: 8

PROVISIONS FOR THE MUESLI BARS

2/3 cup almond butter

2/3 cup honey

2 cups old-fashioned oats

1/2 cup dried cranberries

1/3 cup raisins

1/2 cup unsweetened coconut, shredded

1/3 cup pepitas

1/2 cup almonds, roughly chopped

3 tablespoons sesame seeds

1/2 teaspoon ground cinnamon

Pinch of kosher salt

PROVISIONS FOR THE YOGURT GLAZE

1/4 cup plain Greek yogurt, room temperature

1/2 cup powdered sugar

1/8 teaspoon almond extract

1/8 teaspoon vanilla extract

DIRECTIONS FOR THE MUESLI BARS

1. In a small pot over medium-low heat, add the almond butter and honey. Begin stirring with a wooden spoon as the mixture heats up to a simmer. Continue to stir to avoid burning as the mixture thickens and simmers. Then continue to thicken for 1 more minute. Remove from heat.
2. In a large mixing bowl, add the oats, cranberries, raisins, coconut, pepitas, almonds, sesame seeds, cinnamon, and salt. Mix together.
3. Add the almond butter–honey mixture to the dry mixture in the large mixing bowl. Quickly stir to coat all of the ingredients before the honey cools and hardens.
4. Press the mixture into an ungreased 9-by-9-inch square cake pan, making sure the mixture is flat and even.
5. Cover with plastic wrap and place the pan in the refrigerator to cool completely, approximately 1 hour.
6. Once cool, remove the bars from the refrigerator and cut into rectangles.

DIRECTIONS FOR THE YOGURT GLAZE

1. In a small mixing bowl, add the yogurt, powdered sugar, almond extract, and vanilla extract. Whisk until smooth.
2. When the bars have cooled, drizzle with the yogurt glaze.

Alternate Course: Instead of the raisins and cranberries, use any dried fruit of your choice. Instead of the almonds and pepitas (roasted, salted pumpkin seed kernels), go nuts with any variety!

Kiel, Germany

CABBAGE ROLLS

Cabbage is so underrated and deserves to be elevated to celebrity status. Low in cost but high in nutritional value, this cruciferous vegetable is a staple in my galley refrigerator. Rich in fiber and vitamins C and K, cabbage was historically used by European sailors to prevent scurvy during long sea voyages.

TOTAL TRIP: 1 hour, 15 minutes

CRUISING TIME: 45 minutes

IDLE TIME: 30 minutes

SERVES: 4

PROVISIONS FOR THE CABBAGE ROLL

- 1 head green cabbage
- 2 cups white bread, 1/2-inch cubes
- 1/2 cup whole milk
- 1 pound ground beef
- 1 cup yellow onion (1/2 medium), small diced
- 1 egg, beaten
- 1 teaspoon kosher salt
- 1/2 teaspoon freshly ground black pepper
- 1 teaspoon garlic powder
- 1 teaspoon paprika
- 1 teaspoon caraway seeds
- 1/2 teaspoon marjoram
- 1/2 cup plain bread crumbs
- 1/4 cup salted butter (1/2 stick), divided, for frying
- 1/4 cup fresh flat-leaf parsley, chopped, for garnish

PROVISIONS FOR THE SAUCE

- 2 cups beef stock
- 1 tablespoon cornstarch
- 1 tablespoon water

DIRECTIONS FOR THE CABBAGE ROLL

1. Fill a large pot 3/4 full with water and bring to a boil.
2. Prepare the cabbage for boiling by using a knife to cut out the core at the bottom of the head while keeping the leaves attached. Place the cored whole cabbage into the boiling water. After 5 minutes, use tongs to remove the large outer leaves as they soften. Continue boiling, removing the layers of leaves as they soften over the next 5 minutes, until 12 to 15 leaves are extracted. Place on a large sheet tray and let cool (save the smaller leaves to throw into any future soup to ward off scurvy).
3. In a medium mixing bowl, add the bread cubes, and pour the milk over them to soak. Use your hands to mush the bread into a paste.
4. Add the beef, onion, egg, salt, pepper, garlic powder, paprika, caraway seeds, marjoram, and bread crumbs to the bowl. Mix with your hands until the filling is blended.
5. To assemble each cabbage roll, use 1 leaf and fill with 1/3 cup of the filling. Like a burrito wrap, fold the 2 sides inward to cover the filling and then roll up. Tie up each roll with kitchen twine and, after drying the large sheet tray, return the tied cabbage rolls to it.
6. In a large skillet over medium-high heat, melt half of the butter for the first batch. Once melted, use tongs to add the cabbage rolls and cook until browned, approximately 2 minutes on each side. Return to the sheet tray and repeat the process with the second batch.

Alternate Course: Instead of the ground beef, use ground pork, chicken, or turkey.

DIRECTIONS FOR THE SAUCE

1. Once the cabbage rolls are browned, return them all to the skillet and add the beef stock. Cover and simmer over medium heat for 10 minutes or until the filling is fully cooked through.
2. Once cooked, turn off the heat and remove the cabbage rolls, setting them on the clean, large sheet tray while you finish the sauce in the skillet.
3. In a small mixing bowl, combine the cornstarch and water to make a slurry. Add the slurry into the skillet, returning the heat to medium. Stir until bubbly and thick, 2 to 4 minutes, then reduce the heat to low.
4. Return the cabbage rolls to the sauce to briefly reheat. Use tongs to flip the cabbage rolls until evenly coated in the sauce.
5. Using kitchen shears, remove the kitchen twine and serve the cabbage rolls on a platter, spooning extra sauce over the rolls and garnishing with the parsley.

RADLER

What a rad term! *Radler* is German for "cyclist." As the story goes, a bunch of bicyclists in the 1920s needed a light libation after their ride in the Bavarian countryside. The combination of beer with lemon soda provided the perfect solution to stretch the amount of beer that was available. How genius! And how refreshing!

TOTAL TRIP: 1 minute

SERVES: 4

PROVISIONS

8 cups German beer, refrigerated

4 cups lemon-lime or grapefruit soda, refrigerated

DIRECTIONS

1. In a pitcher, combine the beer and soda.
2. Pour into steins, lift them high, and toast with a "*Prost!*"

Throttle Control: Adjust the amount of soda (sweet) based on taste preferences.

Alternate Course: Instead of the German beer, use any wheat beer such as a lager, but make sure to look someone in the eye as you make a toast with a "*Prost!*" to Germany.

SCHNITZEL SLIDERS

Say that three times fast! Schnitzel sliders will have you tongue-tied. What won't be difficult, though, is getting the pork dredged (coated) for the shallow-frying process. It's as simple as 1, 2, 3. This crowd-pleasing appetizer is worth yodeling about. *Guten appetit!*

TOTAL TRIP: 45 minutes

SERVES: 4

PROVISIONS FOR THE AIOLI

1/4 cup whole-grain mustard

1/4 cup mayonnaise

1 tablespoon fresh lemon juice (1/2 medium lemon)

PROVISIONS FOR THE DREDGING

Bowl 1

1 cup all-purpose flour

2 teaspoons kosher salt

1 teaspoon freshly ground black pepper

Bowl 2

2 eggs, beaten

Bowl 3

1 cup plain bread crumbs

PROVISIONS FOR THE SCHNITZEL

1 pound pork cutlets, thinly sliced

2 cups canola oil, for frying

1/2 teaspoon finishing salt, for sprinkling

PROVISIONS FOR THE SLIDER ASSEMBLY

8 pretzel slider buns

1 cup baby arugula

1 whole fresh lemon, cut into quarter wedges

DIRECTIONS FOR THE AIOLI

1. In a small mixing bowl, add the mustard, mayonnaise, and lemon juice. Stir with a spoon until the aioli is blended.

DIRECTIONS FOR DREDGING AND PREPARING THE SCHNITZEL

1. In a large skillet, preheat the oil to 350°F over medium-low heat.
2. Gather 3 small kitchen bowls for dredging. In the first bowl, mix the flour, salt, and pepper. In the second bowl, whisk the eggs. In the third bowl, add the bread crumbs.
3. Prepare the pork cutlets for dredging, cutting them into 2 1/2-by-2 1/2-inch pieces. Place the pork pieces between 2 pieces of plastic wrap and beat with a meat hammer (or the bottom of a heavy pot) until each is 1/8- to 1/4-inch thick.
4. Coat each piece with the flour mixture (bowl 1) and shake before dipping into the beaten eggs (bowl 2). Allow excess egg to drain off and then coat with the bread crumbs (bowl 3). Repeat and lay each dredged piece onto a sheet tray in a single layer.
5. Using tongs, place the cutlets into the hot oil, making sure to keep them a single layer so the skillet is not overcrowded. Shallow-fry each side for approximately 1 minute or until golden brown.
6. Remove from the oil and drain on a sheet tray lined with paper towels. Immediately sprinkle with the finishing salt. Repeat the frying process for each batch of pork.

DIRECTIONS FOR THE SLIDER ASSEMBLY

1. Spread the aioli on the inside of each of the slider buns. Place the arugula next, followed by the pork schnitzel, and then the bun top.
2. Serve hot with one of the lemon wedges on the side.

Alternate Course: Instead of the pork, use chicken breasts or veal cutlets.

Kiel, Germany

CUCUMBER AND DILL SALAD

Dilly, dilly, dilly do! I always incorporate dill in German salads, vegetable dishes, seafood meals, and herb butter. With a taste similar to celery and anise mixed together, dill makes cucumbers come to life, especially when fresh. I love to grow it on the windowsill in my yacht galley.

TOTAL TRIP: 10 minutes

SERVES: 4

PROVISIONS

2 cups English cucumbers (1 large), sliced in semicircles

2/3 cup sour cream

4 teaspoons apple cider vinegar

2 tablespoons fresh dill, chopped, for the dressing

1 teaspoon granulated sugar

1 1/2 teaspoons kosher salt

1 teaspoon freshly ground black pepper

4 sprigs fresh dill, for garnish

DIRECTIONS

1. In a medium mixing bowl, add the cucumbers, sour cream, vinegar, dill, sugar, salt, and pepper. Stir with a spoon to combine.
2. Serve immediately at room temperature or place in the refrigerator to serve cold later, garnishing with fresh dill.

Kiel, Germany

CRISPY PORK KNUCKLES WITH BRAISED RED CABBAGE

This isn't your average cut of pork, but it is nonetheless available in regular grocery stores. Sometimes called a pork shank or a ham hock, pork knuckle is a fistful of flavorful, with fatty yet delicate meat hiding beneath a crusty exterior and bold look. You, like my guests, will probably opt to use your hands to fully enjoy devouring this succulent meat. I say go for it!

TOTAL TRIP: 4 hours

CRUISING TIME: 30 minutes

IDLE TIME: 3 hours, 30 minutes

SERVES: 4

PROVISIONS FOR THE PORK KNUCKLES

4 pounds pork knuckles (4 small), bone-in

1 large yellow onion, cut into quarters

5 cloves garlic, peeled

3 bay leaves

2 tablespoons kosher salt

1 teaspoon caraway seeds

1 teaspoon fennel seeds

1/2 teaspoon whole black peppercorns

5 allspice cloves

Water, to cover pork

PROVISIONS FOR THE ROASTING BROTH

1 cup pork broth, reserved from boiling the pork in water

1 1/2 cups German beer

PROVISIONS FOR THE PORK SEASONING

2 tablespoons extra virgin olive oil

1 1/2 teaspoons kosher salt

1/2 teaspoon freshly ground black pepper

1 teaspoon garlic powder

PROVISIONS FOR THE CABBAGE

6 strips uncooked bacon, sliced into 1/4-inch portions

8 cups red cabbage (1 medium), thinly sliced

2 cups Granny Smith apples (2 medium), peeled, cubed

1/2 cup apple cider vinegar

1/4 cup water (plus more if needed)

1/2 cup light brown sugar

2 teaspoons kosher salt

1 teaspoon freshly ground black pepper

8 whole cloves

DIRECTIONS FOR THE PORK KNUCKLES, ROASTING BROTH, AND PORK SEASONING

1. In a large pot, add the pork knuckles, onion, garlic, bay leaves, salt, caraway seeds, fennel seeds, peppercorns, and allspice cloves and enough water to cover the pork by 1/2 inch.
2. Cover the pot and simmer the pork over medium heat for 60 minutes, adding water as needed to keep the knuckles covered. After 45 minutes, preheat the oven to 300°F.
3. After 60 minutes, remove the knuckles to a cutting board. Pour the reserved pork broth into an 11-by-15-inch roasting pan. Add the beer.
4. Use a slotted spoon to retrieve the onion and garlic from the pot and add to the pork broth and beer in the roasting pan.
5. Use a sharp knife to score the skin of the pork with shallow, diagonal cuts in two directions

to create a crisscrossed, $^1/_2$-inch diamond pattern. Then drizzle with the olive oil and season with the salt, pepper, and garlic powder.

6. Place a roasting rack on top of the liquid (or place several whole carrots in the pan if without a rack) in the roasting pan. Place the pork on the rack (or carrots). The pork should be above the liquid.
7. Bake the pork for $1^1/_2$ hours, basting every 30 minutes.
8. Turn the temperature up to 475°F and bake for another 20 to 30 minutes or until the pork is crispy. Check at 5-minute intervals to ensure there is no burning.
9. Start the red cabbage preparation in the meantime, but be sure to remove the pork when crisp.

DIRECTIONS FOR THE CABBAGE

1. In an unheated large skillet, add the sliced bacon. Turn the heat to medium to render the bacon, stirring occasionally, approximately 8 minutes.
2. Once the bacon is crispy, add in the red cabbage and apples. Sauté together for 5 minutes.
3. Add in the vinegar, water, brown sugar, salt, pepper, and cloves. Cover and braise for 30 minutes over medium-low heat, stirring occasionally. Add more water if needed.
4. Remove the cloves and plate the cabbage. Place the pork knuckles on top.
5. Feast!

Alternate Course: Instead of crisping the pork in the oven, fry the pork in oil on the stovetop to make it extra crispy.

Rogue Wave: Avoid a scrawny bite by getting a pork knuckle that is extra meaty, such as the rear leg portion.

Kiel, Germany

APPLE MARZIPAN CAKE

When I am in Germany, I find marzipan everywhere. Marzipan is a smooth, pliable paste made of almonds and sugar with a 1:2 ratio. Almond paste, with a 1:1 ratio of almonds and sugar, is understandably coarser but has a richer nuttiness. Either way, the almond flavor comes through. This recipe makes extra for the freezer, ready for the next celebration.

TOTAL TRIP: 1 hour, 30 minutes

CRUISING TIME: 30 minutes

IDLE TIME: 1 hour

SERVES: 8

PROVISIONS FOR THE CAKE

3/4 cup almond paste, or marzipan

1 cup salted butter (2 sticks), softened

2/3 cup granulated sugar

1 teaspoon vanilla extract

1 teaspoon ground cinnamon

1/4 teaspoon kosher salt

1/2 cup whole milk

4 eggs, beaten

1 2/3 cups all-purpose flour

1 tablespoon baking powder

PROVISIONS FOR THE APPLE-ALMOND TOPPING

2 cups Granny Smith apples (2 large), peeled, sliced

2 tablespoons fresh lemon juice (1 medium lemon)

1/2 cup almonds, sliced

2 tablespoons powdered sugar, for dusting

DIRECTIONS FOR THE CAKE

1. Preheat the oven to 350°F. Grease a 9-inch round springform pan (or a 9-inch round cake pan).
2. In a large mixing bowl, add the almond paste (or marzipan), butter, and sugar. Beat with a hand mixer until creamy, approximately 5 minutes.
3. Once light and fluffy, add in the vanilla, cinnamon, salt, milk, and eggs. Beat to combine for 1 additional minute.
4. In a medium mixing bowl, add the flour and baking powder. Whisk to blend the dry ingredients.
5. Add the dry ingredients into the large mixing bowl with the wet ingredients. Gently fold in with a rubber spatula until the batter is just combined.
6. Pour the batter into the greased pan.

DIRECTIONS FOR THE APPLE-ALMOND TOPPING

1. In a small mixing bowl, toss the apples in the lemon juice to coat.
2. Place the apples on top of the batter in a circular pattern. Discard the lemon juice.
3. Sprinkle the almonds on top.
4. Bake for 60 minutes or until a toothpick inserted comes out clean.
5. Remove the cake from the oven and let it cool before unmolding from the pan and dusting with the powdered sugar.
6. Cut into 8 slices and serve.

Alternate Course: Instead of the almond paste that is readily available, use marzipan if you can find it. Rest assured, both almond paste and marzipan work wonders in showcasing an awesome almond flavor.

FRANCE

Nice, France

You gotta love the French way of living. *Joie de vivre* works for me, as I find "joy in life" wherever it takes me.

Our next port of call is Nice, France, the ultimate destination for those who live the good life (but very discreetly, of course). Yachts are everywhere on the French Riviera and are part of the rich experience of this Mediterranean region.

Take in the scene with me, Little Chef: Art deco buildings line the labyrinthine lanes. Baroque church steeples aspire to reach the sky. Old Town markets spread out sun-kissed fruits and vegetables under striped yellow tents. Wide-tired bikes with fresh flowers in their baskets lean against lampposts. Bright-blue beach umbrellas with fancy white tassels dance in the ocean breeze.

Colors and shapes intensify as the last rays of light hit the horizon. Beautiful people, strolling and sipping, complete this masterpiece that is painted in front of us.

From the galley window, this view of the French Riviera is a dream. I imagine myself as an artist conjuring this Mediterranean landscape into reality as I look out from the kitchen galley—the window trim serving as the perfect frame.

French ingredients are the tools we will use to create a masterfully *magnifique* meal. I love to sample different wines as I cook. And I always ask my guests if they want to join me in the fun if they are in the kitchen with me. Try a few of the top grape varieties planted in the country to complement your French meal: merlot, ugni blanc, grenache, Syrah, cabernet sauvignon, pinot noir, chardonnay, sauvignon blanc, cabernet franc, Carignan.

And don't forget to throw in a sparkling wine from Champagne to make any meal a special occasion!

Mangez bien, riez souvent, aimez beaucoup. Eat well, laugh often, love a lot.

Even our mascot Thurston approves of the French Riviera tablescape.

Nice, France

BREAKFAST

Quiche Lorraine

LUNCH

Fish en Papillote with Fennel

COCKTAIL HOUR

French 75

Coquilles Saint-Jacques

DINNER

French Onion Soup

Seared Duck Breast with Poppy Seed Salad

Chocolate Éclairs

Nice, France

QUICHE LORRAINE

I don't think you could ever go wrong with putting your eggs in one basket when rich cream and a flaky pastry are involved. The French are lucky to claim the quiche as their own, as "Lorraine" in the title originates from the lovely region of the same name in the northeast part of France. Here we elevate the wonderfulness with Gruyère cheese, a real crowd-pleaser on the yacht.

TOTAL TRIP: 1 hour, 15 minutes

CRUISING TIME: 30 minutes

IDLE TIME: 45 minutes

SERVES: 8

PROVISIONS

1 frozen 9-inch deep-dish piecrust

4 strips uncooked bacon, chopped

3/4 cup shallots (3 medium), small diced

5 eggs

1 1/3 cups heavy whipping cream

3/4 teaspoon kosher salt

Pinch of cayenne pepper

Pinch of ground nutmeg

3/4 cup Gruyère cheese, shredded

1/4 cup fresh flat-leaf parsley, chopped, for garnish

DIRECTIONS

1. Preheat the oven to 375°F.
2. Poke holes in the bottom of the frozen piecrust with a fork, then prebake the crust for 10 minutes.
3. While the piecrust is prebaking, in an unheated large skillet, add the chopped bacon. Turn on medium heat to render the bacon until crispy, stirring occasionally with a wooden spoon, approximately 8 minutes.
4. Remove the piecrust from the oven and set aside.
5. Add the shallots to the bacon and drippings in the skillet. Sauté, stirring occasionally with a wooden spoon until the shallots are translucent, approximately 5 minutes.
6. Remove from heat and allow to cool for 5 minutes.
7. Once cool, transfer the bacon, shallots, and drippings to a medium mixing bowl. Add the eggs, cream, salt, cayenne pepper, nutmeg, and cheese and whisk until the quiche filling is combined.
8. Pour the quiche filling into the piecrust.
9. Return the filled piecrust to the oven and bake for 40 minutes or until the center is just slightly set.
10. Allow to cool for 10 minutes. Garnish with parsley, then serve hot or cold.

Rogue Wave: Be sure to watch the crust to ensure it does not burn. To prevent this, place a ring of aluminum foil around the edge of the piecrust.

Nice, France

FISH EN PAPILLOTE WITH FENNEL

Parchment paper, the "papillote" part of this dish's name, provides the magic. This is such a special fish preparation! If you wrapped me up in a warm blanket with some wine and butter, I would be tender too. Guests love this French specialty. The fish just melts in your mouth.

TOTAL TRIP: 40 minutes

CRUISING TIME: 20 minutes

IDLE TIME: 20 minutes

SERVES: 4

PROVISIONS

3 cups fennel (1 bulb), thinly sliced

1½ cups shallots (6 medium), thinly sliced

1½ teaspoons garlic (2 cloves), minced

2 pounds whitefish (like flounder, halibut, cod, or sea bass), cut into 4 portions

1 teaspoon kosher salt, divided

1 fresh lemon, unpeeled, thinly sliced

1 fresh blood orange, unpeeled, thinly sliced

¼ cup salted butter (½ stick), cut into 4 equal pieces

4 sprigs fresh thyme (or 1 teaspoon dried)

½ cup dry white wine

¼ cup fresh flat-leaf parsley, chopped, for garnish, as desired

DIRECTIONS

1. Preheat the oven to 400°F.
2. On a large baking sheet, create 4 "packages" for the fish, using four 12-by-15-inch pieces of parchment paper. Distribute the fennel, shallots, and garlic evenly onto each package, making sure the mixture is 3 inches off-center on the parchment for the proper folding process in step 6.
3. Place each portion of the fish on top of the bed of the fennel, shallots, and garlic.
4. Season each package with ¼ teaspoon of the salt. Then shingle the lemon and orange slices equally on top of each piece of fish.
5. On top of the shingled fruit, add 1 piece of butter and 1 sprig of the thyme to each packet.
6. To ensure that the package is sealed properly to steam the fish, fold the parchment paper over the contents so that the two edges of paper come together. Then, just like an empanada is sealed into a semicircle, make 1-inch folds inward and continue crimping until three-quarters of the package is sealed. At this point, pour 2 tablespoons of the wine into each package, and then finish the crimps until the mixture is completely sealed.
7. Bake for 15 to 20 minutes or until the fish is cooked through and flakes easily with a fork.
8. Once done, remove from the oven and transfer each package onto an individual plate. Provide a knife or scissors so guests can cut open the packages to release the steam and to add the parsley as desired.

Alternate Course: Instead of the fennel, use thinly sliced potatoes. Instead of the white wine, use chicken stock. Instead of the blood orange, use any variety of orange.

Rogue Wave: Be sure not to overcook the fish, as it will lose its buttery beautifulness. Pay attention to the thickness of the fish to adjust the baking time accordingly. If you have to check for doneness, make sure to reseal the package so that the steaming process remains in effect. As soon as the fish flakes with a fork, it's done.

Nice, France

FRENCH 75

You'll feel the power of the French 75, just as you would when firing a 75mm howitzer field gun back in 1915. That's the connection! Make sure to keep this in mind when partaking of this potent potion of champagne and gin that is booming with history.

TOTAL TRIP: 10 minutes

SERVES: 4

PROVISIONS

1 fresh lemon, unpeeled, whole

1/2 cup gin

1/4 cup fresh lemon juice (2 medium lemons)

1/4 cup simple syrup

2 cups champagne

DIRECTIONS

1. Wash the whole lemon and then gently peel the yellow exterior, trying to avoid the white pith. Use 1/4-inch-wide by 2-inch-long rinds to make 4 lemon twists. Save for garnishing.
2. Squeeze the peeled lemon for the lemon juice in the cocktail.
3. In a pitcher with ice, add the gin, lemon juice, simple syrup, and champagne.
4. With a long spoon, stir to combine.
5. Serve in flute glasses and garnish each glass with one of the lemon twists. *Santé!* Cheers!

Vineyards make chefs (and guests) so happy.

Nice, France

COQUILLES SAINT-JACQUES

What a glamorous name for scallops, right? Coquilles Saint-Jacques is beautifully French. The simplicity of this dish parallels the simplicity of the original Saint-Jacques, also known as Saint-James, a saintly pilgrim who reportedly used a scallop shell to collect simple food and drink.

TOTAL TRIP: 45 minutes

CRUISING TIME: 30 minutes

IDLE TIME: 15 minutes

SERVES: 4

PROVISIONS FOR THE SCALLOPS

1 pound sea scallops (12 large)

2 teaspoons kosher salt

3 tablespoons salted butter (3/8 stick)

PROVISIONS FOR THE SAUCE

1/4 cup salted butter (1/2 stick)

3/4 cup shallots (3 medium), small diced

2 cups white button mushrooms (8 ounces), thinly sliced

1/2 teaspoon kosher salt

Pinch of freshly ground black pepper

2/3 cup dry white wine

1/2 cup heavy whipping cream

4 teaspoons fresh tarragon, chopped

1 teaspoon fresh lemon zest (1/2 medium lemon)

1 egg yolk

Pinch of cayenne pepper

PROVISIONS FOR THE ASSEMBLY

1/4 cup Gruyère cheese, shredded

12 scallop shells, for presentation

2 sprigs fresh tarragon, for garnish

DIRECTIONS FOR THE SCALLOPS

1. On a large sheet tray lined with paper towels, place the scallops in a single layer and season with the salt. Let the scallops rest for 10 minutes to draw out the moisture.
2. After 10 minutes, pat the scallops dry with paper towels.
3. Heat a large skillet over high heat. Once hot, quickly add the butter. Add the scallops immediately to the sizzling butter to sear.
4. Cook for approximately 2 minutes on each side, turning with tongs, until golden brown and just cooked through. Remove the scallops from the skillet to a plate.

DIRECTIONS FOR THE SAUCE

1. In the same skillet, melt the butter over medium heat, and add the shallots. Cook until they are translucent, about 3 minutes, using a wooden spoon to stir occasionally.
2. Add the sliced mushrooms, salt, and pepper. Cook and stir until the mushrooms are soft and any liquid has evaporated, 5 to 7 minutes.
3. Pour in the wine and bring to a simmer. Cook until the wine has reduced by half, approximately 5 minutes, stirring occasionally.
4. Stir in the cream, tarragon, and lemon zest.
5. Simmer and stir for another 2 to 3 minutes, until the sauce thickens slightly. Turn off the heat and set aside.

Alternate Course: Instead of using the individual scallop shells, use oven-safe ramekins. Or use a cast-iron skillet for a communal plating of the dish.

6. In a small mixing bowl, whisk together the egg yolk and cayenne pepper.
7. Slowly add a few tablespoons of the warmed sauce to the egg yolk mixture, whisking constantly to temper the yolk.
8. Turn on the heat again to medium. Gradually whisk the egg yolk mixture back into the skillet with the sauce.
9. Reduce the heat to low and cook for another 1 to 2 minutes, stirring constantly, until the sauce thickens further without boiling. Remove from the heat.

DIRECTIONS FOR THE ASSEMBLY

1. Preheat the broiler.
2. Place the cooked scallops (along with their juices on the plate) into the sauce, using a spoon to gently coat each scallop.
3. Arrange the scallop shells on a large sheet pan and then place 1 scallop and a bit of the sauce mixture into each shell.
4. Evenly sprinkle the shredded cheese over the top of each filled scallop shell.
5. Place the baking sheet under the broiler for 2 to 3 minutes, until the cheese is bubbly and golden brown.
6. Serve immediately, garnishing with additional tarragon.

Alternate Course: Instead of the traditional Gruyère and Parmesan cheese pairing, use mozzarella for extra gooeyness.

Rogue Wave: Be aware that "low and slow" is key. If the onions are hastily heated, they will burn and lose the sweet flavor that occurs only with caramelization. The same is true with watching the heat of the cheeses under the broiler. Avoid burning the cheeses by checking the broiler every few seconds. The moment the cheeses are bubbly and golden brown, remove from the oven.

Nice, France

FRENCH ONION SOUP

French bread soaking up oniony, cheesy, beefy broth—could there be anything more satisfying in a soup? This is an absolute must in my kitchen, both at home and on the yacht. Experience the sublime. May your appetite be completely satisfied. *Bon appétit!*

TOTAL TRIP: 1 hour, 30 minutes

CRUISING TIME: 30 minutes

IDLE TIME: 1 hour

SERVES: 4

PROVISIONS FOR THE SOUP

4 tablespoons salted butter (1/2 stick)

10 cups sweet onions (5 medium), 1/4-inch julienne cut

2 teaspoons kosher salt

1 tablespoon garlic (4 cloves), minced

1 cup dry white wine

6 cups beef stock

2 bay leaves

4 sprigs fresh thyme (or 1 teaspoon dried)

1/2 teaspoon freshly ground black pepper

2 teaspoons Worcestershire sauce

1 tablespoon dry sherry

PROVISIONS FOR THE ASSEMBLY

1 loaf of French bread, sliced

2 cups Gruyère cheese, grated

1 1/2 cups Parmesan cheese, grated

Sprigs of fresh thyme (or dried), for garnish

DIRECTIONS FOR THE SOUP

1. In a large pot, melt the butter over medium heat. Add the onions and salt. With a wooden spoon, stir to coat the onions with the butter.
2. Cook the onions, stirring occasionally, until they become soft and caramelized, 30 to 40 minutes. Make sure to stir more frequently toward the end to prevent burning.
3. After the onions are caramelized, add the garlic and cook for another 2 minutes.
4. Pour in the wine, stirring to deglaze the pot and loosen any browned bits from the bottom. Cook until the wine is reduced by half, approximately 5 minutes.
5. Add the beef stock, bay leaves, thyme sprigs, and pepper.
6. Bring the soup to a simmer and cook for 20 to 30 minutes, allowing the flavors to meld.
7. Remove the bay leaves and thyme sprigs from the soup.
8. Stir in the Worcestershire sauce and sherry.

DIRECTIONS FOR THE ASSEMBLY

1. Preheat the oven to broil.
2. Ladle the hot soup into soup crocks or other oven-safe bowls.
3. Place a slice of the bread on top of each bowl of soup.
4. Evenly distribute the cheeses over the bread.
5. Set the bowls on a large sheet tray and place under the broiler.
6. Broil until the cheeses are melted, bubbly, and golden brown, 2 to 4 minutes.
7. Remove from the oven and garnish with fresh thyme sprigs to serve.

Nice, France

SEARED DUCK BREAST WITH POPPY SEED SALAD

If you have never tried duck, you should. One bite of the full-bodied flavor will melt away any misgivings you may have. So tender, so earthy, duck is a French favorite for good reason. Savor this regional delicacy with light greens and fresh berries to balance out the richness.

TOTAL TRIP: 40 minutes

SERVES: 4

PROVISIONS FOR THE SALAD DRESSING

- 1/4 cup extra virgin olive oil
- 1 tablespoon red wine vinegar
- 2 teaspoons Dijon mustard
- 1 tablespoon granulated sugar
- 1/2 teaspoon kosher salt
- Pinch of freshly ground black pepper
- 1/2 teaspoon poppy seeds
- 1 teaspoon mayonnaise

PROVISIONS FOR THE SALAD

- 6 cups spring mix lettuce
- 1 cup fresh blackberries (14 medium), halved vertically
- 1/4 cup radishes (2 large), sliced
- 1/4 cup pecans, chopped
- 1/4 cup Gorgonzola cheese, crumbled
- 1/4 cup red onion (1/8 medium), sliced

PROVISIONS FOR THE DUCK

- 4 duck breasts, skin-on, boneless
- 4 teaspoons herbes de Provence
- 4 teaspoons kosher salt
- 2 tablespoons salted butter (1/4 stick)
- 2 tablespoons honey

DIRECTIONS FOR THE SALAD DRESSING AND THE SALAD

1. In a small mixing bowl, add the oil, vinegar, mustard, sugar, salt, pepper, poppy seeds, and mayonnaise. Whisk until well combined. Set aside the salad dressing.
2. In a large serving bowl, add the lettuce, blackberries, radishes, pecans, Gorgonzola, and onion. Set aside the salad.

DIRECTIONS FOR THE DUCK AND ASSEMBLY

1. To begin the duck preparation, use a sharp knife to score the fatty-skin side of the duck with shallow diagonal cuts in two directions to create a crisscrossed, 1/2-inch diamond pattern.
2. Using your hands, rub each side of the breasts with the herbes de Provence and salt.
3. In an unheated large skillet, place the breasts skin side down. Then begin rendering the duck over medium heat. Cook until the skin is crispy and golden brown, 8 to 10 minutes, occasionally draining off the fat into a bowl as needed.

4. Use tongs to turn the breasts over and cook for an additional 4 to 6 minutes on the other side. Once the internal temperature is 130°F, set the duck on a large sheet tray and allow it to rest for 5 minutes.
5. Meanwhile, in a small microwave-safe mixing bowl, microwave the butter and honey for 45 seconds. Whisk to combine.
6. Slice the rested breasts thinly and drizzle the honey butter over the slices.
7. Pour the prepared salad dressing over the mixed salad and toss gently to coat.
8. Divide the dressed salad among 4 plates. Top each salad with slices of the glazed duck breast.

Throttle Control: Adjust the amount of mayonnaise (creamy) in the salad dressing based on taste preferences.

Alternate Course: Instead of the blackberries, use fresh raspberries, cherries, grapes, or figs. Instead of the duck, use chicken. (It's okay to admit that you are a chicken for not using duck.)

Rogue Wave: Be sure not to overcook the duck. Even though duck is in the poultry family, it is not chicken. In most high-end restaurants, you will see a slightly pink center with an internal temperature of 135°F. Check food safety guides and decide accordingly. Be sure to reserve the precious duck fat in the refrigerator for up to 6 months as a decadent substitute for butter or olive oil.

Nice, France

CHOCOLATE ÉCLAIRS

I would never call myself a French pastry chef, but anyone can master this particular French pastry process in creating a dough known as *pâte à choux*. Simple ingredients are transformed. The magic of steam creates the airy "puff" of the pastry when it bakes. Trust me on this one. You'll amaze yourself—and your guests too.

TOTAL TRIP: 2 hours, 30 minutes

CRUISING TIME: 30 minutes

IDLE TIME: 2 hours

SERVES: 8

PROVISIONS FOR THE PASTRY

1 cup water

1/2 cup salted butter (1 stick)

2 teaspoons granulated sugar

1 cup all-purpose flour

4 eggs

PROVISIONS FOR THE PASTRY CREAM

1 cup whole milk

2 egg yolks

2 tablespoons cornstarch

1/4 cup granulated sugar

2 teaspoons vanilla extract

2 tablespoons salted butter (1/4 stick)

PROVISIONS FOR THE GLAZE

1 cup dark chocolate chips

DIRECTIONS FOR THE PASTRY

1. Preheat the oven to 425°F.
2. In a small pot, add the water, butter, and sugar. Bring to a boil over medium-high heat, approximately 5 minutes.
3. Once boiling, remove from the heat and add the flour all at once. Stir vigorously with a wooden spoon until the mixture forms a ball and pulls away from the sides of the pot.
4. Return the pot to the heat and cook, stirring constantly, for 1 to 2 minutes to dry out the dough slightly, and then transfer the dough to a medium mixing bowl and let cool for 5 to 10 minutes.
5. When the dough has cooled, add the eggs one at a time, beating well with a hand mixer for approximately 30 seconds after each egg. Ultimately, the dough should be wet, sticky, and shiny once all 4 eggs are incorporated.
6. Line a large sheet tray with parchment paper.
7. Transfer the dough from the mixing bowl into a gallon-size plastic food-storage bag with a 1/2-inch diameter hole that you cut for piping (or a pastry bag with a 1/2-inch plain piping tip). On the sheet tray lined with parchment paper, carefully pipe the dough into 4-inch-long strips with 2 inches of spacing between each strip.
8. Bake the pastry dough for 25 to 30 minutes until the éclairs have risen and are golden brown. While they are baking, prepare the pastry cream.
9. When they are done baking, turn off the oven and let the éclairs sit in the oven with the door slightly ajar for another 10 minutes to dry out further.
10. After 10 minutes, remove the éclairs from the oven to cool completely on a cooling rack.

Alternate Course: Instead of the vanilla extract, try almond, lemon, or another flavor for a delectable pastry cream.

Rogue Wave: Be sure to leave the éclairs in the oven for the specified time after they are done baking, as the temperature change from hot to room temperature should be gradual. Do not risk deflation of your puff! Patience is key.

DIRECTIONS FOR THE PASTRY CREAM

1. In a small pot, heat the milk over medium heat until it begins to simmer, whisking constantly. Once simmering, remove from heat.
2. In a small heat-safe mixing bowl, whisk together the egg yolks, cornstarch, and sugar until smooth and pale.
3. Gradually pour the hot milk into the egg mixture, whisking constantly to prevent the eggs from curdling.
4. Pour the mixture back into the pot and return to the stove to cook over medium heat. Whisk constantly until the mixture thickens and begins to simmer, approximately 3 minutes.
5. Once simmering, continue to cook for another 1 to 2 minutes, whisking constantly until the mixture is very thick. Remove from heat and whisk in the vanilla and butter until fully incorporated.
6. Transfer the pastry cream to a small mixing bowl and cover with plastic wrap directly on the surface of the cream to prevent a skin from forming. Let your pastry cream cool completely in the refrigerator.

DIRECTIONS FOR THE GLAZE

1. Once the éclairs and pastry cream are completely cooled, slice the éclairs in half lengthwise and set aside the tops to be glazed (step 4).
2. Spoon or pipe the pastry cream onto the bottom half of each éclair.
3. In a small microwave-safe mixing bowl, melt the chocolate chips in the microwave in 20-second intervals. Stir after each interval until smooth and fully melted.
4. Dip the top halves of the éclairs into the chocolate, allowing any excess to drip off.
5. Place the top halves of the éclairs onto the filled bottom halves.
6. Place the éclairs on a cooling rack to let the chocolate set, approximately 15 minutes.

ITALY

Cinque Terre, Italy

Are you ready for a *riposo* along the Italian Riviera, Little Chef? "Resting" on deck is the the perfect way to soak up the scenery.

Our journey continues into Italy, where rugged cliffs meet the sea. Olive trees from the Middle Ages cling to the earth's edge. Lemon trees flourish, their fresh scent as pervasive as the salty ocean spray. Grapes hang in rows. Ancient villages are dotted with terraces, where people are sitting at patio tables, feasting on life.

This land, its people, and the food Italy gives us . . . well, it takes my breath away actually. I am so proud that this is my heritage. I belong here. When we drop anchor off the coast of Cinque Terre, I take the time to look through my nana and gigi's handwritten recipes (lovingly stained with tomato sauce splashes) and relive childhood memories.

Mangiamo! "Let's eat!"

Growing up, I would hear the call and be the first to run to the kitchen table where our big Italian family would enjoy a first course of antipasto with prosciutto, mozzarella, olives, red peppers (roasted every Saturday night), eggplant (grilled on the porch that morning), and fresh tomatoes, sprinkled with sprigs of basil (picked from my gigi's garden that hour). My plate was always teeming with goodness, and my heart was teeming with love. Childhood was a special time for me, especially on Sunday afternoons, when we all gathered to *mangiare*—to eat—our food together.

I liked helping in the kitchen at all stages in the process, from the cutting of vegetables and herbs beforehand, to the making of a "catchall" soup afterward. You see, leftovers are the next great meal! *Tutto fa brodo*, as they say in Italy. Everything makes broth.

On the yacht, I throw the leftover zucchini into the Tuscan soup. I add extra sautéed mushrooms to the risotto, which comes to life with freshly grated Parmigiano-Reggiano. I even repurpose the cold coffee into a tantalizing tiramisu. The possibilities are endless when you allow yourself to explore.

I've heard guests literally moan over authentic Italian food. I like to think it's because it tastes like rustic resourcefulness. It uses the best ingredients that the land can provide and creates magic in the mixing. *Ottimi*. The best. Let's feast together as we explore the very best of Italy.

Chill time for this Little Chef!

Lake Garda, Italy

Cinque Terre, Italy

BREAKFAST

Cappuccino

LUNCH

Mushroom Risotto

COCKTAIL HOUR

Aperol Spritz

Crispy Prosciutto Panini

DINNER

Cioppino

Chicken Duo: Pollo al Marsala and Pollo al Tarragon

Tiramisu

Cinque Terre, Italy

CAPPUCCINO

When in Italy, do as the Italians do. Grab a *cornetto* from the market and enjoy it with a cappuccino. I like to add Nutella to my pastry, but others enjoy cream or jam. Any cornetto will be great with your cappuccino as you take a morning walk, a *passeggiate*, like Italians do as part of a healthy lifestyle.

TOTAL TRIP: 15 minutes

SERVES: 4

PROVISIONS

2 cups whole milk

2 cups prepared espresso

DIRECTIONS

1. In a small pot over medium heat, warm the milk to approximately 150°F, just until it starts steaming, but before a simmer. Constantly stir to avoid burning the milk, 5 to 7 minutes.
2. Pour 1 cup of the milk into a French press and plunge 15 to 30 times to froth the milk. The milk should double in volume due to the incorporation of air. Pour the frothed milk into a small pitcher. Repeat with the remaining cup of milk.
3. Pour 1/2 cup of the espresso into each mug, and top with the cup of the hot frothed milk. Use any leftover coffee for tiramisu.

Throttle Control: Adjust the amounts of espresso and milk based on taste preferences. Here, the classic Italian cappuccino is equal parts espresso, milk foam, and steamed milk.

Rogue Wave: Stick to tradition while in Italy. Drink your cappuccino before or during breakfast, and never after eleven in the morning.

Alternate Course: Instead of an espresso machine, use a moka pot on the stovetop to brew an intensely strong coffee with finely ground beans. Or use an Italian instant espresso. Instead of cow's milk, use any milk alternative, but note that it may not froth as effectively.

Cinque Terre, Italy

MUSHROOM RISOTTO

Perfect risotto requires patience. Gradually stir in the warm broth to coax the starches out of the rice. Then sauté the three mushroom varieties to enrich the creamy risotto. Feel free to take an afternoon nap afterward.

TOTAL TRIP: 45 minutes

SERVES: 4

PROVISIONS

6 cups chicken stock

1/4 cup salted butter (1/2 stick)

2 tablespoons extra virgin olive oil

1 cup shallots (4 medium), small diced

2 cups baby bella mushrooms (8 ounces), sliced

2 cups shiitake mushrooms (8 ounces), sliced

1 cup oyster mushrooms (4 ounces), sliced

1 teaspoon kosher salt

1/4 teaspoon freshly ground black pepper

2 tablespoons garlic (6 small cloves), minced

2 teaspoons fresh thyme leaves (or 1 teaspoon dried)

2 cups Arborio rice, unrinsed

1 cup dry white wine

1/2 cup Parmesan cheese

1/2 cup heavy whipping cream

1/4 cup fresh flat-leaf parsley, chopped, for garnish

DIRECTIONS

1. In a medium pot over low heat, add the chicken stock and keep it warm, ready to be used for the risotto preparation in step 7.
2. Meanwhile, in a large pot over medium heat, melt the butter and olive oil together.
3. Once the butter is melted, add the shallots and stir with a wooden spoon until translucent, approximately 5 minutes.
4. Add in all of the mushrooms and the salt, pepper, garlic, and thyme. Sauté while stirring occasionally until browned, approximately 8 minutes.
5. Add the rice and toast for 5 minutes, stirring constantly.
6. Add the wine to deglaze the pan. Stir until the wine is absorbed into the rice.
7. Once absorbed, ladle 1 cup of the hot chicken stock into the rice. Stir just enough to keep the rice from sticking to the bottom and until the stock is absorbed into the rice, 3 to 4 minutes. Repeat until all of the stock has been used and the rice is cooked, 15 to 25 minutes in total.
8. Take the risotto off the heat to add the Parmesan and cream. Stir until the cheese is melted. Garnish with the parsley and serve immediately.

Throttle Control: Adjust the amount of mushrooms (flavor) based on taste preferences.

Alternate Course: Instead of the mushrooms, add in peas or asparagus.

Rogue Wave: For risotto preparation, never wash your rice beforehand, as this removes the starch that is responsible for its smooth texture. And do not hasten the slow yet perfect process of stirring regularly to agitate the grains of rice so they rub against each other to create creaminess as the starch is released. But don't overstir the rice too much either! This adds excess air, which cools down the risotto, making it gluey. Stirring "just enough" is an art, a labor of love.

Cinque Terre, Italy

APEROL SPRITZ

Aperol, an Italian bitter apéritif made with gentian, rhubarb, and cinchona, lights up the room with its vibrant orange color. I love to brighten up the deck with this famous spritz when in the Italian Riviera. *Saluti!* Best wishes!

TOTAL TRIP: 5 minutes

SERVES: 4

PROVISIONS

3 cups prosecco

2 cups Aperol apéritif liqueur

1 cup club soda

4 fresh orange slices (1/4 orange), for garnish

DIRECTIONS

1. In a pitcher, combine the prosecco, Aperol, and club soda. Mix with a long spoon.
2. Pour the cocktail into large wineglasses filled with ice.
3. Garnish each wineglass with one of the orange slices.

Alternate Course: Instead of the club soda, use a fun sparkling water flavor. Instead of the Aperol apéritif liqueur, use Campari, its older "sibling" with a darker color and twice as much alcohol. Just reduce the amount of the stronger Campari, and you will be right where you need to be with this refreshingly bright spritz.

Cinque Terre, Italy

CRISPY PROSCIUTTO PANINI

Everyone loves a good sandwich, especially when it has prosciutto squeezed inside. Prosciutto dates back to pre-Roman times, when villagers would dry-age pork legs to extend the shelf life of meat available during wintertime. Now, prosciutto perfection is enjoyed in Italy—and around the world—all year long.

TOTAL TRIP: 15 minutes

SERVES: 4

PROVISIONS

1/4 pound prosciutto, thinly sliced

1 loaf focaccia, cut in half horizontally

1 cup baby arugula

1/2 cup fresh basil leaves

8 ounces burrata Italian cheese, rough-pulled into 1-inch pieces

1 large heirloom tomato, thickly sliced

1/2 teaspoon kosher salt

1 tablespoon balsamic glaze

DIRECTIONS

1. In an unheated large sauté pan, lay half of the prosciutto flat.
2. Turn the burner to medium-low heat, and cook the prosciutto until crispy, approximately 4 minutes per side, using tongs to turn.
3. Drain the prosciutto on a large sheet tray lined with paper towels. Repeat with a second batch.
4. To assemble the sandwich, on the bottom half of the focaccia bread, place the arugula, basil, cheese, sliced tomato, salt, balsamic glaze, and crispy prosciutto. Then cover with the top half.
5. Cut the sandwich into 4 equal pieces and serve on a platter.

Throttle Control: Adjust the amounts of arugula (peppery), basil (sweet spiciness), tomato (tangy), and balsamic glaze (sweet tartness) based on taste preferences.

Alternate Course: Instead of the heirloom tomato, use beefsteak, which is easier to find (but not as colorful). Rather than the balsamic glaze, use pesto or sundried tomatoes. Instead of the burrata cheese, use mozzarella (but expect less creaminess). Instead of making a room temperature sandwich, consider using a panini press to toast.

Cinque Terre, Italy

CIOPPINO

As the descendant of Italian immigrants, I like to pay homage to cioppino. Resourceful fishermen invented this hearty tomato-based seafood stew composed of any available fish they could find for sale on the docks. The type of fish is not integral to the essence of cioppino. Throw in leftover wine, and you'll really capture the "poor" beginnings of this rich soup. You might find yourself saying, *"Buon appetito, piatto pulito!"* which means "good appetite, clean plate!"

TOTAL TRIP: 40 minutes

CRUISING TIME: 25 minutes

IDLE TIME: 15 minutes

SERVES: 4

PROVISIONS FOR THE CIOPPINO

2 tablespoons salted butter (1/4 stick)

2 tablespoons extra virgin olive oil

3 cups fennel (1 bulb), thinly sliced

1 cup shallots (4 medium), thinly sliced

2 tablespoons garlic (6 small cloves), thinly sliced

1 teaspoon red pepper flakes

1 tablespoon kosher salt

1/4 cup tomato paste (half of a 6-ounce can)

3 1/2 cups diced tomatoes (or one 28-ounce can), with juice

2 cups dry white wine

3 cups seafood stock

2 cups clam juice

2 bay leaves

2 pounds fresh clams, cleaned, in shell

1 pound fresh mussels, cleaned, in shell

1 pound jumbo shrimp, peeled, deveined, tail on

1 pound whitefish fillet (like halibut, cod, snapper, or grouper), cubed in 1-inch pieces

1/4 cup fresh flat-leaf parsley, chopped, for garnish

DIRECTIONS

1. In a large pot over medium heat, melt the butter and olive oil together.
2. Add the fennel, shallots, garlic, red pepper flakes, and salt. With a wooden spoon, stir and cook until the fennel is tender, approximately 8 minutes.
3. Add the tomato paste and stir for 2 minutes, until the paste is warmed and fragrant.
4. Add the tomatoes, wine, seafood stock, clam juice, and bay leaves. Simmer for 15 minutes, stirring occasionally.
5. Add the clams in their shells and cook for 3 minutes, stirring constantly.
6. Add in the mussels in their shells, the shrimp, and the fish. Stir and cook for 5 minutes, until the mussels open and the seafood is cooked.
7. Remove immediately to avoid overcooking the seafood. Serve in bowls and garnish with the parsley.

Throttle Control: Adjust the amount of red pepper flakes (spicy) based on taste preferences.

Alternate Course: Instead of the clams, mussels, shrimp, and whitefish, use your favorite seafood combination. Instead of the seafood stock, use clam juice.

Rogue Wave: Watch the seafood carefully as it cooks since you will not want it to be overdone and rubbery.

Alternate Course: Instead of the pasta, use mashed potatoes, which also soak up the sauce beautifully. Instead of the tarragon (known as *dragoncello* in Italy), use fresh basil or fresh rosemary (but expect a completely different taste).

Cinque Terre, Italy

CHICKEN DUO: POLLO AL MARSALA AND POLLO AL TARRAGON

Since guests rave about the Marsala and tarragon sauces for the chicken cutlets, I've included both recipes. Take your pick depending on your preferences or provisions (I sometimes make both). Onion, garlic, chicken stock, wine, and cream are the commonalities in the two sauces. From there, they take off in different directions. Each sauce is unique, so you will want to try both!

TOTAL TRIP: 1 hour

SERVES: 4

PROVISIONS FOR THE CHICKEN

1 cup all-purpose flour

1 tablespoon kosher salt

1 teaspoon freshly ground black pepper

1/4 cup salted butter (1/2 stick), divided

1/4 cup extra virgin olive oil, divided

2 pounds chicken breast cutlets, boneless, skinless, thinly sliced

PROVISIONS FOR THE PASTA

Salt, for water

1 pound fettuccine, linguine, pappardelle, or any broad, flat-shaped noodle

PROVISIONS FOR THE MARSALA SAUCE

1/4 cup extra virgin olive oil

2 cups yellow onion (1 medium), thinly sliced

4 cups portabello mushrooms (16 ounces), thinly sliced

2 teaspoons kosher salt

2 tablespoons garlic (8 cloves), thinly sliced

2 tablespoons all-purpose flour

1 cup chicken stock

1 cup Marsala wine

1 cup heavy whipping cream

2 teaspoons fresh thyme leaves (or 1 teaspoon dried)

Pinch of freshly ground black pepper

1/4 cup fresh flat-leaf parsley, chopped, for garnish

PROVISIONS FOR THE TARRAGON SAUCE

1/4 cup extra virgin olive oil

2 cups yellow onion (1 medium), sliced

1/2 teaspoon kosher salt

1 tablespoon garlic (4 cloves), minced

1 cup chicken stock

1 cup dry white wine

1 1/3 cups heavy whipping cream

1/2 cup fresh tarragon leaves

1/4 cup fresh flat-leaf parsley, chopped, for garnish

DIRECTIONS FOR THE CHICKEN

1. In a medium bowl, add the flour, salt, and pepper to create seasoned flour.
2. Using tongs or your hands, coat each chicken cutlet in the seasoning and set aside on a large sheet tray.
3. In a large sauté pan over medium heat, add 2 tablespoons of the butter and 2 tablespoons of the olive oil.
4. Once the butter and olive oil are hot, use tongs to gently add half of the chicken cutlets. Do not crowd the pan. Brown each side for 2½ to 3 minutes or until golden brown. Remove to a clean, large sheet tray lined with paper towels. Repeat with the remaining butter, olive oil, and chicken cutlets.
5. Save the drippings from the pan to make the sauce of your choice.

DIRECTIONS FOR THE PASTA

1. In a large pot, cook the pasta in heavily salted boiling water until al dente, according to the directions on the package.
2. Meanwhile, prepare the sauce of your choice.
3. Once the pasta is cooked, drain in a colander.

Choose one or both of the sauces below.

DIRECTIONS FOR THE MARSALA SAUCE

1. In the large sauté pan with the chicken drippings, set to medium heat, add the oil, onion, mushrooms, salt, and garlic. Sauté while stirring occasionally with a wooden spoon until the onion is translucent, approximately 5 minutes.
2. Add in the flour and stir constantly for 1 minute.
3. Add in the chicken stock and wine and bring to a boil to thicken the sauce, stirring often, approximately 5 minutes.
4. Add the cream, thyme, and pepper. Stir to combine.
5. Return the chicken with juices to the pan to reheat and coat with the sauce.
6. Serve the chicken and sauce over the pasta and garnish with the parsley.

DIRECTIONS FOR THE TARRAGON SAUCE

1. In the large sauté pan with the chicken drippings, set to medium heat, add the olive oil, onion, and garlic. Sauté while stirring occasionally until the onion is translucent, approximately 5 minutes.
2. Add in the chicken stock and wine. Simmer and stir until reduced by half, 8 to 10 minutes.
3. Once reduced, add in the cream and simmer for 5 minutes, until the sauce coats the spoon, stirring occasionally.
4. Remove the sauce from the heat and add the tarragon. Stir to combine.
5. Return the chicken with juices to the pan to reheat and coat with the sauce.
6. Serve the chicken and sauce over the pasta and garnish with the parsley.

Cinque Terre, Italy

TIRAMISU

Tiramisu means "pick me up." And boy, it does just that with espresso and Kahlúa soaked into the crisp, airy Italian *savoiardi* ladyfingers. (Heck, I like to use my own "lady fingers" to lap up extra mascarpone cream, so I make more than is needed!) This recipe makes enough for you to sneak some for a midnight snack after the guests have left the party. Enjoy *la dolce vita*—the sweet life!

TOTAL TRIP: 1 hour, 30 minutes (up to 12 hours)

CRUISING TIME: 30 minutes

IDLE TIME: 1 hour (or more, to soak)

SERVES: 8

PROVISIONS

2 cups heavy whipping cream

1 cup mascarpone cheese (8 ounces)

1/4 cup granulated sugar

3 tablespoons powdered sugar

2 teaspoons vanilla extract

1/2 cup Kahlúa

1 cup prepared espresso, cold

1 package ladyfingers (8 ounces)

1 tablespoon cocoa powder, for dusting

DIRECTIONS

1. In a large mixing bowl, add the cream, mascarpone, sugar, powdered sugar, and vanilla. Use a hand mixer to whisk to soft peaks, 1 to 2 minutes.
2. In a separate small mixing bowl, pour the liqueur and espresso (perhaps some extra from breakfast). Stir with a wooden spoon until well combined.
3. One by one, use tongs or your hands to fully dip each ladyfinger in the liquid for a split second. Lay the ladyfingers in a single layer in a 9-by-13-inch casserole dish until the bottom is completely covered.
4. Pour half of the mascarpone mixture over the ladyfingers. With a rubber spatula, spread the mixture evenly, but gently.
5. Repeat a second layer of dipped ladyfingers, followed by the mascarpone mixture.
6. On the top of the tiramisu, use a fine-mesh strainer to dust with the cocoa powder.
7. Place the tiramisu in the refrigerator for 1 hour or more (even overnight) to allow the layers to set.
8. Serve chilled.

Mykonos, Greece

We've arrived in the land of the gods, Little Chef.

As our yacht pulls in to port in Mykonos, guests stand on the deck and simply gaze at Greece in all its splendor. The island's white houses stand in contrast to the deep azure of the Aegean Sea. These simple cubic structures, adorned with iconic cobalt-blue shutters and vibrant bougainvillea, lure us into the ongoing story of its people living in a fantastical land. Winding staircases and terraced balconies complete the surreal vision of this magical village, set on "a mass of stones," from which the name Mykonos may be derived.

Mykonos's nickname is "The Island of the Winds" due to its typically strong winds that blow regularly and power the sixteenth-century windmills perched on the hills overlooking the sea. With whitewashed facades and conical roofs, the windmills tell a story of the island's rich maritime history as their rotating sails flap gently in the breeze.

And the chapels. There are so many. Whitewashed like the homes (and even the grout of the walkway stones), these white structures dot the landscape as a reminder to say thank you, as did the Greek sailors, to God. How cool that these sea folk might have built the bell-towered chapels for their *tamata* (votive offerings) to show gratitude for safe passage. How sacred and special. I know our guests and I feel blessed by this land that popular legend claims is named after Mykons, descendant of the mythological god Apollo.

Whether from mythology or the Greek Orthodox church, the magic and mystery of Mykonos cannot be denied. Imagine all the church bells ringing at once. I know that this occurs on religious holidays but have yet to experience it myself. It's on my bucket list to return during the Easter season, when celebration heightens to its fullest in this spiritually rooted place.

Until then, this is a great place to secure authentic provisions that guests are sure to enjoy. My favorite is kopanisti cheese, a tangy and creamy blend of cow and goat milk that will thrill the guests at an afternoon cocktail hour. I also provision some local honey and grapes for the charcuterie board, along with a guest favorite, spanakopita. We serve martinis with fresh lemon to complement the local ouzo flavored with anise, fennel, cinnamon, and cardamom.

While our guests spend the day walking the labyrinthine streets to shop and sightsee, I usually slip into the myth that is Mykonos, visible from my galley window. I imagine that the guests gaze back out at the sea (and our yacht) from the pergola-shaded terraces dotting the landscape. They know that a beautiful meal awaits them when they return from the village.

The magic of Mykonos makes me smile.

Mykonos, Greece

BREAKFAST

Sfougato

LUNCH

Chicken Gyros

COCKTAIL HOUR

Ouzo Martini

Spanakopita

DINNER

Avgolemono Soup

Moussaka

Baklava

Mykonos, Greece

SFOUGATO

Is it a frittata, an open-faced omelet, a soufflé, or a crustless quiche? However you compare it with other egg-based dishes, *sfougato* is Greece's specialty and can be served warm or chilled. The Greek word *sfougari* means "sponge," so we'll soak up the freshness in this breakfast dish with a plethora of fresh herbs and vegetables.

TOTAL TRIP: 1 hour, 30 minutes

CRUISING TIME: 30 minutes

IDLE TIME: 1 hour

SERVES: 4

PROVISIONS

1 tablespoon extra virgin olive oil, for sautéing

1½ cups yellow squash (2 small), grated, drained in cheesecloth

2 cups zucchini (2 small), grated, drained in cheesecloth

½ cup green onions (4 stalks), sliced

1 teaspoon kosher salt, for vegetables

¼ teaspoon freshly ground black pepper, for vegetables

2 tablespoons fresh flat-leaf parsley, chopped

2 tablespoons fresh dill, chopped

1 tablespoon fresh mint leaves, chopped

1 teaspoon dried oregano

8 eggs

¼ cup whole milk

2 tablespoons extra virgin olive oil, for egg mixture

1 teaspoon kosher salt, for the eggs

¼ teaspoon freshly ground black pepper, for the eggs

½ cup feta cheese

1 cup Roma tomatoes (2 medium), sliced

DIRECTIONS

1. In a large sauté pan over medium-high heat, add the olive oil.
2. Once hot, add in the squash, zucchini, green onions, salt, and pepper. Using a wooden spoon, stir and sauté for approximately 8 minutes.
3. Transfer the vegetable mixture into a large bowl and allow to cool for 15 minutes.
4. Preheat the oven to 350°F. Grease a 9-by-9-inch square cake pan.
5. Once the vegetable mixture is cool, add in the parsley, dill, mint, oregano, eggs, milk, olive oil, salt, pepper, and feta. Whisk until the egg mixture is combined.
6. In the greased pan, pour in the egg mixture and then decorate the top with the sliced tomatoes.
7. Bake until the eggs are set, approximately 35 minutes.
8. Allow to cool for 10 minutes, then slice and serve.

Throttle Control: Adjust the amounts of vegetables (flavor) and cheese (creamy) based on taste preferences.

Alternate Course: Instead of the squash and zucchini, use any grated vegetables of your choice.

Mykonos, Greece

CHICKEN GYROS

Gyro meat is traditionally cooked on a vertical rotisserie, then sliced and wrapped in pita bread. Our spin on this Greek giant is to marinate the chicken and then brown it on the stovetop. We'll serve it with tzatziki, the quintessential dip of Greek culture with its cultured yogurt base. Healthy, yes. Addictive, even bigger yes.

TOTAL TRIP: 1 hour, 45 minutes (up to 12 hours)

CRUISING TIME: 45 minutes

IDLE TIME: 1 hour (or more, to marinate)

SERVES: 4

PROVISIONS FOR THE CHICKEN

2 pounds chicken thighs, boneless, skinless, cut into strips

1 tablespoon garlic (4 cloves), minced

4 teaspoons red wine vinegar

1/4 cup fresh lemon juice (2 medium lemons)

4 teaspoons extra virgin olive oil, for marinade

1/4 cup plain Greek yogurt

2 teaspoons dried oregano

1 tablespoon kosher salt

1/2 teaspoon freshly ground black pepper

2 tablespoons extra virgin olive oil, for searing

PROVISIONS FOR THE TZATZIKI

2 cups English cucumbers (1 large), skin-on

1 cup plain Greek yogurt

2 tablespoons fresh lemon juice (1 medium lemon)

4 teaspoons extra virgin olive oil

1 1/2 teaspoons garlic (2 cloves), minced

2 tablespoons fresh flat-leaf parsley, chopped

2 tablespoons fresh dill, chopped

4 teaspoons fresh mint leaves, chopped

1/2 teaspoon kosher salt

Pinch of freshly ground black pepper

PROVISIONS FOR THE SALAD

2 cups Roma tomatoes (4 medium), medium diced

1 1/2 cups English cucumber (1 medium), medium diced

1 cup red onion (1/2 medium), medium diced

2 tablespoons fresh flat-leaf parsley, chopped

4 teaspoons extra virgin olive oil

1 teaspoon kosher salt

Pinch of freshly ground black pepper

PROVISIONS FOR THE ASSEMBLY

4 Greek pitas, 8-inch rounds

DIRECTIONS FOR THE CHICKEN

1. In a large mixing bowl, add the chicken strips, garlic, vinegar, lemon juice, olive oil, yogurt, oregano, salt, and pepper. Mix together and then cover with a lid or plastic wrap to marinate in the refrigerator for 1 hour or more (overnight is great). While the chicken is marinating, work on the tzatziki (which can also be stored overnight) and the salad (prepare only when ready to serve).
2. Once the chicken has marinated, heat a large sauté pan over medium-high heat. Add in the olive oil and heat for 30 seconds before using tongs to add the marinated chicken strips in a single layer. Allow the chicken to brown, and then flip to brown the second side, approximately 3 minutes on each side.
3. To keep the chicken hot while preparing the rest of the meal, transfer to a 9-by-13-inch casserole dish covered with aluminum foil. Place in the oven on the lowest setting (170°F) until ready to assemble.

DIRECTIONS FOR THE TZATZIKI

1. Grate the cucumber and place into a 12-by-12-inch square of cheesecloth. Wrap and squeeze out as much water as possible.
2. In a small mixing bowl, add the grated cucumber, yogurt, lemon juice, olive oil, garlic, parsley, dill, mint, salt, and pepper. Mix until the tzatziki sauce is combined.
3. Serve immediately or cover with plastic wrap and place in the refrigerator for up to 8 hours (or overnight).
4. When ready to assemble, top the gyro with as much tzatziki as desired.

DIRECTIONS FOR THE SALAD AND ASSEMBLY

1. In a medium mixing bowl, add the tomatoes, cucumber, onion, parsley, olive oil, salt, and pepper. Using a spoon, mix all of the ingredients together.
2. To assemble the gyro, place one of the pitas on a dish, followed by some of the chicken, salad, and tzatziki on top.
3. Fold like a taco and enjoy!

Mykonos, Greece

OUZO MARTINI

Ouzo is an anise-flavored liqueur produced from grape must (the leftovers after making wine). You "must" (get it?) try it, especially in this martini infused with lemon, honey, and mint. It pairs well with our spanakopita appetizer and is perfect for enjoying on the deck after a glorious day in Mykonos. *Yia mas!* To our health, Little Chef!

TOTAL TRIP: 10 minutes

SERVES: 4

PROVISIONS

1¼ cups fresh lemon juice (10 medium lemons)

2 cups ouzo liqueur

¼ cup honey

Ice, for shaking

4 sprigs fresh mint, for garnish, if desired

DIRECTIONS

1. In a large shaker, add the lemon juice, ouzo, and honey and some ice. Shake until the container is ice-cold, approximately 15 seconds.
2. Pour into 4 chilled martini glasses and garnish each glass with 1 sprig of the mint.

Mykonos, Greece

SPANAKOPITA

Spinach has never tasted so good as when wrapped in phyllo dough. What makes the spanakopita pop? The feta. The spices. The perfect size to savor while sipping.

TOTAL TRIP: 1 hour

CRUISING TIME: 35 minutes

IDLE TIME: 25 minutes

SERVES: 4

PROVISIONS FOR THE FILLING

2 cups frozen spinach, thawed, measured after draining in cheesecloth (or 1 pound fresh spinach, cooked, drained in cheesecloth)

1½ cups fresh flat-leaf parsley, chopped

2 tablespoons fresh dill, chopped

2 cups yellow onion (1 medium), small diced

2 tablespoons garlic (6 small cloves), minced

2 tablespoons extra virgin olive oil

5 eggs, beaten

½ teaspoon kosher salt

½ teaspoon freshly ground black pepper

2 cups feta cheese, crumbled

PROVISIONS FOR THE SPANAKOPITA

⅔ cup extra virgin olive oil

8 ounces phyllo dough (½ package), thawed

Flaked salt, for finishing

DIRECTIONS FOR THE FILLING

1. In a large mixing bowl, use a wooden spoon to mix the spinach, parsley, dill, onion, garlic, olive oil, eggs, salt, pepper, and feta. Set aside.

DIRECTIONS FOR THE SPANAKOPITA

1. Pour the olive oil into a small mixing bowl. Unroll the phyllo and cover with a damp towel to prevent it from drying out. Take one sheet of the phyllo and place it on a clean, dry surface. Using a pastry brush, lightly brush the sheet with 1 tablespoon of the olive oil.
2. Place another phyllo sheet on top of the first one and brush it with another tablespoon of the olive oil. Using a knife, cut the dough down the center to split the width in half to create long strips (now the dough should be approximately 4½ inches wide, and the same original length).
3. Place a small spoonful of spinach filling, approximately the size of a golf ball, near one end of the phyllo strip.
4. Take the bottom right corner of the strip and fold it over the filling to form a triangle. The bottom edge should align with the left edge of the strip when folded. Continue folding the triangle up along the strip, maintaining the triangle shape, similar to folding a flag. Fold up to the left, then to the right, then to the left again, and so on, until the end of the strip is reached.
5. Place the finished triangle on a large sheet tray lined with parchment paper, seam side down.
6. Meanwhile, preheat the oven to 375°F.

7. Continue the folding process to make all of the triangles. Once all of the spanakopita are complete, brush the tops with more olive oil.
8. Bake the triangles until golden brown and crispy, 20 to 25 minutes.
9. Remove the spanakopita from the oven, and immediately sprinkle them with the flaked salt.
10. Let the pastries cool slightly before serving.

Rogue Wave: Be sure to watch the overall salt level based on the varying saltiness of different feta cheeses.

Mykonos, Greece

AVGOLEMONO SOUP

Avgolemono, a mix of eggs and lemon, thickens and brightens this creamy Greek chicken soup to perfection. Preparation is so easy that you'll find yourself making it regularly, even if you aren't on a yacht in Mykonos.

TOTAL TRIP: 30 minutes

SERVES: 4

PROVISIONS FOR THE RICE

1 cup long-grain white rice, rinsed 3 to 4 times

1½ cups water

PROVISIONS FOR THE SOUP

1 tablespoon salted butter (⅛ stick)

1 tablespoon extra virgin olive oil

1½ cups yellow onion (¾ medium), small diced

1 cup celery (2 large stalks), small diced

2 teaspoons kosher salt

½ teaspoon freshly ground black pepper

6 cups chicken stock

2 eggs

¼ cup fresh lemon juice (2 medium lemons)

2 cups rotisserie chicken, store-bought, cooked, shredded

2 tablespoons fresh dill, chopped

4 sprigs fresh dill, for garnish

Lemon wedges, for garnish

DIRECTIONS FOR THE RICE

1. In a small pot or a rice cooker, use the recipe's ratio to cook the rice in the water, or follow the directions on the package. Once cooked, remove from heat.

DIRECTIONS FOR THE SOUP

1. While the rice cooks, in a large pot on medium-high heat, melt together the butter and olive oil.
2. Once melted, add the onion, celery, salt, and pepper. Using a wooden spoon, stir and sauté until the onion is translucent, approximately 5 minutes.
3. Add the chicken stock and bring to a simmer, 5 to 8 minutes. Once simmering, reduce the heat to low.
4. Meanwhile, in a small heat-safe mixing bowl, beat the eggs with a whisk. Temper the eggs by gradually adding 1 cup of the warm stock to the eggs while whisking continuously.
5. Once the full cup has been added, pour the tempered eggs into the pot. Keep the temperature on low until the mixture slightly thickens, 1 to 2 minutes. Then turn off the heat and add in the cooked rice, lemon juice, shredded chicken, and dill.
6. Serve in bowls with the sprigs of dill and lemon wedges for garnish.

Throttle Control: Adjust the amounts of lemon juice (acidic) and rice (thickness) based on taste preferences.

Alternate Course: Any kind of rice will work, but try jasmine or basmati if available.

Rogue Wave: Avoid scrambling the eggs in the tempering process by whisking continuously over low heat. Reheating the soup will make the rice gummy. To prepare for a later meal, store the soup without the rice, adding it only when ready to eat.

Mykonos, Greece

MOUSSAKA

For those who have seen (and love, as I do) the movie *My Big Fat Greek Wedding*, you can have fun with this word. Admit it, you want to! This eggplant casserole is a staple in my galley. It reminds me of lasagna but with lamb (rather than beef and sausage) and eggplant (rather than noodles). *Kalí óreksi!* Happy eating!

TOTAL TRIP: 1 hour, 30 minutes

CRUISING TIME: 1 hour

IDLE TIME: 30 minutes

SERVES: 4

PROVISIONS FOR THE EGGPLANT

2 large eggplants, sliced longways

1 tablespoon kosher salt

3 tablespoons extra virgin olive oil

PROVISIONS FOR THE MEAT SAUCE

1 tablespoon extra virgin olive oil

1 pound ground lamb

2 teaspoons kosher salt

1/2 teaspoon freshly ground black pepper

1 tablespoon plus 1 teaspoon garlic (5 cloves), minced

2 cups yellow onion (1 medium), small diced

2 tablespoons tomato paste

1/3 cup dry red wine

1 cup canned crushed tomatoes, with juice

2/3 cup beef stock

2 bay leaves

2 teaspoons granulated sugar

2 teaspoons dried oregano

1/4 teaspoon ground cinnamon

PROVISIONS FOR THE BÉCHAMEL SAUCE

1/4 cup salted butter (1/2 stick)

1/4 cup all-purpose flour

3 cups whole milk

1/4 teaspoon ground nutmeg

1 teaspoon kosher salt

1/4 teaspoon freshly ground black pepper

2 eggs

PROVISIONS FOR THE TOPPING

1/2 cup grated Parmesan cheese

1/2 cup panko bread crumbs

DIRECTIONS FOR THE EGGPLANT

1. Preheat the oven to 375°F.
2. Lay out the sliced eggplant on 2 large sheet trays lined with paper towels.
3. Sprinkle half of the salt evenly on all of the eggplant. Flip and repeat with the remaining salt. Then allow the slices to sit for 10 minutes.
4. Once the salt has drawn the water out of the eggplant, use paper towels to dry off the eggplant. Then remove the paper towels and place parchment paper on the sheet trays.
5. Line the eggplant evenly in a single layer on the sheet trays. Disperse the olive oil evenly on top of the eggplant.

6. Place the eggplant in the oven and bake it until tender, approximately 25 minutes.
7. While the eggplant is baking, work on the meat sauce.
8. Once the eggplant is tender and slightly browned, remove from the oven.

DIRECTIONS FOR THE MEAT SAUCE

1. In a large sauté pan over medium-high heat, add the olive oil. Heat the oil for 30 seconds.
2. Add the lamb, salt, pepper, garlic, and onion and cook until the lamb is browned, approximately 8 minutes. Use a wooden spoon to stir occasionally.
3. Add in the tomato paste and stir constantly for 2 minutes.
4. Reduce the heat to medium-low. Add in the wine, tomatoes, beef stock, bay leaves, sugar, oregano, and cinnamon. Stirring occasionally, simmer for 15 minutes.
5. While the meat sauce is simmering, make the béchamel sauce.

DIRECTIONS FOR THE BÉCHAMEL SAUCE

1. In a medium pot over medium heat, melt the butter, approximately 1 minute.
2. Once melted, whisk in the flour and cook for 1 minute.
3. Gradually add the milk while whisking constantly. Add the nutmeg, salt, and pepper. Whisking constantly for 8 to 10 minutes, bring to a simmer or until thickened to form the sauce.
4. As soon as the sauce hits a simmer, remove from the heat to cool for 20 minutes.
5. Once the sauce is cool, whisk in the eggs.

DIRECTIONS FOR THE TOPPING AND ASSEMBLY

1. Preheat the oven to 375°F.
2. In an ungreased 9-by-13-inch casserole dish, ladle in a small portion (approximately ½ cup) of the meat sauce on the bottom of the dish to ensure the eggplant does not stick.
3. Begin layering with a single layer of the eggplant, followed by ⅓ of the meat sauce and then ⅓ of the béchamel.
4. Repeat the layering process 2 more times, ending with the béchamel sauce as the top layer.
5. Sprinkle the Parmesan and panko on top of the béchamel sauce.
6. Bake the moussaka until bubbly and browned on top, approximately 30 minutes.

Alternate Course: Instead of the lamb, which is a gamey (and wonderful) meat, use beef.

Rogue Wave: Be sure to set timers to coordinate the various steps in this multitasking recipe.

Mykonos, Greece

BAKLAVA

Sweet, flaky baklava is a classic Greek dessert. The honey, lemon, and nuts layered between buttery-thin phyllo dough make my mouth water. Are you with me? We are in good company since there's a "sweet" reference to a bread served with honeyed wine in Homer's masterpiece *The Odyssey*, written more than 2,600 years ago. It's a classic for a reason.

TOTAL TRIP: 7 hours (up to 12 hours)

CRUISING TIME: 25 minutes

IDLE TIME: 6 hours, 35 minutes (or more, to soak)

SERVES: 8

PROVISIONS FOR THE ASSEMBLY

1/2 cup salted butter (1 stick), melted

8 ounces phyllo dough (1/2 package), thawed

PROVISIONS FOR THE WALNUT FILLING

2 cups walnuts, finely crushed

1 1/2 teaspoons ground cinnamon

1/4 cup granulated sugar

PROVISIONS FOR THE SYRUP

2/3 cup water

1/2 cup granulated sugar

1/2 cup honey

1 teaspoon fresh lemon zest (1/2 medium lemon)

1 tablespoon fresh lemon juice (1/2 medium lemon)

DIRECTIONS FOR THE WALNUT FILLING

1. In a medium mixing bowl, add the walnuts, cinnamon, and sugar. Mix well.

DIRECTIONS FOR THE ASSEMBLY

1. Preheat the oven to 350°F. Grease a 9-by-9-inch square cake pan with some of the melted butter.
2. Unroll the phyllo and cover with a damp towel to prevent it from drying out.
3. Place one sheet of the phyllo on the bottom of the greased pan. Using a pastry brush, coat the sheet lightly with some of the melted butter.
4. Repeat this buttering process until you have 8 layers of phyllo in the pan.
5. Sprinkle 1/3 of the walnut filling over the 8 layers of phyllo.
6. Add 4 more layers of buttered phyllo, followed by 1/3 of the filling.
7. Repeat step 6, then finish with 8 layers of buttered phyllo.
8. Before placing the pan in the oven, use a sharp knife to cut the baklava into 2-inch squares. Be sure to cut completely through to the bottom to aid in portioning once cooked.
9. Bake the baklava until golden brown and crispy, 35 to 40 minutes.

DIRECTIONS FOR THE SYRUP

1. When the baklava is almost done baking, in a small pot, add the water, sugar, honey, lemon zest, and lemon juice.
2. Use high heat to bring the mixture to a boil for 3 minutes, stirring constantly with a wooden spoon.
3. Reduce the heat to low while waiting for the baklava to finish baking.
4. Once the baklava is done, remove it from the oven and immediately pour the hot syrup evenly over the entire dish.
5. Let the baklava soak in the syrup for at least 6 hours or longer on the counter.
6. With the syrup fully absorbed, the baklava is ready to be served. Drizzle with extra honey once plated, if desired.

Alternate Course: Instead of adding the lemon juice and lemon zest, use a 1/2 teaspoon of rosewater. Instead of the walnuts, use any nuts of your choice.

Rogue Wave: Patience! Let it soak. The syrup needs to absorb fully for the baklava to be its best.

INDIA

Mumbai, India

India and spices. They belong together in the culinary world.

In the market near the port in Mumbai, India, you can experience the staggering selection of spices in all shades of yellow, orange, red, brown, green, and more in various baskets and jars. I stand in awe. Speechless.

Let's honor this country and its amazing cuisine by letting the spices speak for themselves:

Cardamom: I am cool like mint, yet strong and smoky. My intense fragrance impacts many Indian dishes.

Clove: I am warm and very aromatic. I am part of the evergreen family and love pairing up with cinnamon, nutmeg, and star anise to make the best curries and desserts.

Coriander: I am nutty with a tart, citrusy flavor. I am the dried seed of the cilantro plant.

Cumin: I am warm, earthy, and aromatic. I am a popular member of the parsley family, and I outrank many others in Indian cooking.

Curry Leaves: I am bitter and pungent, reminiscent of lemongrass and citrus.

Fennel: I am your breath's best friend, with an aroma like licorice.

Garam Masala: I add a little warmth, heat, and sweetness to Indian food. I am a special mix of spices that are ground together: coriander, cumin, cardamom, cloves, black pepper, cinnamon, and nutmeg.

Indian Green Chili: I am full of heat and work well in Indian curries, chutneys, and pickled dishes. I am hard to find, so many use the Thai green chili in my place.

Saffron: I am rich, and I am magic with my mix of honey and hay flavors. My red threads come from the *Crocus sativus* flower, a precious find.

Star Anise: I am strong, and I smell like licorice. Use me in traditional Indian specialties such as biryani and masala chai.

Turmeric: I am warm, peppery, and earthy. My yellowness stains fabric, fingers, and wooden spoons!

These spices distinctly elevate ingredients to a one-of-a-kind experience. Little Chef, I urge you to invest in this richness for your pantry. Even from your own kitchen, just a few pinches of authentic Indian spices will transport you and your guests to another world.

Relaxing after a busy day at the spice market

Mumbai, India

BREAKFAST

Masala Dosa

LUNCH

Chicken Biryani

COCKTAIL HOUR

Mango Rum Lassi

Potato and Pea Samosas

DINNER

Curried Carrot Salad

Indian Butter Shrimp

Pistachio and Cardamom Kulfi

Mumbai, India

MASALA DOSA

We'll season our potatoes with garlic, ginger, cumin, chilies, and other Indian spices. We'll then stuff the masala potatoes in a dosa that is traditionally made with fermented rice and lentil batter. Crispier than a regular savory crepe, the dosa provides the magic for this gorgeous dish.

TOTAL TRIP: 14 hours, 45 minutes (up to 24 hours)

CRUISING TIME: 45 minutes

IDLE TIME: 14 hours (or more, to ferment)

SERVES: 4

PROVISIONS FOR THE DOSA

2 cups basmati rice

2/3 cup urad dal Indian lentils, whole or split, dried

4 cups water, for soaking

2 teaspoons salt

1 1/2 cups water or more, for batter

1/4 cup extra virgin olive oil

PROVISIONS FOR THE MASALA POTATOES

6 cups Yukon Gold potatoes (6 medium), peeled, 1-inch cubes

3 tablespoons extra virgin olive oil, or ghee

1 Thai green chili (1 teaspoon), finely chopped

1 tablespoon plus 1 teaspoon garlic (5 cloves), grated

1 tablespoon plus 1 teaspoon fresh ginger, peeled, grated

2 cups yellow onion (1 medium), small diced

2 teaspoons kosher salt

2 teaspoons dried mustard seeds

2 teaspoons cumin seeds

15 curry leaves

2 teaspoons ground turmeric

1/4 cup fresh cilantro leaves, for garnish

DIRECTIONS FOR THE DOSA

1. Rinse the rice and urad dal under cold water until the water runs clear.
2. In a large mixing bowl, soak the rice and urad dal in the water on the counter, covered in plastic wrap, for 6 hours or more (even overnight).
3. Drain the water and transfer the rice and urad dal to a blender, along with the 1 1/2 cups of water. Blend to a crepe-batter consistency (but not completely smooth since small bits of rice and urad dal remain). Add more water if needed to create this crepe-batter consistency.
4. Once blended, pour into a large mixing bowl and cover with a damp towel. Let it ferment for 8 to 12 hours (or longer).
5. After the fermentation, the batter should be foamy and slightly sour. Add in the salt and stir with a wooden spoon to combine. (Before cooking the fermented batter, prepare the masala potatoes.)
6. Heat a medium sauté pan on medium-high heat. Pour a ladleful of the batter onto the center of the hot pan and spread it out in a circular motion, using the bottom of the ladle.

7. Cook the dosa on one side only, until the edges start to lift from the pan and turn golden brown, 2 to 3 minutes.
8. Drizzle 1½ teaspoons of the olive oil (or melted ghee, for authenticity) on the top.
9. Using a metal spatula, remove the dosa from the pan. Roll up or fold the dosa in half and place on a serving platter. Repeat the dosa preparation for the remaining the batter, for a total of 8 dosas.

DIRECTIONS FOR THE MASALA POTATOES

1. In a medium pot, boil the potatoes until fork-tender, 12 to 15 minutes. Drain and set aside.
2. While the potatoes boil, heat a large sauté pan over medium heat, then add the oil (or ghee).
3. Once the oil (or ghee) is hot, add the chili, garlic, ginger, onion, salt, mustard seeds, cumin seeds, curry leaves, and turmeric. Sauté while stirring occasionally until the onion is translucent, approximately 5 minutes.
4. Once done, add the cooked potatoes and stir to break them up slightly. Remove from heat while the dosa is prepared.
5. Once ready, garnish the potatoes with the cilantro and place on the platter to the side of (or wrapped in) the dosa.

Throttle Control: Adjust the amount of Thai green chili (heat of 50,000 to 100,000 Scoville heat units, or SHU) based on taste preferences.

Alternate Course: Instead of the Thai green chili, use Indian jwala chili peppers, which are milder at 30,000 to 50,000 SHU. Even milder heat options include jalapeño peppers (2,500 to 5,000 SHU) or serrano peppers (10,000 to 23,000 SHU).

Rogue Wave: Be patient. The urad dal (found online or at Indian markets) and the rice need to ferment. The longer the mix sits, the more sour tasting and bubbly it becomes. Flavor, baby.

Mumbai, India

CHICKEN BIRYANI

Traditional biryani can be made in three different ways: the *dum pukht* method (slow-cooking the meat and vegetables over a low flame to release all of the flavors), the *kacchi* method (layering the raw, marinated meat with uncooked rice and then cooking), and the *pukka* method (partially cooking the meat and rice separately and then steaming together). All three work beautifully, but here we'll use the *pukka* method as I don my favorite "puka" shells . . . a different word altogether but a fun way to choose, right?

TOTAL TRIP: 2 hours, 30 minutes (up to 12 hours)

CRUISING TIME: 1 hour, 30 minutes

IDLE TIME: 1 hour (or more, to marinate)

SERVES: 4

PROVISIONS FOR THE CHICKEN MARINADE

2 pounds chicken breasts, boneless, skinless, 1-inch cubes

2 teaspoons kosher salt

½ teaspoon red pepper flakes

2 tablespoons fresh ginger, peeled, grated

1 tablespoon plus 1 teaspoon garlic (5 cloves), grated

1 Thai green chili (1 tablespoon), finely chopped

2 tablespoons fresh mint leaves, roughly chopped

¼ cup plain Greek yogurt

1 tablespoon fresh lemon juice (½ medium lemon)

PROVISIONS FOR THE RICE

1½ cups basmati rice, rinsed 3 to 4 times

2¼ cups water

PROVISIONS FOR THE BIRYANI

¼ cup butter, or ghee

4 cups yellow onions (2 medium), thinly sliced

2 teaspoons kosher salt

1 teaspoon cumin seeds

2 teaspoons turmeric

½ teaspoon cayenne pepper

1½ cups Roma tomatoes (3 medium), medium diced

3 whole cloves

½ teaspoon cardamom

2 bay leaves

1 teaspoon chili powder

1 cinnamon stick

1 star anise

1 Thai green chili (1 tablespoon), finely chopped

2 teaspoons garam masala

Saffron water (¼ cup warm water plus 1 teaspoon saffron)

1 cup fresh cilantro leaves, for garnish

DIRECTIONS FOR THE CHICKEN MARINADE

1. In a large mixing bowl, add the chicken, salt, red pepper flakes, ginger, garlic, chili, mint, yogurt, and lemon juice. Using a wooden spoon or your hands, stir to combine.
2. Cover the bowl with plastic wrap and place in the refrigerator to marinate for at least 1 hour or more (even overnight).

DIRECTIONS FOR THE RICE

1. In a small pot, use a 1 to 1.5 ratio of rice and water to cook the rice until it is 80 percent cooked, approximately 13 minutes (rather than completely cooked at 17 minutes). Remove from heat. It will not be done at this point since the completion occurs in the oven later.

DIRECTIONS FOR THE BIRYANI

1. Preheat the oven to 375°F.
2. In a large pot over medium-high heat, melt the butter (or ghee, for authenticity).
3. Once melted, add in the onions, salt, cumin seeds, turmeric, cayenne pepper, tomatoes, cloves, cardamom, bay leaves, chili powder, cinnamon stick, star anise, chili, and garam masala. Stir with a wooden spoon, cooking until the onions are translucent, approximately 5 minutes.
4. Add in the marinated chicken and sauté until browned, 8 to 10 minutes.
5. Add the partially cooked rice on top of the chicken and sauce.
6. Sprinkle the saffron water (with the saffron itself) on top of the rice, then cover with a lid or aluminum foil. Transfer to the oven and bake until the rice and chicken are fully cooked, approximately 30 minutes.
7. Turn the entire contents upside down onto a large serving platter. Remove the whole cloves. Garnish with the cilantro.

Throttle Control: Adjust the amounts of red pepper flakes and Thai green chili (heat) and garlic and ginger (the most awesome flavor pairing–bump it up!) based on taste preferences.

Rogue Wave: Watch out for yellow staining from the turmeric, a natural dye. Create a paste of baking soda and lemon juice to soak on the stain, and then scrub it after it sits for 5 minutes.

Alternate Course: Instead of the pricy saffron, use turmeric and sweet paprika for color. Instead of the Thai green chili (heat of 50,000 to 100,000 Scoville heat units, or SHU), use Indian jwala chili peppers, which are milder at 30,000 to 50,000 SHU. Even milder heat options include jalapeño peppers (2,500 to 5,000 SHU) or serrano peppers (10,000 to 23,000 SHU).

Mumbai, India

MANGO RUM LASSI

Around 1000 BC, in Punjab, India, the lassi was born, with both salty and sweet versions utilizing the native mango. Blending yogurt with fruits and seasonings into a sweet smoothie is the tastiest way to cut the heat of the day and the spiciness of the food in India. And in this case, with our added rum not found in a traditional lassi, we might be tempted to get to the cocktail party even sooner!

TOTAL TRIP: 1 hour, 10 minutes

CRUISING TIME: 10 minutes

IDLE TIME: 1 hour

SERVES: 4

PROVISIONS

1 cup plain yogurt

2 cups frozen or fresh mango

1/4 cup heavy whipping cream

1/4 teaspoon cardamom

1 tablespoon granulated sugar

3/4 cup mango rum

Pinch of cardamom, for garnish

DIRECTIONS

1. In a blender, mix the yogurt, mango, cream, cardamom, sugar, and rum, just until the mango is blended, approximately 30 seconds to 1 minute.
2. Pour into a pitcher, cover, and place in the refrigerator until chilled, approximately 1 hour.
3. Serve in a handleless clay cup called a *kulhar*, then garnish with a sprinkle of cardamom.

Throttle Control: Adjust the amount of sugar (sweet) based on taste preferences.

Alternate Course: Instead of the mango rum, use any flavor of rum.

Rogue Wave: Whip alert! Be sure not to overblend the heavy whipping cream, unless you are up for a whipped cream lassi instead of a cocktail drink.

Mumbai, India

POTATO AND PEA SAMOSAS

Whether triangular, conical, or crescent in shape, samosas are a savory pastry snack filled with vegetables, potatoes, onions, peas, or more. Samosas, an iconic symbol of Indian cuisine, demand center stage, so we'll make them the star of our cocktail party.

TOTAL TRIP: 1 hour

SERVES: 4

PROVISIONS FOR THE MINT CHUTNEY

1 cup fresh cilantro leaves

1/2 cup fresh mint leaves

1 tablespoon fresh ginger, peeled, grated

1 teaspoon garlic (1 small clove), roughly chopped

1/4 teaspoon cumin seeds

1/2 Thai green chili (1 1/2 teaspoons), finely chopped

1 tablespoon fresh lemon juice (1/2 medium lemon)

2 tablespoons plain yogurt

1 teaspoon kosher salt

2 tablespoons water

PROVISIONS FOR THE DOUGH

3 cups all-purpose flour

2 teaspoons kosher salt

1/4 cup salted butter (1/2 stick), melted

1 cup water

PROVISIONS FOR THE PEA AND POTATO FILLING

4 cups russet potatoes (4 medium), peeled, 1/2-inch cubes

1/4 cup extra virgin olive oil

2 teaspoons cumin seeds

2 teaspoons mustard seeds

1 cup yellow onion (1/2 medium), medium diced

1 Thai green chili (1 tablespoon), finely chopped

2 tablespoons garlic (8 cloves), thinly sliced

2 tablespoons fresh ginger, peeled, grated

2 teaspoons chili powder

2 teaspoons cumin

2 teaspoons turmeric

1 cup frozen peas, thawed

PROVISIONS FOR THE FRYING

5 cups canola oil, for frying

DIRECTIONS FOR THE MINT CHUTNEY

1. In a blender, blend the cilantro, mint, ginger, garlic, cumin seeds, chili, lemon juice, yogurt, salt, and water until smooth.
2. Pour into a small mixing bowl, cover with plastic wrap, and place in the refrigerator.

DIRECTIONS FOR THE DOUGH

1. In a large mixing bowl, add the flour, salt, and butter. Use your hands to rub the melted butter into the flour until it resembles coarse bread crumbs.
2. Gradually add the water, using your hands to knead until the dough is smooth and firm, approximately 5 minutes.
3. Cover the bowl with a damp cloth and let it rest, approximately 30 minutes.

DIRECTIONS FOR THE PEA AND POTATO FILLING

1. Add the potatoes to a medium pot of water and cook over medium-high heat. Boil until fork-tender, 8 to 12 minutes. Drain.
2. In a large sauté pan, heat the olive oil over medium heat. Add in the cumin seeds and mustard seeds. Cook until they pop, approximately 30 seconds.
3. Quickly add in the onion, chili, garlic, ginger, chili powder, cumin, and turmeric. Using a wooden spoon, sauté until the onion is translucent, approximately 5 minutes.
4. Add in the peas and potatoes. Stir together and cook until heated through.
5. Remove from the heat.

DIRECTIONS FOR THE SAMOSAS ASSEMBLY AND FRYING

1. Portion the dough into 12 equal balls on a clean, lightly floured, flat surface.
2. Using a rolling pin, flatten each ball into a 1/4-inch-thick disk approximately 6 inches in diameter.
3. Cut each disk in half to form 2 semicircles.
4. Using your fingers, moisten the straight portion of the semicircle with a little water. Then fold the semicircle into a cone shape, like a waffle cone. Seal the overlapping edges.
5. Fill the cone with 2 tablespoons of the pea and potato filling.
6. Using your wet fingers, seal the open edge by pressing the dough together to form a triangular samosa shape.
7. Repeat with the remaining dough and filling. Place the filled triangles on a large sheet tray lined with parchment paper.
8. In a large skillet, preheat the oil to 350°F. Gently place the samosas into the hot oil. Fry until golden brown, approximately 8 minutes.
9. Drain the samosas on a large sheet tray lined with paper towels.
10. Serve 3 hot samosas for each plate with the mint chutney.

Throttle Control: Adjust the amounts of Greek yogurt (creamy) and Thai green chili (heat of 50,000 to 100,000 Scoville heat units, or SHU) based on taste preferences.

Alternate Course: Instead of the Thai green chili, use Indian jwala chili peppers, which are milder at 30,000 to 50,000 SHU. Even milder heat options include jalapeño peppers (2,500 to 5,000 SHU) or serrano peppers (10,000 to 23,000 SHU).

Rogue Wave: Ouch! Frying mustard seeds can be dangerous if they pop in your direction. Try holding a large pot lid in front of you as a shield, or don safety glasses for extra protection.

Mumbai, India

CURRIED CARROT SALAD

This special salad is made as orange as possible: carrots, orange zest, turmeric, and curry. It is balanced with the warmth of cloves and ginger, the sweetness of raisins and honey, and the nuttiness of cashews. I make it for friends and family on the boat or off—it's always a hit!

TOTAL TRIP: 15 minutes

CRUISING TIME: 15 minutes

SERVES: 4

PROVISIONS

4 cups pre-shredded carrots

2 teaspoons fresh orange zest (1/2 medium orange)

1 tablespoon garlic (4 cloves), minced

2 teaspoons fresh ginger, peeled, grated

1/2 cup raisins

3/4 cup cashews, roughly chopped

1/2 cup fresh cilantro leaves, chopped

3 tablespoons fresh lime juice (1 1/2 medium limes)

4 teaspoons honey

1 teaspoon turmeric

2 teaspoons curry powder

Pinch of cayenne pepper

1/2 cup yellow onion (1/4 medium), small diced

3 tablespoons extra virgin olive oil

2 teaspoons kosher salt

DIRECTIONS

1. In a large mixing bowl, add the carrots, orange zest, garlic, ginger, raisins, cashews, cilantro, lime juice, honey, turmeric, curry powder, cayenne pepper, onion, olive oil, and salt. Use tongs to mix until combined. So easy! So fresh!

Mumbai, India

INDIAN BUTTER SHRIMP

The spices bring this dish to life. You can make your own garam masala spice blend with cloves, cinnamon, cardamom, cumin, coriander, nutmeg, bay leaf, mace, and black pepper. You can also buy it as a blend on the international aisle or in a specialty market. Either way, you will be transported to India.

TOTAL TRIP: 30 minutes

SERVES: 4

PROVISIONS FOR THE RICE

- 1½ cups basmati rice, rinsed 3 to 4 times
- 2¼ cups water

PROVISIONS FOR THE SHRIMP

- 2 pounds jumbo shrimp, peeled, deveined, tail off
- 2 tablespoons garlic (8 cloves), grated
- 2 tablespoons fresh ginger, peeled, grated
- 1 teaspoon cayenne pepper
- 2 teaspoons kosher salt
- ¼ cup salted butter (½ stick)

PROVISIONS FOR THE SAUCE

- ¼ cup salted butter (½ stick)
- 1⅓ cups yellow onion (⅔ medium), small diced
- ¼ cup cashews
- 1 cup tomato sauce
- ½ cup Roma tomato (1 medium), medium diced
- ½ teaspoon kosher salt
- 1 teaspoon ground coriander
- 1 teaspoon garam masala
- 2 teaspoons turmeric
- ¼ cup heavy whipping cream
- 2 teaspoons honey
- ¼ cup cilantro, for garnish

DIRECTIONS FOR THE RICE

1. In a small pot or a rice cooker, use the recipe's ratio to cook the rice in the water, or follow the directions on the package. Once cooked, remove from heat.

DIRECTIONS FOR THE SHRIMP

1. While the rice cooks, in a large mixing bowl, add the shrimp, garlic, ginger, cayenne pepper, and salt. Mix to season and coat the shrimp.
2. In a large skillet over medium-high heat, melt the butter.
3. Add in the seasoned shrimp. Cook for 1½ minutes on each side, using tongs to turn. Clean the bowl.
4. Put the shrimp and liquids from the pan into the now-clean, large mixing bowl.

DIRECTIONS FOR THE SAUCE

1. In the same large skillet, using medium-low heat, add in the butter, onion, cashews, tomato sauce, tomato, salt, coriander, garam masala, and turmeric. Stirring occasionally with a wooden spoon, simmer until the sauce has thickened and onion is tender, 10 to 15 minutes.
2. Use an immersion blender in the skillet to puree the sauce (or a regular blender, returning the sauce to the skillet).
3. Add the cream and honey to the sauce. Simmer for 3 more minutes.
4. Stir the shrimp with juices back into the sauce. Simmer for 2 more minutes.
5. Serve with the rice. Garnish with the cilantro on top.

Throttle Control: Adjust the amounts of tomato (acidic) and cream/butter (creamy) based on taste preferences.

Alternate Course: Instead of the shrimp, use chicken.

Rogue Wave: Avoid rubbery shrimp! Be sure to watch the timing of your shrimp simmering in the sauce. No more than 2 minutes!

Mumbai, India

PISTACHIO AND CARDAMOM KULFI

From as early as the sixteenth century in Delhi, India, kulfi has been enjoyed after a hot meal to cool the palate. *Kulfi* comes from the Persian word *qulfi,* which means "covered cup." Made with pistachios, spices, and condensed milk, this kulfi version is done in the Popsicle style for fun and for ease of eating.

TOTAL TRIP: 3 hours, 15 minutes (up to 12 hours)

CRUISING TIME: 15 minutes

IDLE TIME: 3 hours (or more, for freezing)

SERVES: 4

PROVISIONS

1/2 teaspoon saffron

1 tablespoon hot water

1 cup whole milk

1/3 cup heavy whipping cream

1/4 cup dried milk powder

1/4 cup condensed milk

1/3 cup unsalted pistachios, crushed

1/4 teaspoon cardamom

DIRECTIONS

1. In a blender, add the saffron and hot water to steep for 1 minute without any blending.
2. Add the milk, cream, milk powder, condensed milk, pistachios, and cardamom. Blend until the mixture is smooth.
3. Strain the mixture through a fine-mesh strainer to remove nuts that are too grainy for our Popsicle.
4. Pour the strained mixture into Popsicle molds (or simply use cups with wooden sticks, a reminder of childhood!).
5. Place in the freezer until completely frozen, 3 hours or more (even overnight).

Throttle Control: Adjust the amount of condensed milk (sweet) based on taste preferences.

Alternate Course: Instead of saffron, pistachios, and cardamom, be creative with your flavors! Rosewater and mango are great options.

THAILAND

Phuket, Thailand

Clear waters, soft sand, and fresh coconuts—welcome to Thailand!

The vibrant landscape unfolds like a postcard. Turquoise-blue seas. Powdery-white sand beaches. Lush green vegetation. Rain-forested mountains. You'll definitely write home about this place.

And then there are the friendly people and phenomenal foods. This is a highlight on our world tour with *vacation* written all over it, Little Chef!

On the yacht, Thai dishes are a hot item with the guests, literally and figuratively. I provision my galley with loads of curry and coconut milk from Phuket's plentiful markets. And I always make lots of extra Thai meals for myself since Thai food is my favorite. I know I'm not alone in this. Thailand's palate-pleasing cuisine knocks our socks off, which is perfect since bare feet are ideal for digging our toes in the sand.

In particular, there are three curries that make my toes (and tongue) tingle—yellow, red, and green. I appreciate their different heat levels when combined into a curry blend with regulars like lemongrass, ginger, garlic, shallots, shrimp paste, cumin, coriander seeds, and turmeric.

Yellow curry is easy to love. Mild yellow chilies are mixed with the regular blend of spices, along with vegetables, potatoes, or rice, and a protein such as chicken or tofu. To this end, start with mild-mannered yellow curry if you and your guests are new to our curry party.

Thailand's most popular blend with my guests is red curry. Spicier than yellow, our red curry dish starts with a paste of crushed red chilies that will have your toes tapping in no time. Mellow out the heat of the red chilies with our much-needed coconut milk and a fruit such as mango or pineapple to round out the flavor profile.

In fresh-coconut land, I'm ready for my curry creation.

And finally, there's our hottest blend, green curry. You'd think that the color green might be as innocent as grass, but it is the spiciest of them all. When composing a green curry dish, consider your audience. Make sure to add plenty of coconut milk to balance out the intensity and keep the curry party going strong.

Notice the common ingredient in all three curry blends? Coconut milk! It's the coolest staple I know to keep handy in my galley. Coconut milk makes every Thai curry possible. Sweet and creamy, coconut milk is easy to find in any grocery store. Or grab a fresh coconut from a tree, if possible, as we dock in Phuket. The beach is loaded with them. We break open our coconut right on the deck and then use simple tools to grate the meat and extract the liquid.

Whether you're cracking open a fresh coconut or simply a can of coconut cream, you will quickly feel these recipes transport you to beautiful Thailand, where sunsets and smiles are surreal and spectacular. What a dream destination.

Phuket, Thailand

BREAKFAST

Thai Omelet

LUNCH

Pad See Ew

COCKTAIL HOUR

Sabai Sabai

Green Papaya Salad

DINNER

Tom Yum Soup

Beef Thai Red Curry

Mango Sticky Rice

Phuket, Thailand

THAI OMELET

Our Thai omelet, or *khai jiao,* is a centuries-old staple in Thai cuisine. No wonder, since everyone loves a good omelet. And who doesn't love fried foods? Score both with our Thai breakfast omelet. This nationally beloved Thai street food is the perfect way to start the morning.

TOTAL TRIP: 30 minutes

CRUISING TIME: 20 minutes

IDLE TIME: 10 minutes

SERVES: 4

PROVISIONS FOR THE RICE

1 cup jasmine rice, rinsed 3 to 4 times

1½ cups water

PROVISIONS FOR THE OMELET

12 eggs

½ cup green onions (4 stalks), thinly sliced

2 tablespoons fish sauce

Pinch of kosher salt

4 teaspoons light brown sugar

2 Thai red chilies, sliced

1 cup canola oil, for frying

¾ cup English cucumber (½ large), sliced in semicircles

DIRECTIONS FOR THE RICE

1. In a small pot or a rice cooker, use the recipe's ratio to cook the rice in the water, or follow the directions on the package. Once cooked, remove from heat.

DIRECTIONS FOR THE OMELET

1. While the rice cooks, in a medium mixing bowl, add the eggs, green onions, fish sauce, salt, brown sugar, and chilies. Whisk until combined.
2. In a medium sauté pan, preheat the oil to 350°F over medium-high heat.
3. Working in 4 batches, ladle ¼ of the egg mixture into the hot oil. Fry each side for 2 minutes or until golden brown.
4. Remove the omelets and place on a large sheet tray lined with paper towels to drain the oil. Repeat with the remaining mixture to make 4 omelets in total.
5. Serve with the cooked rice and sliced raw cucumber.

Throttle Control: Adjust the amount of Thai red chilies (heat) based on taste preferences, or use a less intense pepper since Thai red chilies have a heat of 50,000 to 100,000 Scoville heat units, or SHU. Less intense peppers include jalapeño (2,500 to 5,000 SHU), serrano (10,000 to 23,000 SHU), red pepper flakes (15,000 to 45,000 SHU), and cayenne (30,000 to 50,000 SHU).

Alternate Course: Instead of the green onions, add any vegetables of your choice. Instead of the fish sauce, add extra salt, but note that the umami (savory and rich) flavor is then compromised.

Rogue Wave: Thai red chilies are spicy hot! To tame the heat of the pepper, remove the seeds, veins, and pith when preparing.

Alternate Course: Instead of the chicken, add any protein of your choice. Instead of the Chinese broccoli, use regular broccoli, but use half the amount since the Chinese version is leafier. Instead of the regular soy sauce, use traditional Thai or black soy sauce version, which is darker but not as salty (add salt as needed).

Phuket, Thailand

PAD SEE EW

Noodle stir-frying is a must in Thailand. Translated to mean "fried with soy sauce," pad see ew is a glorious celebration of umami and texture. It's also a celebration of early 1900s Chinese immigrants, who allegedly brought the dish to the Thai culture. So easy and super satisfying, this dish will have you in a celebratory mood when it is on the table is less than an hour.

TOTAL TRIP: 40 minutes

CRUISING TIME: 35 minutes

IDLE TIME: 5 minutes

SERVES: 4

PROVISIONS FOR THE NOODLES

14 ounces wide rice noodles, uncooked

PROVISIONS FOR THE STIR-FRY

1/4 cup soy sauce

1/4 cup oyster sauce

1/4 cup canola oil

2 tablespoons fish sauce

1/4 cup granulated sugar

1 tablespoon plus 1 teaspoon garlic (6 cloves), minced

2 chicken breasts, boneless, skinless, thinly sliced

2 eggs, beaten

8 cups Chinese broccoli (2 large heads), cut into 1/2-inch pieces

DIRECTIONS FOR THE NOODLES

1. Prepare the rice noodles as directed on the package, until tender. Set aside to cool. If the packaging is a different size, dry noodles can be stored in the pantry for later.

DIRECTIONS FOR THE STIR-FRY

1. In a small mixing bowl, add the soy sauce, oyster sauce, oil, fish sauce, sugar, and garlic. Mix to combine.
2. In a large skillet, heat half of the sauce over medium-high heat, then add the chicken. Cook the chicken, turning with tongs, until browned, approximately 5 minutes. Remove from the skillet and set aside on a large sheet tray.
3. In the same skillet, add the eggs to scramble by stirring constantly, 1 to 2 minutes.
4. Once the eggs are cooked, add in the Chinese broccoli and cook for 3 minutes, stirring occasionally. Remove from the skillet and place on the same tray as the chicken.
5. Add the remaining sauce and the cooked noodles to the skillet. Stirring only occasionally with tongs, allow the noodles to stick as they brown, almost burn, with the caramelization of the sugars in the sauce to add a smoky taste, approximately 5 minutes.
6. Add back in the chicken, eggs, and broccoli to reheat and toss together with tongs.
7. Serve and enjoy!

Phuket, Thailand

SABAI SABAI

Comfortable, content, relaxed, cozy. These are all appropriate translations of the Thai word *sabai,* which is often said twice for full effect. You can get to this not-a-care-in-the-world state of mind with Thai rum, basil, and citrus, I promise. *Sabai sabai!* And cheers too! *Chok dee!*

TOTAL TRIP: 5 minutes

SERVES: 4

PROVISIONS

3/4 cup Thai rum

3/4 cup fresh lemon juice (6 medium lemons)

1/2 cup simple syrup

3/4 cup club soda

4 sprigs fresh Thai basil, for garnish

DIRECTIONS

1. Into a pitcher, add the rum, lemon juice, simple syrup, and club soda.
2. Add ice and stir with a long spoon.
3. Serve in your favorite glasses filled with ice, and garnish each glass with one of the basil sprigs.

Alternate Course: Instead of the Thai rum, use any type of white or dark rum, but note that the distinct Thai taste will be forfeited. Instead of Thai basil, use regular basil, but again, note that the flavor will be less sabai sabai-style.

Phuket, Thailand

GREEN PAPAYA SALAD

This unique salad will surprise everyone with its crispy shreds of unripened papaya. The tangy lime juice and the peanut crunch set this dish apart from any other salad out there.

TOTAL TRIP: 20 minutes

SERVES: 4

PROVISIONS

1 green (unripe) papaya, peeled

1 cup Chinese long beans, cut into 1/2-inch pieces

1 cup cherry tomatoes (10 medium), halved

1 tablespoon garlic (4 cloves), roughly chopped

1/4 cup peanuts, chopped

4 Thai red chilies, chopped

4 teaspoons granulated sugar

1/4 cup fish sauce

1/4 cup fresh lime juice (2 medium limes)

2 tablespoons peanut butter

2 tablespoons peanuts, chopped, for garnish

DIRECTIONS

1. Use a julienne peeler (or a knife or mandoline) to make long, thin shreds of the green papaya. Set aside in a large mixing bowl, and combine with the beans and tomatoes.
2. In a small mixing bowl, add the garlic, peanuts, chilies, sugar, fish sauce, lime juice, and peanut butter. Using an immersion blender (or a regular blender, returning to the bowl afterward), puree the mixture until smooth.
3. Pour the sauce into the papaya mixture. Toss with tongs.
4. Garnish with chopped the peanuts and serve.

Throttle Control: Adjust the amount of peanut butter (nutty and creamy) based on taste preferences.

Alternate Course: Instead of the Chinese long beans, use regular green beans.

Rogue Wave: Do not use a ripe papaya, as the soft texture and sweetness will not work. Asian and Mexican grocery stores, and even some regular markets, carry the green, unripened version.

Phuket, Thailand

TOM YUM SOUP

Yum is right! Lemongrass, ginger, kaffir lime leaves, and other fabulous Thai flavors round out this perfect soup. If you can't get to Asia by boat, visit your nearest Asian market for the best and freshest ingredients. Bring Thailand to you!

TOTAL TRIP: 30 minutes

CRUISING TIME: 10 minutes

IDLE TIME: 20 minutes

SERVES: 4

PROVISIONS

2 tablespoons canola oil

2 lemongrass stalks, cut in thirds

2 tablespoons fresh ginger, peeled, grated

8 kaffir lime leaves, whole

Thai red chilies, thinly sliced

2 tablespoons garlic (8 cloves), minced

1 cup Roma tomatoes (2 medium), medium diced

2 cups oyster mushrooms (8 ounces), sliced

2/3 cup sweet onion (1/3 medium), thinly sliced

4 teaspoons granulated sugar

2 tablespoons fish sauce

6 cups chicken stock

20 jumbo shrimp, peeled, deveined, tail on

2 tablespoons fresh lime juice (1 medium lime)

1/2 cup fresh cilantro leaves, whole, for garnish

DIRECTIONS

1. In a large pot, heat the oil over medium-high heat. Using the blunt side of a knife, bang the lemongrass to split it. Then add the bruised lemongrass, ginger, lime leaves, chilies, garlic, tomatoes, mushrooms, and onion. Using a wooden spoon, sauté until the tomatoes start to break down, 8 to 10 minutes.
2. Add in the sugar, fish sauce, and chicken stock. Reduce the heat to medium-low and simmer for 10 minutes, stirring occasionally.
3. Remove the lemongrass and discard.
4. Add in the shrimp to cook fully, stirring occasionally, approximately 3 minutes.
5. Turn off the heat and add in the lime juice.
6. Serve hot in a bowl and garnish with the cilantro.

Throttle Control: Adjust the amount of Thai red chilies (heat) based on taste preferences, or use a less intense pepper since Thai red chilies have a heat of 50,000 to 100,000 Scoville heat units, SHU. Less intense peppers include jalapeño (2,500 to 5,000 SHU), serrano (10,000 to 23,000 SHU), red pepper flakes (15,000 to 45,000 SHU), and cayenne (30,000 to 50,000 SHU).

Alternate Course: Instead of the oyster mushrooms, use any mushrooms of your choice. Instead of the lemongrass stalks, use lemongrass paste, which can be found in most grocery stores (1 stalk: 2 teaspoons paste).

Rogue Wave: Don't be surprised if you can't find kaffir lime leaves in your regular grocery store since they are imported as dried leaves. Look online to secure this very distinct and wonderful flavor. And remember: Thai red chilies are spicy hot! To tame the heat of the pepper, remove the seeds, veins, and pith when preparing.

Throttle Control: Adjust the amounts of brown sugar (sweet) and Thai red curry paste (heat) based on taste preferences.

Alternate Course: Instead of the mango, use pineapple. Instead of the zucchini and red bell pepper, use any vegetables of your choice.

Rogue Wave: Don't be surprised if you can't find kaffir lime leaves in your regular grocery store. Look online to secure this very distinct and wonderful flavor.

Phuket, Thailand

BEEF THAI RED CURRY

Welcome to my favorite meal, not just in Asia but maybe in the whole world. If you can't experience it for yourself in Thailand, be sure to make this at home. The red curry is mellowed perfectly with coconut milk and mango, transporting you to a tropical paradise. *Gin hâi a-ròi!* Enjoy your delicious meal!

TOTAL TRIP: 40 minutes

SERVES: 4

PROVISIONS FOR THE RICE

1½ cups jasmine rice, rinsed 3 to 4 times

2¼ cups water

PROVISIONS FOR THE CURRY

2 tablespoons canola oil

½ cup Thai red curry paste (4-ounce can)

1 pound sirloin steak, boneless, thinly sliced

2 teaspoons kosher salt

3½ cups coconut milk (two 13.5-ounce cans), unsweetened

¼ cup light brown sugar

2 tablespoons fish sauce

2 kaffir lime leaves

2 cups zucchini (2 small), cut into thin semicircles

1 cup bamboo shoots (8-ounce can), drained

1 cup fresh mango (1 small), cubed

1½ cups red bell pepper (1 large), matchstick cuts

½ cup fresh Thai basil leaves, chiffonade cut, for garnish

DIRECTIONS FOR THE RICE

1. In a small pot or a rice cooker, use the recipe's ratio to cook the rice in the water, or follow the directions on the package. Once cooked, remove from heat.

DIRECTIONS FOR THE CURRY

1. While the rice cooks, in a large sauté pan, add the oil and curry paste. Using medium heat and stirring with a wooden spoon, heat until fragrant, 1 to 2 minutes.
2. Once fragrant, add in the steak and salt. Brown the meat, 3 to 4 minutes.
3. Once browned, add in the coconut milk, brown sugar, fish sauce, and lime leaves. Stirring occasionally, simmer for 5 minutes.
4. Add in the zucchini, bamboo shoots, mango, and bell pepper. Stirring occasionally, simmer the vegetables in the coconut milk until tender, 3 to 5 minutes.
5. Remove from the heat and add the Thai basil garnish.
6. Serve with the rice.

Phuket, Thailand

MANGO STICKY RICE

When in Thailand, take advantage of the sweet tropical fruit found right outside your window. Did you know that there is a Thai sweet green mango that is actually not sweet but rather nutty and crunchy like a Granny Smith apple? Whether you choose a Thai mango or one from your local store that is as sweet and juicy as a peach, this dessert will showcase our mango friend just the same.

TOTAL TRIP: 1 hour, 45 minutes

CRUISING TIME: 15 minutes

IDLE TIME: 1 hour, 30 minutes

SERVES: 4

PROVISIONS FOR THE RICE

1 cup glutinous rice (sweet or sticky rice), rinsed 3 to 4 times

1 cup water

PROVISIONS FOR THE COCONUT SAUCE

2/3 cup coconut milk, unsweetened

1/3 cup granulated sugar

Pinch of kosher salt

PROVISIONS FOR THE COCONUT GLAZE

2/3 cup coconut milk, unsweetened

1 tablespoon granulated sugar

2 teaspoons cornstarch

PROVISIONS FOR THE ASSEMBLY

1 tablespoon sesame seeds, for garnish

2 cups fresh mangoes (2 small), sliced, for garnish

DIRECTIONS FOR THE RICE

1. In a small pot or a rice cooker, use the recipe's ratio to cook the rice in the water according to the directions for a sticky rice. Once cooked, remove from heat.

DIRECTIONS FOR THE COCONUT SAUCE

1. While the rice cooks, in a medium microwave-safe mixing bowl, add the coconut milk, sugar, and salt. Heat in the microwave until the sugar is dissolved, approximately 1 minute.
2. Once the rice is cooked, pour the coconut sauce over it. Gently incorporate the sauce and the rice with a rubber spatula. Set aside to cool for 20 minutes.
3. After 20 minutes, cover the bowl with plastic wrap. Place it in the refrigerator to chill for 1 hour.

DIRECTIONS FOR THE COCONUT GLAZE

1. In an unheated small pot, add the coconut milk, sugar, and cornstarch. Whisk to combine.
2. Bring to a boil over medium-high heat while continuing to whisk. Once boiling, immediately turn off the heat, transferring the thickened coconut glaze into a small heat-safe mixing bowl.
3. Cool in the refrigerator for 30 minutes.

DIRECTIONS FOR THE PLATING

1. Once the rice and the coconut glaze are cooled, scoop the rice onto plates.
2. Garnish the rice with the coconut glaze, sesame seeds, and fresh mango slices.

Alternate Course: Instead of the glutinous rice, use any type of short- or medium-grain white rice, which will be less sticky and starchy, but still tasty.

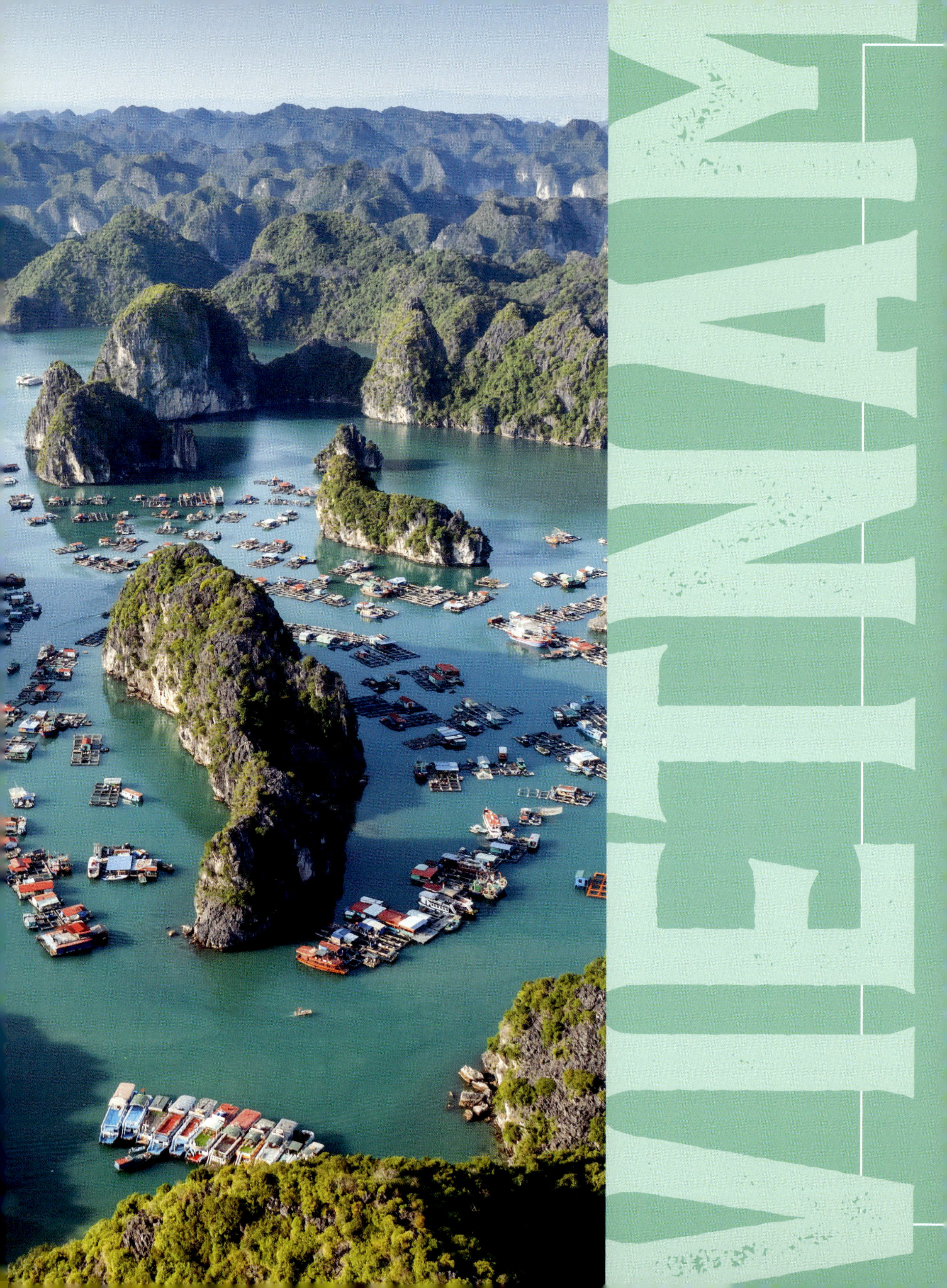
VIETNAM

Hạ Long Bay, Vietnam

Prepare to be mesmerized by the landscapes and tastes of Southeast Asia!

Limestone towers rise up from the emerald waterways as junk boats and sea kayaks explore in Hạ Long Bay, Vietnam. Watch the rock climbers scaling karst formations, the scuba divers exploring coral reefs, and the day hikers roaming rain forests and caves.

But don't miss the Vietnamese food, Little Chef! I seek adventure beyond my yacht galley by exploring the village markets to learn how to combine the five fundamental tastes, called *ngũ vị* in Vietnamese: sweet, salty, bitter, sour, and spicy. I gather the freshest ingredients and return to my yacht galley carrying baskets of local specialties: lemongrass, mint, ginger, coriander, cinnamon, chili, lime, Thai basil, sriracha, hoisin, and fish sauce. With these unique flavors, I create traditional Vietnamese meals that transform any vegetable, starch, or protein into an absolute showstopper.

Vietnamese cooking maximizes the use of ingredients and wastes nothing. I love the resourcefulness. Our scallion's stalk will flavor our soup stock and "crunchify" the stir-fry, plus the root will grow more babies when we replant it. The same is true with other vegetables and proteins too. Why waste anything so yummy?

I like to serve Vietnamese food to the guests traditionally, where other than an individual bowl of rice (*cơm trắng*), everyone shares in the bowls set in the center of the table. Family style, my favorite way to enjoy a meal, makes the dining experience communal and communicative. In Vietnam, the younger people wait for their elders to start eating first. Then everyone at the table invites the others to enjoy the meal as they serve each other fish (*cá*), meat (*thịt*) and/or tofu (*đậu phụ*), vegetables (*rau*), and broth (*canh*).

The Vietnamese dining experience really takes on its most notable character trait with the addition of the condiments and relishes that are set on the table. The *nước chấm* condiments include pure fish sauce, ginger fish sauce, tamarind sauce, soy sauce, *muối tiêu chanh* (salt and pepper with lime juice), and *muối ớt* (salt and chili), which are used for dipping. The relishes include salted eggplant, pickled white cabbage, pickled papaya, pickled garlic, and pickled bean sprouts.

Now the feast begins. Dip it, relish it, love it!

Hạ Long Bay, Vietnam

BREAKFAST

Bánh Mì

LUNCH

Barbecue Short Rib Vermicelli

COCKTAIL HOUR

Egg Coffee Cocktail

Shrimp Summer Rolls

DINNER

Crunchy Chicken Salad

Pho

Honeycomb Cake

Hạ Long Bay, Vietnam

BÁNH MÌ

This Vietnamese sandwich packs tantalizing Asian flavors between two slices of bread (*bánh mì*). Traditionally baked with wheat flour, the crisp baguette (a bread style inspired by the French) provides the perfect vehicle for on-the-go eating at any time of day. I like to serve it up first thing in the morning as I watch the sun rise outside my galley window.

TOTAL TRIP: 3 hours, 20 minutes

CRUISING TIME: 20 minutes

IDLE TIME: 3 hours

SERVES: 4

PROVISIONS FOR THE PORK BELLY

2 pounds pork belly

1/4 cup fish sauce

1/4 cup light brown sugar

1 tablespoon garlic (4 cloves), minced

4 teaspoons sesame oil

4 teaspoons soy sauce

1/2 teaspoon freshly ground black pepper

1/4 cup green onions (2 stalks), sliced

PROVISIONS FOR THE PICKLED VEGETABLES

1/4 cup rice vinegar

1/4 cup water

2 teaspoons kosher salt

2 teaspoons granulated sugar

1 cup red onion (1/2 medium), thinly sliced

1 cup carrots (2 medium), shredded

PROVISIONS FOR THE SPICY MAYONNAISE

1/4 cup mayonnaise

1 tablespoon sriracha

PROVISIONS FOR THE ASSEMBLY

2 baguettes (12- to 14-inch lengths)

1/4 cup hoisin sauce

1 cup English cucumber (1 small), matchstick cuts

1/2 cup jalapeño peppers (2 medium), thinly sliced

1 cup fresh cilantro leaves

DIRECTIONS FOR THE PORK BELLY

1. Preheat the oven to 300°F.
2. In a 9-by-13-inch casserole dish, add the pork belly, fish sauce, brown sugar, garlic, sesame oil, soy sauce, pepper, and green onions. Mix with your hands to coat the pork belly. Cover with aluminum foil and bake until tender, approximately 3 hours.
3. When the pork belly is done, remove from the oven onto a cutting board to rest for 10 minutes. Thinly slice the pork belly.

DIRECTIONS FOR THE PICKLED VEGETABLES AND SPICY MAYONNAISE

1. While the pork belly is baking, in a medium microwave-safe mixing bowl, add the rice vinegar, water, salt, and sugar. Microwave until boiling, approximately 3 minutes. Carefully remove from the microwave.
2. Immediately add the red onion and carrots into the boiling vinegar mixture, stirring until submerged. Let the vegetables marinate until ready to assemble the bánh mì.
3. In a small mixing bowl, add the mayonnaise and sriracha. Stir to combine.

DIRECTIONS FOR THE ASSEMBLY

1. Slice the baguettes in half horizontally and toast them.
2. Spread the hoisin and the spicy mayo on the bottom half of the baguettes.
3. Layer the sliced pork belly, cucumber, pickled vegetables (drained), jalapeños (to taste), and cilantro on the bottom half of the baguette. Top with other half of the baguette.
4. Slice the bánh mì sandwiches in half to serve 4.

Throttle Control: Adjust the amount of fresh jalapeño peppers (heat). Or consider placing the jalapeños in the pickling juice (instead of raw) to reduce the heat.

Alternate Course: Instead of the pork belly, use thinly sliced pork cutlets that are seared on the stovetop or grill. This quick method bypasses slow-roasting so the sandwich is ready much sooner, but the taste is quite different.

Rogue Wave: Thai red chilies are spicy hot! To tame the heat of the pepper, remove the seeds, veins, and pith when preparing.

Hạ Long Bay, Vietnam

BARBECUE SHORT RIB VERMICELLI

As in many Vietnamese dishes, noodles play an important role here. Long, thin, round rice noodles lay the foundation for our fabulous short rib creation. The term *vermicelli* is assigned to this shape of noodle, but you won't find this name in Vietnam. Think spaghetti, but made with rice instead of semolina flour and called *bún*. I call it "fun bún" since the hot ribs on top of it make for a celebration indeed.

TOTAL TRIP: 1 hour, 30 minutes (up to 12 hours)

CRUISING TIME: 30 minutes

IDLE TIME: 1 hour (or more, to marinate)

SERVES: 4

PROVISIONS FOR THE SHORT RIBS

2 pounds beef short ribs, flanken style

1 tablespoon garlic (4 cloves), minced

1/4 cup fish sauce

1 tablespoon thick (or regular) soy sauce

6 tablespoons dark brown sugar

3 tablespoons lemongrass (2 stalks), tender inner heart parts only, finely chopped

2 tablespoons canola oil, for frying

PROVISIONS FOR THE DIPPING SAUCE

3 tablespoons fish sauce

3 tablespoons granulated sugar

1/4 cup water

1 tablespoon rice vinegar

2 tablespoons fresh lime juice (1 medium lime)

1 teaspoon garlic (1 small clove), minced

1 tablespoon fresh ginger, peeled, grated

1 Thai red chili, thinly sliced

PROVISIONS FOR THE NOODLES

14 ounces vermicelli rice noodles, uncooked

PROVISIONS FOR THE ASSEMBLY

2 cups green leaf lettuce (3/4 of a head), roughly chopped

1 cup carrots (2 medium), shredded

1 cup daikon radish (1 large), matchstick cuts

1/4 cup fresh cilantro leaves

1/4 cup fresh Thai basil leaves

1/4 cup fresh mint leaves

1 cup bean sprouts

1/2 cup green onions (4 stalks), sliced, for garnish

1/2 cup peanuts, chopped, for garnish

Thai red chili, thinly sliced, for garnish

DIRECTIONS FOR THE SHORT RIBS

1. In a gallon-size plastic food-storage bag, add the short ribs, garlic, fish sauce, soy sauce, brown sugar, and lemongrass. Seal and mix around until the beef is coated, and marinate in the refrigerator for 1 hour or more (even overnight).
2. Meanwhile, prepare the dipping sauce and noodles.
3. Once the beef is marinated, heat a large skillet over medium-high heat. When hot, add the oil and sear the beef until browned, approximately 2 minutes on each side.

DIRECTIONS FOR THE DIPPING SAUCE AND NOODLES

1. In a small mixing bowl, add the fish sauce, sugar, water, rice vinegar, lime juice, garlic, ginger, and chili. Stir to combine. Pour into a small cup.
2. Prepare the rice noodles according to the directions on the package. Store any leftover dry noodles in the pantry for other dishes.
3. Once the noodles are tender, cool them quickly by submerging the noodles into an ice bath in a medium mixing bowl. For 2 minutes, move the noodles around with tongs to ensure they cool. Drain the water and ice.

DIRECTIONS FOR THE ASSEMBLY

1. Assemble each plate with individual portions of each item, starting with 1/4 of the cooled rice vermicelli covering approximately 40 percent of the plate.
2. To the other side of the plate, add 1/4 of the lettuce, followed by 1/4-size portions of the carrots, daikon radish, cilantro, Thai basil, mint, and bean sprouts.
3. Place 1/4 of the hot short ribs on top of the rice vermicelli on each plate.
4. Garnish the entire plate with the green onions, peanuts, and Thai red chili. Serve with the dipping sauce in a small cup that can be poured on top if desired.

Throttle Control: Adjust the amount of Thai red chili (heat) based on taste preferences, or use a less intense pepper since Thai red chilies have a heat of 50,000 to 100,000 in Scoville heat units, SHU. Less intense peppers include jalapeño (2,500 to 5,000 SHU), serrano (10,000 to 23,000 SHU), red pepper flakes (15,000 to 45,000 SHU), and cayenne (30,000 to 50,000 SHU).

Alternate Course: Instead of the short ribs, use any protein based on your preferences. Instead of the Thai basil with a spicy licorice flavor, use sweet basil. Instead of the fresh lemongrass, use 2 teaspoons of the paste version. If without the daikon radishes, increase the amount of carrots for the crunch factor.

Hạ Long Bay, Vietnam

EGG COFFEE COCKTAIL

Here is a celebratory spin on the popular egg coffee enjoyed in Vietnam. I add Kahlúa to make it a cool cocktail to pair with our spring roll appetizer, elevating it to a new level of fun. One, two, three, drink! *Một, hai, ba, dzô!*

TOTAL TRIP: 15 minutes

CRUISING TIME: 10 minutes

IDLE TIME: 5 minutes

SERVES: 4

PROVISIONS

4 pasteurized egg yolks

1/3 cup condensed milk

1 teaspoon vanilla extract

1/3 cup Kahlúa

4 cups prepared coffee, strongly brewed, chilled

DIRECTIONS

1. In a small mixing bowl, whisk the egg yolks, condensed milk, and vanilla until fluffy, approximately 3 minutes.
2. In a pitcher, mix the Kahlúa and chilled coffee (perhaps some extra from breakfast). Add ice.
3. To serve, pour the spiked coffee into 4 glasses and top with the sweet egg mixture.

Throttle Control: Adjust the amount of Kahlúa (sweet and coffee forward) based on your preferences.

Rogue Wave: Be sure the egg is pasteurized since serving raw.

Hạ Long Bay, Vietnam

SHRIMP SUMMER ROLLS

Do you see what I see? We can peek inside our summer roll since it is a translucent rice wrap that is served cool, rather than a fried spring roll made of flour that is served hot. In any season, summer rolls bring a light freshness to the table, perfect for a sunshiny day on the deck.

TOTAL TRIP: 45 minutes

SERVES: 4

PROVISIONS FOR THE NOODLES

7 ounces vermicelli rice noodles, uncooked

PROVISIONS FOR THE DIPPING SAUCE

1/4 cup peanut butter, smooth

4 teaspoons hoisin sauce

2 teaspoons sesame oil

4 teaspoons soy sauce

2 teaspoons crunchy garlic chili oil or sriracha

1 teaspoon light brown sugar

2 tablespoons water

PROVISIONS FOR THE ROLLS

8 sheets rice paper, circular

Water, for softening the rice paper

32 medium shrimp, cooked, peeled, deveined, tail off

2 cups carrots (4 small), shredded

3 cups butter lettuce (1 head), shredded

1 cup red cabbage (1/8 head), shredded

32 fresh Thai basil leaves

32 fresh mint leaves

2 cups fresh cilantro leaves

1 cup English cucumber (3/4 small), matchstick cuts

DIRECTIONS FOR THE NOODLES

1. Prepare the rice noodles according to the directions on the package. Store any leftover dry noodles in the pantry for other dishes.
2. Once the noodles are cooked, cool them quickly by submerging the noodles into an ice bath in a medium mixing bowl. For 2 minutes, move the noodles around with tongs to ensure they cool. Drain the water and ice.

DIRECTIONS FOR THE DIPPING SAUCE

1. In a small mixing bowl, add the peanut butter, hoisin, sesame oil, soy sauce, garlic chili crunch or sriracha, brown sugar, and water. Mix the dipping sauce until combined.

DIRECTIONS FOR THE ROLLS

1. Fill a large skillet with 2 inches of cold water.
2. Working with one sheet at a time, quickly submerge the rice paper in the water for 15 to 20 seconds. Place the wet rice paper on a large sheet pan. Line the first rice paper sheet with 4 shrimp in a row, followed by 1/8 of the carrots, lettuce, red cabbage, Thai basil, mint, cilantro, cucumber, and rice vermicelli. Fold the sides in, then roll up tightly like a burrito. If necessary, rewet the edges so they seal.
3. Repeat step 2 until all 8 rolls are complete.
4. Serve the rolls cold or at room temperature with dipping sauce.

Alternate Course: Instead of the vegetables used in this recipe for the filling, use any salad-type fixings inside the wrap.

Rogue Wave: Be sure to not oversoak the rice paper, as it will become too gummy.

Hạ Long Bay, Vietnam

CRUNCHY CHICKEN SALAD

Peanuts and fried shallots add a bunch of crunch. I always make extra of this extraordinary salad since the crew comes in hungry after working on the deck. It is a staple on the yacht, especially because cabbage can keep in the refrigerator for weeks. Perfect for any long voyage!

TOTAL TRIP: 15 minutes

SERVES: 4

PROVISIONS FOR THE SALAD

3 tablespoons light brown sugar

3 tablespoons fish sauce

3 tablespoons fresh lime juice (1½ medium limes)

2 tablespoons rice vinegar

2 tablespoons serrano pepper (1 medium), finely diced

1½ teaspoons garlic (2 cloves), minced

5 cups green cabbage, pre-shredded "angel hair" thinness

1 cup carrots (2 medium), shredded

½ cup fresh cilantro leaves, chopped

¼ cup fresh mint leaves, chopped

2 cups store-bought rotisserie chicken, cooked, shredded

½ cup peanuts, chopped, for garnish

PROVISIONS FOR THE SHALLOTS

1 cup canola oil, for frying

¾ cup shallots (3 medium), sliced, for garnish

¼ teaspoon kosher salt

DIRECTIONS FOR THE SALAD

1. In a large mixing bowl, add the brown sugar, fish sauce, lime juice, rice vinegar, pepper, and garlic. Mix until combined.
2. Add the green cabbage, carrots, cilantro, mint, and chicken. Toss until combined.

DIRECTIONS FOR THE SHALLOTS AND ASSEMBLY

1. In a small pot, add the canola oil and heat on medium high.
2. Once hot, add in the shallots and fry until golden brown and crispy, approximately 5 minutes. Drain on a plate lined with paper towels and sprinkle the fried shallots with the salt before they cool.
3. Distribute the salad onto 4 plates and then garnish with the crispy shallots and chopped peanuts. Enjoy!

Throttle Control: Adjust the amount of serrano pepper (heat of 10,000 to 23,000 Scoville heat units, or SHU) based on taste preferences.

Alternate Course: Instead of the serrano pepper, use ¼ cup of jalapeño pepper (½ large), which is less intense at 2,500 to 5,000 SHU.

Rogue Wave: Serrano chilies are spicy! To tame the heat of the pepper, remove the seeds, veins, and pith when preparing.

PHO

Pho is my favorite three-letter word and coincidentally sounds like "fun" without the *n*. This is a time-consuming recipe, so I start early in the morning with the pho stock and double it so there's extra to freeze for later. *Ăn ngon nhé!* Eat deliciously!

TOTAL TRIP: 8 hours, 30 minutes

CRUISING TIME: 30 minutes

IDLE TIME: 8 hours

SERVES: 8

PROVISIONS FOR THE STOCK

6 pounds beef bones

10 cups water, for blanching

2 yellow onions (medium), cut in half

Fresh ginger, 4-inch knob, peeled, cut in half

1/3 cup granulated sugar

3 tablespoons kosher salt

16 cups water plus 5 cups to replace while evaporating

PROVISIONS FOR THE SPICE MIX

1 food-safe mesh bag (cheesecloth or other material), for adding spices

1 cinnamon stick

5 star anises

2 tablespoons fennel seeds

2 tablespoons coriander seeds

10 whole cloves

PROVISIONS FOR THE NOODLES

14 ounces wide rice noodles, uncooked

PROVISIONS FOR THE ASSEMBLY

Beef, shredded from bones, if available from your stock

2 pounds ribeye steak, raw, shaved

1 cup fresh cilantro leaves

1 cup fresh Thai basil leaves

1 cup fresh mint leaves

2 tablespoons green onion (1 small stalk), small cuts, for garnish

2 limes, cut in wedges

1 cup bean sprouts

2 Thai red chilies, sliced, optional

1/2 cup hoisin sauce, optional

2 tablespoons sriracha, optional

DIRECTIONS FOR THE STOCK AND SPICE MIX

1. In a large pot, add the beef bones and 10 cups of water. Over high heat, bring to a boil for 5 minutes to blanch the bones. Strain the bones and water through a colander. Rinse the bones under cold running water. Use your hands to remove any impurities.
2. Return the bones to the pot and add the onions, ginger, sugar, salt, and 16 cups of water. Over medium heat, bring to a simmer.
3. Simmer for 8 hours, uncovered, adding the 5 additional cups of water halfway through the cooking process. (Go for a swim, take a nap, or stare at the pot.)
4. In the food-safe mesh bag, add the cinnamon, star anise,

fennel seeds, coriander seeds, and cloves. Tie securely. Drop into the stock for the last 2 hours of simmering.

5. Using a colander inside a large mixing bowl, strain out the stock, reserving the bones. Pick the meat off the bones. Discard the bare bones, onions, ginger, and bag of spices.
6. Return the filtered broth to the pot and bring to a boil over high heat.

DIRECTIONS FOR THE NOODLES AND ASSEMBLY

1. Prepare the rice noodles as directed on the package. Store any leftover dry noodles in the pantry for other dishes.
2. Drain the cooked noodles. Divide the noodles and the shredded meat from the bones into 8 individual serving bowls, then add the shaved raw beef on top.
3. Ladle the boiling broth into each bowl. The boiling broth cooks the raw beef.
4. Garnish each pho bowl with a portion of the cilantro, Thai basil, mint, green onion, lime wedges, bean sprouts, and optional Thai red chilies. If using, add the hoisin and sriracha on top, adjusting the amount for individual preferences.

Throttle Control: Adjust the amount of star anise (licorice flavor), Thai red chilies (heat), sriracha (heat), and cloves (numbing effect useful to cool the heat of the Thai red chilies and sriracha) based on taste preferences.

Alternate Course: To bypass the broth preparation, which takes many hours (and usually starts in the early morning), use prepared beef stock, skipping steps 1, 2, 3, and 5. Add the spices for step 4, then pick up with step 6 to complete the process.

Rogue Wave: Since some folks are sensitive to MSG, this fabulous flavor booster is not included in the recipe. However, to really bump up the umami, go rogue and include MSG.

Alternate Course: Instead of the pandan extract, use 1 teaspoon of vanilla extract and 1/4 teaspoon of green food coloring.

HONEYCOMB CAKE

How gorgeous is this green cake? Pandan is a native plant with a fragrant, pointy leaf that is known for its vanilla-like flavor and its distinctive green color. If you are able to get it or grow it fresh, go for it! Otherwise, look online to obtain an extract made with the real plant (rather than artificial). Have a green party with your friends, as there's plenty to share! And since this dessert is gluten-free, the extra effort to secure the ingredients is justifiable for our gluten-free guests, who deserve this exotic extravagance.

TOTAL TRIP: 1 hour, 15 minutes

CRUISING TIME: 30 minutes

IDLE TIME: 45 minutes

SERVES: 8

PROVISIONS

1 cup coconut milk, unsweetened

1/4 teaspoon kosher salt

2/3 cup granulated sugar

1 teaspoon pandan extract

1 1/2 cups tapioca flour

2 tablespoons rice flour

1 1/2 teaspoons baking powder

5 eggs

1 tablespoon canola oil

DIRECTIONS

1. Place a 10-inch Bundt pan (or 9-inch round cake pan) in the oven and heat to 350°F.
2. In a small microwave-safe mixing bowl, add the coconut milk, salt, and sugar. Stir with a fork to combine. Cook in the microwave for 2 minutes, until the sugar is dissolved. Allow to cool for 10 minutes and then add in the pandan extract, stirring in with the fork.
3. In a medium mixing bowl, add the tapioca flour, rice flour, and baking powder and stir with a rubber spatula to combine.
4. Add the wet ingredients into the dry ingredients. Fold with the spatula until just mixed.
5. In a small mixing bowl, add the eggs and very gently break with a fork. Do not add air into the eggs by stirring.
6. Add the eggs to the batter. Whisk gently until combined. Since there will still be lumps, use a fine-mesh strainer over a large mixing bowl to push the batter through with the spatula to break up the lumps.
7. After the batter is smooth, add the oil and use the spatula to fold until combined.
8. Take out the hot Bundt pan, grease, and pour in the batter. Return to the oven to bake until set, approximately 45 minutes.

Rogue Wave: Confirm that your baking powder is still active to ensure that the cake won't deflate. To test before mixing ingredients, place a spoonful of baking powder into a spoonful of room-temperature water, and make sure it bubbles.

SOUTH KOREA

Seoul, South Korea

Do you have a passion for Korean food? Get ready for your own K-drama of feasting in the kitchen, Little Chef!

We have arrived in Seoul, South Korea. The energy is intoxicating. There is a vibrant cultural legacy that takes music, art, literature, dance, architecture, clothing, and cuisine to a whole new level of amazing.

I can't get enough of this dynamic, diverse demographic. I know exactly what I want from the fresh vegetable stalls located in the heart of the city. Kimchi. I usually grab a ready-to-go version for myself, then make a homemade batch for guests using local chilies, onions, scallions, radishes, ginger, garlic, rice flour paste, shrimp paste, and cabbage.

Kimchi dates back over three thousand years and remains a timeless tradition in Korea. Time is an essential ingredient in the art of kimchi since fermentation is required. History repeats itself every year when Korean families come together to produce substantial batches of kimchi in colossal ceramic pots called *onggi*, which are placed underground to keep cool in the summer and warm in the winter. This resourcefulness is rewarded with an ongoing bounty of kimchi available year-round.

In Seoul, there are more than two hundred varieties of kimchi, which start with basics such as napa cabbage, green onions, white onions, carrots, cucumbers, radishes, garlic, and more. So how do these everyday ingredients reach celebrity status? The spices. Easy-to-find ginger and fish sauce are mixed with authentic Korean red pepper flakes (*gochugaru*) and fermented soybean paste (*gochujang*) to create the perfect spicy storm. Even if you have to substitute the gochugaru with chili powder, paprika, crushed chili flakes, cayenne pepper, chipotle flakes, or Aleppo pepper, or the gochujang with miso paste, hot sauce, and sugar, do it. Get to the market and seek out these worth-the-effort ingredients to bring South Korea home to you.

In the true spirit of Korean culture, serve all of these creations from the center of the table so the guests can commune and share the joy of eating together. The shared bowls, known as *banchan*, provide a light and fresh complement to our main dish, beef bulgogi. We'll serve kimchi, boiled eggplant (*gaji namul*), seaweed with salt and vinegar (*miyeok muchim*), radishes with chilies and vinegar (*musaengchae*), steamed spinach with soy and sesame (*sigeumchi namul*), and blanched bean sprouts (*kongnamul*).

My mouth is watering just thinking about this star-studded feast. Is yours? Let your soul be awakened in Seoul.

Seoul, South Korea

BREAKFAST

Gochujang Tofu Egg Skillet

LUNCH

Korean Fried Chicken

COCKTAIL HOUR

Strawberry Soju Coconut Cocktail

Mandu

DINNER

Cucumber Kimchi

Beef Bulgogi

Honey Ginger Cookie

GOCHUJANG TOFU EGG SKILLET

Let tofu and eggs provide the protein, and let Korean spices provide the party of flavor. Sweet, spicy, and savory are introduced to the dish with gochujang (fermented soybean paste), glutinous rice, barley malt powder, and salt. The gochugaru, a coarse powder of Korean red pepper flakes, adds zing to this easy-to-make one-pot breakfast.

TOTAL TRIP: 30 minutes

SERVES: 4

PROVISIONS

2 tablespoons sesame oil

1 cup white onion (1/2 medium), small diced

1 tablespoon garlic (4 cloves), minced

2 teaspoons granulated sugar

Pinch of freshly ground black pepper

1/2 teaspoon kosher salt

3 cups firm tofu, cubed

1 1/3 cups prepared dashi stock

4 teaspoons gochugaru Korean red pepper flakes

2 tablespoons soy sauce

2 tablespoons gochujang Korean red pepper paste

8 eggs

1/4 cup green onions (2 stalks), chopped, for garnish

2 teaspoons sesame seeds, for garnish

DIRECTIONS

1. In a large skillet, heat the sesame oil over medium heat.
2. Once hot, add in the onion, garlic, sugar, pepper, and salt. Sauté while stirring occasionally with a wooden spoon until the onion is translucent, approximately 5 minutes.
3. Add in the tofu, dashi stock, gochugaru, soy sauce, and gochujang. Stir the mixture occasionally to gently break up the tofu while simmering, approximately 5 minutes.
4. Crack the eggs directly into the mixture and then cover. Let the eggs cook until the whites are firm but the yolks are still runny, approximately 4 minutes.
5. Garnish with the green onions and sesame seeds.

Throttle Control: Adjust the amounts of gochugaru and gochujang (heat) based on taste preferences.

Alternate Course: Instead of the dashi, use seafood stock. Or order powdered dashi stock base online.

Rogue Wave: Don't miss the iconic flavor bursts from Korea with authentic gochugaru and gochujang. If not available in your local stores, purchase online, an even easier route than substitutions.

Seoul, South Korea

KOREAN FRIED CHICKEN

These wings are a fan favorite for a tasty lunch on board. Bring the exotic to your next party, whether it is a rooftop gathering, a backyard barbecue, or a couch-based football-watching hangout. Frying chicken is involved—but it's a worthwhile investment of time. Our version provides a crunchy skin with a sweet, spicy, and succulent sauce that will transport your guests to South Korea.

TOTAL TRIP: 1 hour, 30 minutes

CRUISING TIME: 1 hour

IDLE TIME: 30 minutes

SERVES: 4

PROVISIONS FOR THE SAUCE

1/4 cup ketchup

1/4 cup gochujang Korean red pepper paste

1/3 cup honey

1/3 cup dark brown sugar

1/4 cup soy sauce

1 tablespoon garlic (4 cloves), minced

2 tablespoons sesame oil

PROVISIONS FOR THE CHICKEN

5 pounds chicken wings, bone-in, with flaps

1/4 cup rice vinegar

1 tablespoon garlic (4 cloves), minced

2 teaspoons kosher salt

1 teaspoon freshly ground black pepper

8 cups peanut oil, for frying

1 1/2 cups cornstarch

2 teaspoons sesame seeds, for garnish

2 tablespoons green onion (1 small stalk), small cuts, for garnish

DIRECTIONS FOR THE SAUCE

1. In a small microwave-safe mixing bowl, add the ketchup, gochujang, honey, brown sugar, soy sauce, garlic, and sesame oil. Mix with a spoon, and then cook in the microwave (or on the stovetop) until the sugar dissolves, approximately 2 minutes.
2. Set aside and prepare the chicken.

DIRECTIONS FOR THE CHICKEN

1. In a large mixing bowl, add the chicken wings, rice vinegar, garlic, salt, and pepper. Using your hands, coat the chicken evenly with the marinade, then cover with plastic wrap and set aside for 30 minutes on the counter.
2. After the chicken has fully marinated, in a large skillet, preheat the oil over medium-high heat to reach 350°F.
3. Add the cornstarch to a medium mixing bowl. Dredge the chicken wings in the cornstarch and then set on a large sheet tray.
4. Once the oil is hot, use tongs to fry the chicken in several batches for 4 minutes on each side. Drain on a clean, large sheet tray lined with paper towels. Note that the chicken will not yet be golden brown since the process is a double fry.
5. Once the chicken is "single" fried, turn up the oil to reach 375°F and begin to double fry as soon as the temperature is reached. Fry batches for

4 minutes on each side or until golden brown. Drain again for a couple of minutes on a clean, large sheet tray lined with paper towels.

6. Once drained, coat the chicken in the sauce in 2 batches in a large mixing bowl. Add in half of the double-fried chicken and half of the sauce and coat using a large serving spoon. Repeat with the remaining chicken and sauce to finish the dish.
7. Garnish with the sesame seeds and green onion on top for Korean perfection.

Throttle Control: Adjust the amount of gochujang (heat) based on taste preferences, knowing that this iconic, irreplaceable flavor from Korea should not be missed. If not available in your local stores, purchase online, an even easier route than substitutions.

Rogue Wave: Avoid messing with perfection! Do not rock the boat by missing or substituting anything since these wings are finger-licking good with their regional ingredients. Avoid frying in oil that's too hot, as the chicken will burn on the outside and remain undercooked on the inside. And if the oil is not hot enough, the chicken will be soggy.

Seoul, South Korea

STRAWBERRY SOJU COCONUT COCKTAIL

Many consider soju as Korea's national drink since it has gained worldwide popularity with its many fun flavor profiles: original, peach, blueberry, grapefruit, lychee, strawberry, and more. Let's add sparkling water for some extra-fizzy fun. Here, strawberries are showcased for our cocktail since they are in season for more than half of the year in South Korea. *Geonbae!* Bottoms up!

TOTAL TRIP: 5 minutes

SERVES: 4

PROVISIONS

2 2/3 cups strawberry soju

2 2/3 cups club soda

1/4 cup cream of coconut

4 fresh strawberries, sliced

DIRECTIONS

1. In a pitcher, combine the strawberry soju, club soda, and cream of coconut. Stir with a long spoon to dissolve the cream of coconut.
2. Serve in your favorite glassware filled with ice and the strawberries.

Alternate Course: Instead of the club soda, use any flavored sparkling water of your choice to mix things up. Instead of the strawberry soju, go crazy with any of the fun flavors available, complementing with any fresh fruit of your liking.

Seoul, South Korea

MANDU

Never heard of mandu? You might be more familiar with its other name: dumplings. In Korea, dumplings can be steamed, boiled, pan-fried, or deep-fried. Here, we pan-fry on the deck so that we can enjoy the cool port breeze and then whip up an easy and aromatic dipping sauce for added pleasure.

TOTAL TRIP: 1 hour, 30 minutes

SERVES: 4

PROVISIONS FOR THE FILLING

- ½ pound ground pork
- 1½ teaspoons garlic (2 cloves), minced
- 1 teaspoon fresh ginger, peeled, grated
- 2 teaspoons soy sauce
- ½ teaspoon freshly ground black pepper
- 1 teaspoon sesame oil
- ½ cup zucchini (½ small), finely chopped
- 1 cup green cabbage (⅛ head), finely chopped
- ¼ cup oyster mushrooms (1 ounce), finely chopped
- 2 tablespoons yellow onion, finely chopped
- 3 tablespoons Chinese chives, finely sliced
- ½ cup bean sprouts, roughly chopped
- ½ teaspoon kosher salt

PROVISIONS FOR THE NOODLES

- 3 ounces sweet potato noodles, uncooked

PROVISIONS FOR THE MANDU FRYING

- 16 dumpling wrappers (portion 1 package of 3½-inch wheat-flour circles)
- 4 tablespoons canola oil

PROVISIONS FOR THE DIPPING SAUCE

- 3 tablespoons hoisin sauce
- 2 tablespoons soy sauce
- 1 tablespoon sesame oil
- 3 tablespoons green onion (1 large stalk), finely chopped
- 1 stalk green onion, sliced, for garnish

DIRECTIONS FOR THE FILLING

1. Using a large sauté pan over medium-high heat, add the ground pork and brown, approximately 5 minutes. Drain the fat.
2. Add the garlic, ginger, soy sauce, and pepper to the pan. Cook until the pork is done, approximately 4 minutes. Transfer the pork mixture to a medium mixing bowl to cool.
3. In the same sauté pan over medium-high heat, add the sesame oil, zucchini, cabbage, mushrooms, onion, chives, bean sprouts, and salt. Cook until the vegetables are tender, approximately 5 minutes.
4. Add the vegetable mixture into the bowl with the pork to create your mandu filling. Set aside.

DIRECTIONS FOR THE NOODLES

1. Prepare the noodles as directed on the package, using only 3 ounces and storing the rest in the pantry for later.
2. Once the noodles are cooked, chop them into 1-inch portions and add to the mandu filling, now ready for stuffing in the wrappers.

DIRECTIONS FOR THE MANDU FRYING

1. Prepare the mandu by filling each wrapper with 1 tablespoon of the filling. Using wet fingers, moisten the wrapper's outer ring. Then fold the wrapper into a semicircle. Starting from one side, use your fingers to pinch the edge and make small pleats along the seam, pressing down firmly. Work your way across the entire dumpling to seal it completely. Repeat the process for all 16 dumplings, setting them on a large sheet tray to prepare for pan-frying in batches.
2. In the same now-cleaned large sauté pan, add 2 tablespoons of the oil to each batch (I suggest 2 batches of 8 dumplings each), and pan-fry until the mandu is golden brown, 2 to 3 minutes on each side. Return the dumplings to another large sheet tray until all are browned.
3. Keep the mandu warm in the oven on the lowest setting (170°F) while you finish frying and preparing your dipping sauce.

DIRECTIONS FOR THE DIPPING SAUCE AND PLATING

1. In a small mixing bowl, prepare the dipping sauce by whisking together the hoisin, soy sauce, sesame oil, and chopped green onion.
2. Plate the mandu on a serving platter, garnish with the sliced green onion, and serve with the dipping sauce.

Alternate Course: Instead of using the sweet potato noodles, use rice vermicelli. Instead of the oyster mushrooms, use any mushrooms of your choice. Rather than the Chinese chives (also known as garlic chives), use regular chives. Instead of the pork, use chicken or beef, making sure to drain extra liquids from the beef once cooked since it is fattier.

Rogue Wave: Avoid fatigue during this labor of love wrapping the dumplings. Have your friends and family join you in the kitchen to help, just as in the Korean culture, where family bonding and communal eating thrive.

Seoul, South Korea

CUCUMBER KIMCHI

Quick cucumber kimchi is just one of many banchan side dishes traditionally served at a Korean meal. *Banchan*, the small dishes served along with cooked rice in Korean cuisine, create a sense of community since they are shared. We'll set this easy creation in the middle of the table for guests to enjoy with our main dish of beef bulgogi.

TOTAL TRIP: 10 minutes

SERVES: 4

PROVISIONS

2 teaspoons kosher salt

1/4 cup sesame oil

2 tablespoons fresh Thai basil leaves, chopped

2 tablespoons gochugaru Korean red pepper flakes

1 tablespoon garlic (4 cloves), minced

2 teaspoons fresh ginger, peeled, grated

2 teaspoons fish sauce

2 teaspoons granulated sugar

8 small pickling cucumbers (one pound), thinly sliced, skin-on

1/2 cup white onion (1/4 medium), thinly sliced

DIRECTIONS

1. In a medium mixing bowl, add the salt, sesame oil, Thai basil, gochugaru, garlic, ginger, fish sauce, and sugar. Using a whisk, stir until combined.
2. Add the cucumbers and onion. Mix to coat.
3. Serve cold or at room temperature. Or store in the refrigerator for up to a week until needed.

Throttle Control: Adjust the amount of gochugaru (heat) based on taste preferences.

Alternate Course: Instead of the cucumbers, use a mix of sliced daikon radishes and shredded carrots.

Rogue Wave: Don't miss the iconic flavor burst from Korea with authentic gochugaru. If not available in your local stores, purchase online, an even easier route than substitutions.

Seoul, South Korea

BEEF BULGOGI

Our super-popular beef bulgogi has guests returning early to the yacht after their day of exploration. We'll serve this bold, spicy, and earthy meat with banchan and plain white rice to balance out the bang. *Jal meogeo!* Eat well!

TOTAL TRIP: 1 hour, 15 minutes (up to 12 hours)

CRUISING TIME: 15 minutes

IDLE TIME: 1 hour (or more, to marinate)

SERVES: 4

PROVISIONS FOR THE BULGOGI

1/2 cup Asian pear (1/2 medium), peeled, roughly chopped

3 tablespoons soy sauce

3 tablespoons light brown sugar

2 tablespoons sesame oil

1 tablespoon garlic (4 cloves), roughly chopped

1 tablespoon fresh ginger, peeled, roughly chopped

3 tablespoons gochujang Korean red pepper paste

1 1/2 pounds ribeye steak, boneless, thinly sliced

PROVISIONS FOR THE RICE

1 1/2 cups long-grain white rice, rinsed 3 to 4 times

2 1/4 cups water

2 teaspoons sesame seeds, for garnish

2 tablespoons green onion (1 small stalk), sliced, for garnish

DIRECTIONS FOR THE BULGOGI

1. In a blender, add the pear, soy sauce, brown sugar, sesame oil, garlic, ginger, and gochujang. Blend until the sauce is smooth.
2. Transfer the sauce into a medium mixing bowl and then add the beef. Use your hands to coat the beef with the sauce.
3. Cover with plastic wrap. Let the meat marinate in the refrigerator for at least 1 hour or longer (even overnight).
4. After the meat has marinated, heat a large skillet over high heat and use tongs to sear the beef in 2 batches until browned, 2 to 3 minutes on each side.

DIRECTIONS FOR THE RICE AND PLATING

1. Prepare your rice just before cooking the marinated beef. In a small pot or a rice cooker, use the recipe's ratio to cook the rice in the water, or follow the directions on the package. Once cooked, remove from heat.
2. Add a portion of rice to each plate and place the hot bulgogi on the side.
3. Garnish the rice and bulgogi with the sesame seeds and green onion. Serve with your favorite vegetables.

Throttle Control: Adjust the amount of gochujang (heat) based on taste preferences, knowing that this iconic flavor from Korea should not be missed. If not available in your local stores, purchase online, an even easier route than substitutions.

Alternate Course: Instead of the Asian pear, use any pear of your preference, or leave out entirely and add an extra tablespoon of the light brown sugar. Instead of the ribeye, use any cut of beef or chicken.

Rogue Wave: Avoid burning the meat while searing by watching the time and heat. Since there's sugar in the marinade, there is a greater chance of burning.

Alternate Course: Instead of the pine nuts, use any high-fat nuts such as cashews, pecans, walnuts, or macadamias.

Seoul, South Korea

HONEY GINGER COOKIE

If you love sweet fried dough that's crunchy like a cookie, you'll love this Korean treat. The inclusion of pine nuts adds extra density to the texture. For the syrup, we let honey and ginger take the helm. Since this batch makes plenty, you'll have a reserve to keep in the refrigerator, which is a bonus since this dessert tastes even better after time allows the honey glaze to soak in even more.

TOTAL TRIP: 1 hour, 20 minutes (up to 12 hours)

CRUISING TIME: 20 minutes

IDLE TIME: 1 hour (or more, to soak)

SERVES: 8

PROVISIONS FOR THE GINGER SYRUP

1⅓ cups honey

1⅓ cups water

2 tablespoons fresh ginger, peeled, grated

PROVISIONS FOR THE COOKIES

2 cups all-purpose flour, plus more as needed

¼ cup sesame oil

¼ cup honey

¼ teaspoon kosher salt

¼ cup pine nuts, finely crushed, plus more for garnish

¼ cup soju

3 cups canola oil, for frying

DIRECTIONS FOR THE GINGER SYRUP

1. In a small sauté pan, add the honey, water, and ginger. Stir to combine.
2. Over medium-high heat, bring the mixture to a boil for 2 minutes. Remove from heat and set aside.

DIRECTIONS FOR THE COOKIES

1. In a medium mixing bowl, add the flour and sesame oil. Use your palms to rub the oil into the flour until it resembles coarse bread crumbs.
2. Add in the honey, salt, pine nuts, and soju. Use your hands to form the crumbly dough into a ball.
3. On a clean surface lightly dusted with flour, roll out the ball to ½ inch thick. Using a knife, cut into 2-inch triangles.
4. In a large skillet, preheat the oil to 350°F over medium heat. Using tongs, gently place the cookies into the hot oil and fry in 2 batches until golden brown, 1 to 2 minutes on each side. Drain the cookies on a large sheet tray lined with paper towels.
5. Put the cookies into a 9-by-13-inch casserole dish and pour over the ginger honey syrup. Let soak for at least 1 hour, but preferably overnight to allow the syrup to fully absorb.
6. When ready to serve, garnish with the crushed pine nuts.

Rogue Wave: Avoid overfrying the dough by carefully watching the heat and timing. Since there's a lot of sugar in the honey, the cookies can burn easily. If the oil is too hot, the cookies will burn on the outside and remain undercooked on the inside. And if the oil is not hot enough, the cookies will be soggy.

HAWAII

Hawaiian Islands, United States

Aloha to you, dear Hawaii!

Oh, how we appreciate your Polynesian philosophy, where the waves, the sky, and all of nature hold a place of honor. The cool sea breeze from the *moana* (ocean) captivates us. Here at the edge of the world, we are completely mesmerized by your beauty as we approach the rugged coastline of Nā Pali on the island of Kauaʻi.

Our yacht glides past emerald-hued cliffs and massive waterfalls when we travel to the Hawaiian Islands from the mighty Pacific. Our guests are often speechless. Perhaps you can imagine the magnitude of this otherworldly environment as you recall the film *Jurassic Park*, featuring Nā Pali's famous Manawaiopuna Falls and the undulating mountains surrounding it. But I am telling you, Little Chef, there's nothing like being here in person in a mega-yacht that is dwarfed by Mother Nature with her four-thousand-foot cliff faces. It leaves me awestruck.

Nature is indeed awesome, and we have the fiery action of volcanoes to thank for the Hawaiian Islands. Their birth, which began around seventy million years ago, continues to morph into something new with the eruption of Kīlauea on the Big Island of Hawaii. Hawaii is a living museum of Mother Nature at work. There's so much to explore in the many different terrains of the Hawaiian archipelago, with its eight main islands. From north to south, they are:

Niʻihau, known as "The Forbidden Island" (and it will remain so on our journey).
Kauaʻi, "The Garden Isle," famed for its lush landscapes and dramatic cliffs (I love when we anchor here).

O‘ahu, known as “The Gathering Place,” home to the vibrant city of Honolulu, famous for its surfing beaches (I can’t wait to hang ten).

Moloka‘i, called “The Friendly Island,” steeped in time-honored culture with traditional fishing, hunting, and gathering (I like to hike here).

Lāna‘i, known as “The Pineapple Isle,” a serene, luxurious resort destination (sign me up for the spa).

Maui, “The Valley Isle,” celebrated for its stunning beaches and volcanic landscapes (snorkeling the Molokini crater is a must).

Hawai‘i, “The Big Island,” with massively diverse ecosystems and active volcanoes (the youngest and largest of all of the islands, it’s always a thrill).

Kaho‘olawe, an uninhabited island (conservation at its best, so we’ll simply admire it from the yacht).

Each island has so much to teach us. Our time here pays homage to each with fresh pineapples, papayas, bananas, macadamia nuts, coffee, eggs, beef, and dairy. The authentic Hawaiian bounty will elevate our dishes to heights that rival the Manawaiopuna Falls!

Aloha, Little Chef!

Hawaiian Islands, United States

BREAKFAST

Loco Moco

LUNCH

Lomi Lomi Salmon

COCKTAIL HOUR

Mai Tai

Coconut Shrimp

DINNER

Oxtail Soup

Huli Huli Chicken Platter

with Macaroni Salad, Rice, and Grilled Pineapple

Lilikoi Pie

Hawaiian Islands, United States

LOCO MOCO

Local legend has it that this dish originated when surfers in Hilo requested a quick and filling meal that would sustain them for their demanding activity in the waves. And so the loco moco was born, with white rice, beef, fried eggs, and gravy. If you're in Hawaii, use local mushrooms harvested there to elevate your taste buds even more. And then be sure to hit the waves afterward.

TOTAL TRIP: 30 minutes

SERVES: 4

PROVISIONS FOR THE RICE

1 cup long-grain white rice, rinsed 3 to 4 times

1½ cups water

PROVISIONS FOR THE GRAVY

1 tablespoon salted butter (⅛ stick)

1 cup beef stock

1 tablespoon soy sauce

2 teaspoons Worcestershire sauce

1 tablespoon ketchup

1 tablespoon cornstarch

PROVISIONS FOR THE HAMBURGER AND MUSHROOM SAUTÉ

1 pound ground beef

2 teaspoons Worcestershire sauce

2 teaspoons garlic powder

1½ teaspoons kosher salt

¼ teaspoon freshly ground black pepper

1 tablespoon salted butter (⅛ stick)

½ cup yellow onion (¼ medium), thinly sliced

2 cups white button mushrooms (8 ounces), thinly sliced

PROVISIONS FOR THE FRIED EGGS

1 tablespoon salted butter (⅛ stick)

4 eggs

2 tablespoons green onion (1 small stalk), sliced, for garnish

DIRECTIONS FOR THE RICE

1. In a small pot or a rice cooker, use the recipe's ratio to cook the rice in the water, or follow the directions on the package. Once cooked, remove from heat.

DIRECTIONS FOR THE GRAVY

1. While the rice cooks, in an unheated small pot, add in the butter, beef stock, soy sauce, Worcestershire, ketchup, and cornstarch. Turn on medium-high heat to bring to a boil while whisking.
2. Once at a boil, reduce the heat to low and prepare the hamburger.

DIRECTIONS FOR THE HAMBURGER AND MUSHROOM SAUTÉ

1. In a medium mixing bowl, combine the beef, Worcestershire, garlic powder, salt, and pepper. Using your hands, mix and form into 4 patties of ½-inch thickness.
2. Meanwhile, in a large skillet over medium-high heat, melt the butter. Once melted, add in the patties and sear on both sides, using a metal spatula, until cooked to the

desired temperature, 5 to 8 minutes in total. Set aside on a plate covered with aluminum foil to keep warm.

3. In the same skillet with the pan drippings from the beef, add in the onion and mushrooms. Sauté and stir with the spatula until tender, approximately 5 minutes. Remove the mushroom sauté from heat and prepare the fried eggs.

DIRECTIONS FOR THE FRIED EGGS AND ASSEMBLY

1. In a medium sauté pan over medium heat, add the butter to fry the eggs to your liking. Once the butter is melted, cook the eggs for 2 to 3 minutes or until the whites are completely set. Remove the eggs at this point for sunny-side up, or flip with a metal spatula and cook for 30 seconds more for over easy (yolk is still slightly runny), 1 minute more for over medium (yolk is slightly set), or 2 to 3 minutes more for over hard (yolk is hard-set).
2. To assemble, on each plate, start with a bed of the white rice, then add the sautéed onion and mushrooms, followed one of the beef patties, some of the gravy, and finally one of the fried eggs.
3. Garnish with the green onion and enjoy!

Alternate Course: Instead of frying the eggs, poaching or scrambling them works well too.

Rogue Wave: Please note that this fish is not cooked, so there are pathogens that should be avoided by some folks. Yes, the fish is sushi grade (frozen to -20°C/-4°F for seven days or -35°C/-31°F for 15 hours for safer consumption), but you will want to check food safety guides and decide accordingly.

Hawaiian Islands, United States

LOMI LOMI SALMON

Curing salmon sounds so daunting, but it's actually as simple as taking twenty minutes to prep and then letting time do the rest. I love to prepare the salmon the night before so that serving it for lunch the next day is as easy as slicing and accompanying with some rice, just like you'd find at an authentic luau. In Hawaiian, *lomi lomi* means "massage" since you use your hands to rub the spices into the fish. After this easy massage in the kitchen, treat yourself to a lomi lomi massage at a spa while it marinates. Both lomi lomi experiences are pure Hawaii.

TOTAL TRIP: 8 hours, 20 minutes (up to 12 hours)

CRUISING TIME: 20 minutes

IDLE TIME: 8 hours (or more, to cure)

SERVES: 4

PROVISIONS FOR THE SALMON

1 pound salmon fillet, sushi grade, skinless

1½ teaspoons kosher salt

¼ teaspoon freshly ground black pepper

PROVISIONS FOR THE RICE

1½ cups long-grain white rice, rinsed 3 to 4 times

2¼ cups water

PROVISIONS FOR THE VEGETABLES

1½ cups Roma tomatoes (3 medium), small diced

1 cup white onion (½ medium), small diced

½ cup plus 2 tablespoons green onions (5 stalks), sliced

DIRECTIONS FOR CURING THE SALMON

1. In a gallon-size plastic food-storage bag, add the salmon fillet, salt, and pepper. Use your hands to coat the salmon evenly.
2. Allow to cure in the refrigerator for 8 hours (or more, even overnight).
3. After curing, rinse the salt and pepper off the salmon under running water.

DIRECTIONS FOR THE RICE, VEGETABLES, AND ASSEMBLY

1. In a small pot or a rice cooker, use the recipe's ratio to cook the rice in the water, or follow the directions on the package.
2. Once cooked, remove from heat and allow to cool, approximately 20 minutes.
3. While the rice cools, cube the cured salmon into ½-inch cubes and combine with the tomatoes, onion, and green onions.
4. Serve with the cooled rice.

Hawaiian Islands, United States

MAI TAI

The Tahitian word *maita'i* means "good" or "excellence." This sour cocktail, which might have originated from a Tahitian guest sipping it for the first time in the 1940s, lives up to its name. When the drink made its way to Hawaii, orange and pineapple juices were added. Our mai tai here pairs perfectly with coconut shrimp as you watch for whales at cocktail hour.

TOTAL TRIP: 5 minutes

SERVES: 4

PROVISIONS

$1\frac{1}{3}$ cups pineapple juice

$\frac{1}{2}$ cup fresh orange juice (2 small oranges)

$\frac{1}{2}$ cup spiced rum

$\frac{1}{2}$ cup coconut rum

2 teaspoons grenadine syrup

4 fresh orange wedges ($\frac{1}{4}$ orange), for garnish

4 sprigs fresh mint, for garnish

4 maraschino cherries, for garnish, as desired

DIRECTIONS

1. In a pitcher, add the pineapple juice, orange juice, spiced rum, coconut rum, and grenadine. Stir with a long spoon.
2. Serve in glasses with ice, and garnish each glass with an orange wedge, a mint sprig, and a maraschino cherry, if desired.

Hawaiian Islands, United States

COCONUT SHRIMP

What a wonderful way to combine land and sea with our coconut shrimp appetizer. Coconut trees, known as *niu* trees in Hawaii, grow in native groves but are also wild along the beaches. We could harvest a coconut simply by finding it on the ground and cracking it open for our shrimp preparation. Or we could get one from the store and spend the extra time just lounging on the beach instead.

TOTAL TRIP: 45 minutes

SERVES: 4

PROVISIONS FOR THE DREDGING

Bowl 1

1/3 cup all-purpose flour

1 teaspoon garlic powder

1 teaspoon kosher salt

Bowl 2

1 egg

2 tablespoons whole milk

Bowl 3

1 cup shredded coconut, sweetened

2/3 cup panko bread crumbs

PROVISIONS FOR THE DREDGING AND SHRIMP

1 pound jumbo shrimp, peeled, deveined, tail on

4 cups canola oil, for frying

PROVISIONS FOR THE DIPPING SAUCE

1/4 cup apricot jam

1/4 cup sweet Thai chili sauce

1 fresh lime, quartered, for garnish

DIRECTIONS FOR THE SHRIMP

1. Use 3 small kitchen bowls for dredging, an easy process to coat the shrimp. In the first bowl, add the flour, garlic powder, and salt. In the second bowl, add the egg and milk and whisk together. In the third bowl, add the coconut and bread crumbs.
2. Pat dry the shrimp on a large sheet tray lined with paper towels.
3. To dredge the shrimp, hold the tail of the shrimp and dip the body into the flour mixture in the first bowl. Shake off the excess and dip into the egg mixture in the second bowl. Shake off the excess and coat with the coconut and panko in the third bowl, pressing the mixture onto the shrimp with the palm of your hand. Place all of the dredged shrimp on the sheet tray and set aside.
4. In a medium pot, preheat the oil to 350°F.
5. Once the oil is hot, hold the tail of the shrimp and gently place in the oil. Continue to add half of the shrimp into the oil as part of the first batch.
6. Fry until the shrimp are golden brown, 3 to 5 minutes. Using a slotted spoon, move the shrimp around so they do not stick to the bottom. Repeat the process to fry a second batch of shrimp.
7. Remove the fried shrimp with a slotted spoon. Drain on a clean, large sheet tray lined with paper towels.

DIRECTIONS FOR THE DIPPING SAUCE

1. In a small bowl, add the apricot jam and chili sauce. Mix together with a spoon.
2. Place the dipping sauce in a serving bowl, and set on a serving platter, along with the coconut shrimp. Garnish with the lime wedges. Enjoy!

Alternate Course: Instead of the shrimp, use a chicken breast cut into 1-inch cubes.

Rogue Wave: Avoid frying in oil that is too hot, as the breading will burn on the outside and the shrimp will remain undercooked on the inside. And if the oil is not hot enough, the breading will be soggy and fall off.

OXTAIL SOUP

Hawaiian oxtail soup combines local ingredients such as oxtail and onions with unique spices introduced to the culture by Chinese immigrants. Keeping to tradition, we'll slowly simmer the oxtail to extract maximum flavor and nutrients.

TOTAL TRIP: 3 hours, 30 minutes (up to 6 hours)

CRUISING TIME: 30 minutes

IDLE TIME: 3 hours (or more, to slow cook)

SERVES: 4

PROVISIONS

4 pounds oxtails

2 cups yellow onion (1 medium), large diced

Fresh ginger, 2-inch knob, cut in half

2 cinnamon sticks

4 star anises

1 whole orange, peels only

10 cups water, for soup

1½ tablespoons kosher salt

2 tablespoons fish sauce

4 cups bok choy (1 medium head), chopped

¼ cup green onions (2 stalks), sliced, for garnish

1 cup fresh flat-leaf parsley, chopped, for garnish

DIRECTIONS

1. Fill a large pot with water and bring to a boil. Once boiling, add the oxtails, making sure they are submerged in the water, and continue boiling for 2 minutes to clean the bones.
2. Using a colander, drain the oxtails. Rinse the oxtails under cold running water, using your fingers to clean off any impurities.
3. Using the large pot again, now cleaned, add in the oxtails, onion, ginger, cinnamon sticks, star anises, orange peels, water, salt, and fish sauce. Bring to a simmer, cover, and cook until the oxtails are tender, approximately 3 hours.
4. When nearly ready to serve, use a ladle to skim off the excess oil.
5. Then add in the bok choy and cook for 2 minutes, stirring with the ladle to combine.
6. Serve in bowls and garnish with the green onions and parsley.

Alternate Course: Instead of the oxtails, use stew meat, but start at step 3.

Hawaiian Islands, United States

HULI HULI CHICKEN PLATTER

According to this dish's tradition, when the chicken is flipped on the grill, we can shout, *"Huli!"* which is Hawaiian for "turn." From my experience with our yacht guests, the smell of the sweet and fruity marinade is actually what turns heads every time. When you create your huli huli chicken, pair it with macaroni salad (fondly called "mac salad" in Hawaii), cooked rice, and grilled pineapple for the best dinner platter ever, Hawaiian style. *Ono grinds!* Here's to the "delicious food"!

TOTAL TRIP: 3 hours (up to 12 hours)

CRUISING TIME: 1 hour

IDLE TIME: 2 hours (or more, to marinate)

SERVES: 4

PROVISIONS FOR THE CHICKEN

1/2 cup pineapple juice

2 tablespoons fresh ginger, peeled, grated

2 tablespoons garlic (8 cloves), minced

1/4 cup ketchup

1/4 cup soy sauce

2 tablespoons cooking sherry

2 tablespoons light brown sugar

1 teaspoon sriracha

1 teaspoon rice vinegar

2 teaspoons sesame oil

2 pounds chicken thighs, boneless, skinless

PROVISIONS FOR THE MACARONI SALAD

1/2 pound elbow macaroni

1/2 cup carrot (1 medium), shredded

1/4 cup yellow onion (1/8 medium), minced

1 cup mayonnaise

1 1/2 teaspoons granulated sugar

1 teaspoon kosher salt

1/4 teaspoon freshly ground black pepper

2 tablespoons whole milk

1 tablespoon apple cider vinegar

PROVISIONS FOR THE RICE

1 cup long-grain white rice, rinsed 3 to 4 times

1 1/2 cups water

PROVISIONS FOR THE GRILLED PINEAPPLE AND GARNISH

10 pineapple rings (1/2 fresh pineapple), core removed

2 cups iceberg lettuce (1/4 of a head), sliced

2 tablespoons green onion (1 small stalk), sliced

DIRECTIONS FOR THE CHICKEN

1. In a large bowl, combine the pineapple juice, ginger, garlic, ketchup, soy sauce, sherry, brown sugar, sriracha, rice vinegar, sesame oil, and chicken, and mix with your hands until evenly coated. Cover and set aside to marinate for at least 1 hour (or more, even overnight).
2. Meanwhile, prepare the macaroni salad (which can also be stored overnight).
3. Once the chicken is done marinating, preheat the grill to 450°F.
4. Use tongs to place the chicken on the hot grill. After 3 minutes, rotate the chicken 45 degrees to create diamond grill marks and cook for another 3 minutes.
5. Flip the chicken and repeat. Check the internal temperature of the chicken to ensure it reaches 165°F, then set aside.

DIRECTIONS FOR THE MACARONI SALAD

1. While the chicken is marinating, in a large pot, cook the pasta in heavily salted boiling water until al dente, according to the directions on the package.
2. Once the pasta is done, rinse it in a colander under cold running water. Then set aside to cool.
3. Once the pasta is cool, place it in a large bowl with the carrot, onion, mayonnaise, sugar, salt, pepper, milk, and apple cider vinegar.
4. Cover with plastic wrap and let the "mac salad" sit in the refrigerator for 2 hours (or longer, even overnight).

DIRECTIONS FOR THE RICE

1. In a small pot or a rice cooker, use the recipe's ratio to cook the rice in the water, or follow the directions on the package. Once cooked, remove from heat.

DIRECTIONS FOR THE GRILLED PINEAPPLE AND PLATING

1. Grill the pineapple rings on the same hot grill as the chicken.
2. Once the chicken and pineapple are done grilling, assemble the platter with the chicken, macaroni salad, rice, and pineapple rings individually portioned.
3. Garnish with the iceberg lettuce and green onion.

Alternate Course: Instead of the chicken, use any protein of your choice. Instead of the cooking sherry, use red wine or apple cider vinegar. Instead of grilling, use the stovetop on medium-high heat to sear each side until the internal temperature is 165°F.

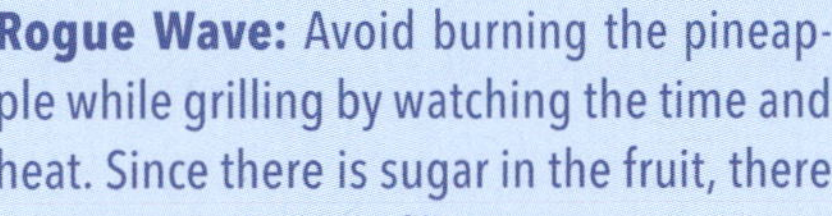

Rogue Wave: Avoid burning the pineapple while grilling by watching the time and heat. Since there is sugar in the fruit, there is a greater chance of burning.

Hawaiian Islands, United States

LILIKO'I PIE

Liliko'i, the Hawaiian word for passion fruit, plays a starring role in this Hawaiian pie. Add local coconut and macadamia nuts to share the stage with our freshly harvested passion fruit, and you'll find that together, they put on a great show.

TOTAL TRIP: 3 hours, 45 minutes (up to 12 hours)

CRUISING TIME: 45 minutes

IDLE TIME: 3 hours (or more, to set)

SERVES: 8

PROVISIONS FOR THE PIE

1 frozen prepared piecrust, 9-inch round

4 pasteurized eggs, separated

1/2 cup passion fruit puree

1/2 cup condensed milk

1/2 teaspoon kosher salt

1 tablespoon unflavored gelatin (one packet)

1/4 cup water

2 teaspoons fresh lemon zest (one medium lemon)

1/2 cup granulated sugar

PROVISIONS FOR THE WHIPPED CREAM TROPICAL TOPPING

1/2 cup heavy whipping cream

2 tablespoons powdered sugar

1/4 cup shredded coconut, sweetened

1/4 cup macadamia nuts, crushed

DIRECTIONS FOR THE PIE

1. Bake the frozen piecrust according to the directions on the package. Set aside and allow to cool while preparing the filling.
2. In a small pot, add the egg yolks (save and set aside the egg whites for step 5), passion fruit puree, and condensed milk. Stirring constantly with a whisk over medium-low heat, bring to a simmer and cook until thickened, 10 to 12 minutes.
3. Add the salt once the egg yolks have thickened, and then take off the heat.
4. Meanwhile, in a small microwave-safe bowl, add the gelatin and water. Heat in the microwave until the gelatin dissolves, 15 to 30 seconds. Stir with a spoon and then add to the custard, along with the lemon zest. With a rubber spatula, stir to combine. Cover with plastic wrap directly on the surface of the custard, then place in the refrigerator to allow it to cool for 45 minutes.
5. Meanwhile, in a medium bowl, use a hand mixer on high to whisk the egg whites until they are foamy, approximately 2 minutes.
6. Add the sugar to the foamy egg whites and continue to whisk until stiff peaks are formed, 2 to 3 minutes.
7. Now add the beaten egg whites into the now-cooled passion fruit custard and use a rubber spatula to gently fold to combine.
8. Once combined, pour the mixture into the baked, cooled piecrust. Place in the refrigerator to set, approximately 3 hours (or more, even overnight).

DIRECTIONS FOR THE WHIPPED CREAM TROPICAL TOPPING AND ASSEMBLY

1. In a medium bowl, use a hand mixer on high to whisk the whipping cream and powdered sugar until stiff peaks are formed, approximately 3 minutes. Set aside.
2. In a small sauté pan over medium heat, toast the coconut, using a spoon to continually move the coconut in the pan to avoid burning, 1 to 2 minutes.
3. To serve, slice the cooled pie. Assemble each slice with a dollop of whipped cream topping and some of the toasted coconut and macadamia nuts.

Alternate Course: Instead of the toasted coconut, use sliced bananas if they are a-peeling!

Rogue Wave: Avoid rushing the egg yolk thickening process or you will end up with cooked eggs. Low, slow, and steady with your whisk is key.

MEXICO

Puerto Vallarta, Mexico

Let the party, or the fiesta, begin!

We have arrived in Puerto Vallarta, Mexico. I try to hit the Malecón, the port's famed boardwalk, in the early morning before the crowds fill up this energetic esplanade of historical landmarks, museums, churches, restaurants, street art, and sculptures. But I always feast on the scenery of the majestic Sierra Madre mountains and forests that surround the streets. It is magical.

I usually set my sights on my favorite taco stand, which in my eyes, is just as majestic. The hand-painted, splintered wooden sign and the clankety-clank of the seasoned cast-iron skillets elevate the place to palatial status for me. Should I pick the *al pastor* savory shaved pork with pineapple? The sweet, sour, slightly spicy breakfast *birria* stew with goat meat? The grilled beef *carne asada* with guacamole? Or the tuna taco with cilantro? Hmmm . . .

With a full belly, I focus on the hunt for fresh tomatoes, peppers, and onions for my authentic salsa featured—along with empanadas and margaritas—in the Mexican cocktail hour back on board. On Saturdays, my ultimate destination is Olas Altas, Puerto Vallarta's finest farmers' market, where I love to catch cooking demonstrations in addition to securing my locally sourced produce.

But in markets skirting the Malecón, I like to select some thick pork and marbled beef from the town butcher. Then I head for a famous local dig that sells all kinds of native corn. *Maize*, which is what the residents in Puerto Vallarta call corn, is revered here—and rightly so. Corn has a history of party-worthy stories of its own.

Stopping for a swim after market

It even shows up on altars during the *Día de Los Muertos* (Day of the Dead) celebration on All Souls' Day. Once second only to rice as the world's most essential harvest, corn is now number one! It is a staple in the Mexican diet and dates back ten thousand years to the first crops. Legend says that farmers can actually hear the corn grow as it bursts from the earth and reaches toward the sunlight. How cool is that, Little Chef? Yellow, red, white, blue, purple—all of these beautiful colors party in the sunshine for us to enjoy.

I like to provision some grilled corn *elotes* still on the cob, as well as hominy that's been *nixtamalized* in an ancient cooking process that softens and dehulls the corn. I anticipate that the corn on the cob will be a big hit, as it always is, with guests sinking their teeth into all of that sweetness and getting butter all over their hands and faces. What a fun scene! And since I buy it ready-to-go for the festive *fiesta*, I can concentrate my time on preparing the salsa for the cocktail hour, along with the *pozole* soup seasoned with chilies and the grilled *pescado zarandeado* with grouper that the crew is so good at catching. Our signal to party is the setting sun being quenched by the horizon.

Puerto Vallarta, Mexico

BREAKFAST

Huevos Rancheros

LUNCH

Birria Tacos

COCKTAIL HOUR

Spicy Margarita

Empanadas

DINNER

Pozole

Pescado Zarandeado

Tres Leches Cake

Puerto Vallarta, Mexico

HUEVOS RANCHEROS

Translated to mean "rancher's eggs," this hearty breakfast uses many Mexican staples in a clever combination. You might not be working hard on a ranch, or sailing the coast of Mexico, but with these tortillas, eggs, tomatoes, cheese, and chilies mixed together, you'll be shouting out *"Increíble!"* at the first incredible bite.

TOTAL TRIP: 45 minutes

SERVES: 4

PROVISIONS FOR THE SALSA

2 tablespoons extra virgin olive oil

2½ cups Roma tomatoes (5 medium), medium diced

2 serrano peppers, small diced

½ cup red onion (¼ medium), small diced

2 teaspoons kosher salt

½ teaspoon freshly ground black pepper

¼ cup water

PROVISIONS FOR THE REFRIED BEANS

2 tablespoons extra virgin olive oil

1½ cups (1 15.5-ounce can) pinto beans, drained, rinsed

1 cube chicken bouillon

¼ teaspoon kosher salt

¼ teaspoon freshly ground black pepper

1 teaspoon garlic powder

1 teaspoon onion powder

1 cup water

1 tablespoon salted butter (⅛ stick)

⅓ cup Monterey Jack cheese, shredded

PROVISIONS FOR THE TORTILLAS, EGGS, AND TOPPINGS

¼ cup canola oil

8 corn tortillas

8 eggs

¼ cup cotija cheese, crumbled

¼ cup fresh cilantro leaves

1 avocado, sliced

¼ cup sour cream

DIRECTIONS FOR THE SALSA

1. In a large sauté pan, heat the olive oil over medium-low heat. Once hot, add in the tomatoes, peppers, onion, salt, pepper, and water. Use a wooden spoon to stir occasionally. Cover and simmer until the tomatoes break down and turn into a thick sauce, approximately 10 minutes.
2. Reduce the heat to low to keep the tomatoes warm while preparing the beans.

DIRECTIONS FOR THE REFRIED BEANS

1. In a small pot, heat the olive oil over medium heat. Once hot, add in the beans, bouillon, salt, pepper, garlic powder, onion powder, and water. Mash the beans with a potato masher while simmering, 5 to 10 minutes.
2. Once the beans are completely broken down, add in the butter and cheese. Stir until combined, then set aside until ready to assemble.

DIRECTIONS FOR THE TORTILLAS, EGGS, AND TOPPINGS

1. In a large sauté pan, heat the olive oil over medium heat. Once hot, add in the tortillas in batches and use

tongs to fry until golden brown, 1 to 2 minutes. Allow to drain on a large sheet tray lined with paper towels.

2. In the same sauté pan, after frying the tortillas, fry the eggs to your liking over medium heat. Cook the eggs for 2 to 3 minutes or until the white is completely set. Remove at this point for sunny-side up, or flip with a metal spatula and cook 30 seconds more for over easy (yolk is still slightly runny), 1 minute more for over medium (yolk is slightly set), or 2 to 3 minutes more for over hard (yolk is hard-set).
3. For assembly, plate the fried tortillas, then the refried beans, the stewed tomato salsa, and fried eggs.
4. Top with the cheese, cilantro, avocado, and sour cream.

Throttle Control: Adjust the amount of water (in the tomatoes and beans) to change to the desired thickness of the sauce. Adjust the amount of serrano peppers (heat), which have a heat of 10,000 to 23,000 Scoville heat units, or SHU. Other peppers include jalapeño (2,500 to 5,000 SHU), red pepper flakes (15,000 to 45,000 SHU), and cayenne (30,000 to 50,000 SHU).

Alternate Course: Instead of the pinto beans, use black beans. Instead of the cotija cheese (salty, dry, and doesn't melt), use feta, queso fresco, or Colby Jack. Instead of the corn tortillas, use flour tortillas.

Puerto Vallarta, Mexico

BIRRIA TACOS

Originally cooked with goat meat, birria is now prepared with various proteins, including pork, lamb, and beef. The secret lies in the ancient preparation method to tenderize and spice the meat that is said to date back to Mesopotamia. The result is *extraordinario* and worth the time. Besides, while it stews, you'll be busy enjoying the beach!

TOTAL TRIP: 3 hours, 45 minutes

CRUISING TIME: 45 minutes

IDLE TIME: 3 hours

SERVES: 4

PROVISIONS FOR THE BIRRIA AND SAUCE

4 dried ancho chili peppers, seeds and stems removed

4 dried guajillo chili peppers, seeds and stems removed

2 dried chile de árbol peppers, seeds and stems removed

3 tablespoons canola oil

3 pounds beef chuck roast, 1-inch cubes

1 tablespoon kosher salt

1 teaspoon freshly ground black pepper

2 cups red onion (1 medium), roughly chopped

1 tablespoon garlic (4 cloves), roughly chopped

1 cup Roma tomatoes (2 medium), medium diced

8 cups beef stock, divided

1 cinnamon stick

4 cloves

1 teaspoon cumin seeds

4 bay leaves

1 tablespoon apple cider vinegar

PROVISIONS FOR THE TACOS AND TOPPINGS

12 corn tortillas, 6-inch rounds

2 cups mozzarella cheese

1 cup white onion (½ medium), small diced

1 cup fresh cilantro leaves, roughly chopped

2 fresh limes, quartered, for garnish

2 radishes, thinly sliced, for garnish

DIRECTIONS FOR THE BIRRIA AND SAUCE

1. Preheat the oven to 325°F.
2. In a small pot, add the chilies and fill with water to cover. Boil over medium-high heat until tender, approximately 20 minutes.
3. Meanwhile, in a large skillet, heat the oil over medium-high heat. Season the meat with the salt and pepper, then use tongs to brown all sides, 8 to 10 minutes. Remove and set aside.
4. In the same skillet with the drippings, add in the onion, garlic, and tomatoes. Using tongs, char the vegetables on all sides, 6 to 8 minutes, then set aside.
5. Once the chilies are cooked, place them in a blender with the charred vegetables and 2 cups of the beef stock. Puree and set aside.
6. Meanwhile, in the same skillet with the drippings, use tongs to toast the cinnamon stick, cloves, cumin seeds, and bay leaves for 2 minutes over medium heat.
7. Once toasted, add the remaining beef stock and the vinegar, as well as

the meat, to the skillet. Using a mesh strainer over the skillet, strain the pureed chilies to add to the sauce and discard the chili skins.

8. Cover the skillet with aluminum foil, followed by a lid, to completely seal the pot for slow roasting in the oven for 3 hours until tender.
9. Once the meat is tender, remove from the oven and discard the cinnamon stick, cloves, and bay leaves. Transfer the meat to a large mixing bowl and use tongs to shred the meat. Set aside both the sauce and the meat separately.

DIRECTIONS FOR THE TACOS AND TOPPINGS

1. Heat a large sauté pan over medium heat. Using tongs, dip the tortilla into the upper fatty layer of the sauce and then place them flat into the pan to brown while filling with a small portion of the beef, cheese, onion, and cilantro. Fold the tortilla in half and use a metal spatula to press and seal.
2. Continue to cook the tortilla on both sides to completely brown, approximately 2 minutes on each side. Repeat the process to make all the tacos.
3. Serve with the lime wedges and radishes and a bowl of the sauce for dipping.

Throttle Control: Adjust the amount of chilies (spicy) based on taste preferences. Ancho chilies, dried from poblano peppers, are mild in heat (heat of 500 to 1,500 Scoville heat units, or SHU), with a sweet, raisin-like, chocolaty flavor. Guajillo chilies, dried from mirasol peppers, are medium in heat (2,500 to 5,000 SHU), similar to mild jalapeños. Chile de árbol peppers are nutty but high in heat (30,000 to 50,000 SHU), similar to spicy cayenne peppers.

Alternate Course: Instead of the beef, use pork shoulder or chicken thighs and adjust the cooking time. Instead of the corn tortillas, use flour tortillas.

Rogue Wave: Corn tortillas break easily. To keep them intact, wrap the tortillas in a damp paper towel and cook in the microwave for 30 seconds before browning in the pan.

Puerto Vallarta, Mexico

SPICY MARGARITA

Tequila, anyone? We can't go to Mexico without a margarita moment! We'll spice up the classic version with Tajín seasoning and jalapeño peppers for heat and then temper it with lime juice and agave. We can also add some salt as garnish to mimic the traditional tequila shot pattern: Salt the hand, lick the salt, swig the tequila, and suck a lime wedge. Then see how rowdy the party gets on deck! *Arriba, abajo, al centro, y para dentro!* Raise your glasses "up, down, and center, and in it goes!"

TOTAL TRIP: 10 minutes

SERVES: 4

PROVISIONS

3/4 cups tequila

1/2 cup fresh lime juice (4 medium limes)

1/4 cup triple sec

1/4 cup agave syrup

1 teaspoon Tajín, for cocktail

1 tablespoon Tajín, for rimming

1 fresh lime, quartered

1 jalapeño pepper, thinly sliced, for garnish

DIRECTIONS

1. In a pitcher filled with ice, add the tequila, lime juice, triple sec, agave, and Tajín. Stir with a long spoon until the agave is dissolved. Set aside.
2. When ready to serve, pour 1 tablespoon of the Tajín onto a flat plate, then use one of the lime wedges to wet the rim of a cocktail glass. Twist the rim of the glass into the Tajín until evenly coated.
3. Pour the margarita mix into each rimmed glass and garnish with the lime wedge and a slice of jalapeño pepper.

Throttle Control: Adjust the amount of jalapeño peppers (heat) based on taste preferences.

Puerto Vallarta, Mexico

EMPANADAS

While the original Spanish recipe uses bread dough, this Mexican version of the empanada calls upon corn masa dough to seal the deal. Serve some with spicy margaritas, and your guests will be dancing the Jarabe Tapatío, the famous Mexican hat dance. Plus, you can freeze any extra empanadas before frying them to start up another dance party whenever you wish.

TOTAL TRIP: 1 hour, 30 minutes

SERVES: 4

PROVISIONS FOR THE DOUGH

2 cups masa corn flour

1 cup all-purpose flour, plus more as needed

1/2 teaspoon kosher salt

2 cups water

PROVISIONS FOR THE FILLING AND ASSEMBLY

1 pound ground beef

1 serrano pepper, finely diced, with seeds

1/2 cup Roma tomato (1 medium), small diced

1 cup red onion (1/2 medium), small diced

1 tablespoon garlic (4 cloves), minced

2 teaspoons kosher salt

1/2 teaspoon freshly ground black pepper

1 cup pepper jack cheese, shredded, divided

4 cups canola or mild oil, for frying

1/4 cup fresh cilantro leaves, roughly chopped, for garnish

DIRECTIONS FOR THE DOUGH

1. In a large bowl, combine the masa corn flour, all-purpose flour, and salt.
2. Add in the water and use a spoon to bring together.
3. Turn out onto a counter dusted with flour and use your hands to knead until smooth and pliable, approximately 5 minutes. Dust with more flour if the dough sticks to your hands or the surface.
4. Wrap the dough with plastic wrap and let it rest for 30 minutes.

DIRECTIONS FOR THE FILLING AND ASSEMBLY

1. While the dough rests, in a large sauté pan over medium-high heat, stir and sauté the beef, serrano pepper, tomato, onion, garlic, salt, and pepper until the beef is browned and the vegetables are tender, 8 to 10 minutes. Remove from heat.
2. On a clean, dry surface dusted with flour, divide the dough into 8 balls. Use a rolling pin to roll out the balls into disks that are 1/8 to 1/4 inch thick and 6 inches in diameter.
3. Place approximately 3 tablespoons of the filling and 2 tablespoons of the cheese into the center of the rolled-out dough. Fold the dough over the filling to create a half circle. Press the edges together with the prongs of a fork to seal.
4. Prepare all of the empanadas for frying (or freeze for frying later). Set aside on a baking sheet lined with parchment paper.

DIRECTIONS FOR FRYING AND PLATING

1. In a large skillet, preheat the oil to 350°F over medium heat. Once hot, gently and carefully lower the empanadas with a slotted spoon into the oil and fry on each side for 2 to 3 minutes or until golden brown. Work in batches until all the empanadas are fried.
2. Remove to drain on a sheet tray lined with paper towels.
3. Plate and garnish with the cilantro leaves.

Throttle Control: Adjust the amount of cheese (creaminess) based on taste preferences.

Alternate Course: Instead of the beef, use ground pork, ground chicken, ground turkey, or beans.

Rogue Wave: Avoid frying in oil that is too hot, as the dough will burn. And if the oil is not hot enough, it will be soggy.

Throttle Control: Adjust the amount of water (consistency) based on taste preferences.

Alternate Course: Instead of the pork shoulder, use stew meat.

Puerto Vallarta, Mexico

POZOLE

This satisfying stew of hominy, meat, broth, chilies, and oregano has been a staple of Mexican cuisine since the sixteenth century. Families pass down their pozole recipes to their children and enjoy it year-round for both regular and celebratory meals. Here we'll serve it as the soup course for our Mexican fiesta night. *Buen provecho!* Good benefit!

TOTAL TRIP: 3 hours

CRUISING TIME: 30 minutes

IDLE TIME: 2 hours, 30 minutes

SERVES: 4

PROVISIONS FOR THE PORK

- 1½ pounds pork shoulder, 1-inch cubes
- 2 cups yellow onion (1 medium), medium diced
- 1 teaspoon garlic (1 small clove), roughly chopped
- 1 tablespoon kosher salt
- 3 bay leaves
- 9 cups water

PROVISIONS FOR THE CHILI SAUCE

- 4 dried guajillo chili peppers, seeds and stems removed
- 1 dried ancho chili pepper, seeds and stems removed
- 2 cups water
- 2 cups yellow onion (1 medium), medium diced
- ½ teaspoon dried oregano
- 1 teaspoon chicken bouillon

PROVISIONS FOR THE ASSEMBLY

- 3 cups white hominy (two 15.5-ounce cans), drained and rinsed
- ¼ cup sour cream
- 1 cup green cabbage, pre-shredded "angel hair" thinness
- ¼ cup radish (2 large), sliced
- ½ cup cilantro
- 1 fresh lime, quartered

DIRECTIONS FOR THE PORK

1. In a large, covered pot over medium-low heat, add the pork shoulder, onion, garlic, salt, bay leaves, and water. Simmer until the pork is tender and shreds easily, approximately 2½ hours.
2. Once tender, reduce the heat to low to keep warm.

DIRECTIONS FOR THE CHILI SAUCE

1. In a medium pot over medium-high heat, add the chili peppers, water, onion, oregano, and bouillon. Simmer until the peppers soften, approximately 15 minutes.
2. Puree all of the contents in the pot using an immersion blender (or remove to puree in a regular blender, returning to the pot afterward).
3. Using a mesh strainer over the pork broth, strain the pureed chilies to add to the sauce and discard the chili skins.

DIRECTIONS FOR THE ASSEMBLY

1. Using tongs, shred the pork in the pot.
2. Add in the hominy and simmer over medium-low heat to warm through, stirring occasionally, approximately 5 minutes.
3. Serve the pozole in bowls and garnish each with the sour cream, cabbage, radish, and cilantro and one of the lime wedges.

Puerto Vallarta, Mexico

PESCADO ZARANDEADO

"Shaken fish"? The translation of this dinner dish makes perfect sense since grilling the fish requires flipping and flopping it over an open flame when sticking to tradition. If you have access to fresh seafood, go for it! In Puerto Vallarta, the crew will be out fishing to land some red snapper or grouper.

TOTAL TRIP: 1 hour, 15 minutes

CRUISING TIME: 30 minutes

IDLE TIME: 45 minutes

SERVES: 4

PROVISIONS FOR THE RICE

1½ cups long-grain white rice, rinsed 3 to 4 times

2¼ cups water

PROVISIONS FOR THE PESCADO

2 dried guajillo chili peppers, seeds and stems removed

2 cups water, for simmering the peppers

1½ teaspoons garlic (2 cloves), roughly chopped

1 cup yellow onion (½ medium), roughly chopped

1 teaspoon dried oregano

1 teaspoon kosher salt

2 tablespoons salted butter (¼ stick)

⅔ cup water, for the pepper sauce

½ teaspoon granulated sugar

2 pounds red snapper fillets, skin-on

PROVISIONS FOR THE ASSEMBLY

2 cups romaine lettuce (¾ head), chopped

¼ cup radishes (2 large), sliced

½ cup Roma tomato (1 medium), small diced

½ cup fresh cilantro leaves, roughly chopped

1 fresh lime, quartered

DIRECTIONS FOR THE RICE

1. In a small pot or a rice cooker, use the recipe's ratio to cook the rice in the water, or follow the directions on the package. Once cooked, remove from heat.

DIRECTIONS FOR THE PESCADO

1. While the rice cooks, in a small pot over medium heat, add the chili peppers and water. Simmer until the peppers are tender, approximately 20 minutes.
2. Preheat the oven to 425°F.
3. Remove the chilies from the water and transfer to a blender. Add the garlic, onion, oregano, salt, butter, water, and sugar. Blend until smooth.
4. Return the mixture to the small pot. Using a mesh strainer, strain the pureed chilies to add to the sauce and discard the chili skins.
5. Stirring occasionally with a wooden spoon, simmer on medium-low until thickened and a deep-red color, 10 to 15 minutes. Set aside the chili sauce.
6. On a large sheet tray lined with aluminum foil, place the fish in a single layer, skin side down.
7. Using a spoon, disperse the chili sauce evenly on top of the fish fillets.
8. Bake the fish until it is nearly done, approximately 10 minutes. Then broil on high heat to finish the cooking and to char the top of the fish, 3 to 5 minutes.

DIRECTIONS FOR THE ASSEMBLY

1. Plate the fish next to a bed of the rice. On the side, add some of the lettuce.
2. Garnish the entirety with some of the radishes, tomato, and cilantro and one of the lime wedges.

Throttle Control: Adjust the amount of chili peppers (heat) based on taste preferences.

Alternate Course: Instead of the red snapper, use grouper or any whitefish of your choice. Instead of broiling, prepare the fish on the grill to keep true to the traditional method.

Rogue Wave: Be sure to watch the broiler! Burning can happen so quickly. Be sure to take out the seeds from the peppers before simmering so that the chili paste is not too spicy. Simply cut off the stems and roll each pepper in your hands to release the seeds out the top.

Puerto Vallarta, Mexico

TRES LECHES CAKE

Perhaps the tradition of soaking cakes in milk originated from the need to make stale bread more palatable. However this unique dessert came to be, we are all lucky for it. *Tres leches* translates to "three milks," referring to the cake's signature soak in a mixture of evaporated, condensed, and cream milks. We'll poke holes in the baked sponge cake to allow the milks to soak in and then top it with whipped cream. *Decadente*. Yes, decadent indeed.

TOTAL TRIP: 3 hours, 45 minutes (up to 12 hours)

CRUISING TIME: 45 minutes

IDLE TIME: 3 hours (or more, to soak)

SERVES: 8

PROVISIONS FOR THE CAKE

- 1½ cups all-purpose flour
- 2 teaspoons baking powder
- ¼ teaspoon kosher salt
- 6 eggs, separated
- 1¼ cups granulated sugar, divided
- ½ cup whole milk
- 1½ teaspoons vanilla extract

PROVISIONS FOR THE MILK MIXTURE

- 1½ cups evaporated milk (one 12-ounce can)
- 1½ cups condensed milk (one 14-ounce can)
- ¼ cup whole milk

PROVISIONS FOR THE WHIPPED TOPPING

- 1½ cups heavy whipping cream
- 2 tablespoons powdered sugar
- 1 teaspoon vanilla extract
- ½ teaspoon ground cinnamon, for garnish

DIRECTIONS FOR THE CAKE

1. Preheat the oven to 350°F. Grease a 9-by-13-inch casserole dish.
2. In a large mixing bowl, add the flour, baking powder, and salt. Whisk together and then set the dry ingredients aside.
3. In a medium mixing bowl, add the egg whites (saving the egg yolks in a separate small mixing bowl for step 4). Use a hand mixer on high to whisk the egg whites until foamy, approximately 2 minutes. Then add ½ cup of the sugar (saving the remaining sugar for step 4) and whisk until stiff peaks are formed, 2 to 3 minutes. Set aside.
4. In the small mixing bowl with the egg yolks, add the remaining ¾ cup of the sugar. Using a hand mixer on high, whisk until fluffy, approximately 2 minutes. Once fluffy, mix in the milk and vanilla until combined.
5. Add the egg yolk mixture into the dry ingredients and fold in with a rubber spatula. Then add in the egg white mixture and gently fold in, until just combined.
6. Pour the batter into the greased casserole dish, and bake until a toothpick inserted comes out clean, approximately 30 minutes.
7. Set aside and allow to cool for 30 minutes.

DIRECTIONS FOR THE MILK MIXTURE

1. In a small mixing bowl, add the evaporated milk, condensed milk, and whole milk. Whisk together until combined.

2. Using a skewer or chopstick, poke approximately 50 holes into the cooled cake.
3. Pour the milk mixture over the cake and let it cool, covered, in the refrigerator for 2 hours or longer (even overnight).

DIRECTIONS FOR THE WHIPPED TOPPING AND GARNISH

1. Within 30 minutes of serving, in a medium bowl, use a hand mixer on high to whisk the cream, powdered sugar, and vanilla until stiff peaks are formed for the whipped topping, 1 to 2 minutes.
2. With the cake still in the baking dish, evenly spread the whipped topping over the entire cake.
3. Sprinkle the cinnamon over the top of the cake as garnish.

Rogue Wave: Be patient. The milks need to soak into the cake, but it is worth the wait.

THANK YOU

The creation of this cookbook has absolutely *everything* to do with the collaborative spirit of my family, friends, industry partners, culinary experts, readers, publishers, and social media followers on TikTok, Facebook, Instagram, and YouTube. I am so very grateful to all of you. The love, support, and enthusiasm you share with me makes my job more like a party of love.

I would not be here if it were not for the unwavering, unconditional love from my mom and dad; it is the essential aid that buoys me up. Truly, they made this publication possible. Together we created many, many monumental memories during the hundreds (and hundreds) of hours spent in the kitchen, at the computer, and in traveling mode. I love you so much, Mom (Janice, manager of the marketing, the creative writing, and all things right-brained) and Dad (Gregg, manager of the business, the logistics, and all things left-brained). You are my world! And to my siblings, uncles, aunts, cousins, in-laws, and extended family who joined in the craziness, I love you oodles and noodles: Andrew, Marlena, Erin, Hanna, Gene, Julie, Aaron, Gracie, Zachary, Jacob, Joshua, Brian, Denny, Rebecca, Caleb, Evan, Brenda, Jay, Aimee, Roger, Will, Hannah, Renée, Josh, Pat, Ralph, Marla, Chris, Lydia, and Lulu.

My heart is full of gratitude to friends whose selfless support and insightful taste testing allowed me to finesse raw recipes into polished products. I reach out a warm hug to you: Jack, Sarah, Tannre, Rachel, Sarah, Nina, Andrew, Kali, Nancy, Myron, Kerry, John, Victor, Nicole, David, Sarah, Patrick, Laura, Greg, Melissa, Dave, Briana, Anne-Marie, Andy, Julianne, Gary, Donna, Pete, Elizabeth, Ken, Giana, Michelle, Ron, Tom, Cathy, Heather, Jim, Megan, Laura, John, Angela, Matt, Jennie Lou, Lisa, Nancee, Alice, Scott, Greg, Leigh, John, Carla, Bill, Diane, Frank, Gloria, Nicki, Alex, Julie, Tim, Angeles, Jim, Karen, Russ, Lee, Bill, Bob, Sally, Susie, David, Christopher, Caitlyn, Lauren, Kevin, Emily, Nancy, Bill, Mary, Jan, Father John, Shamir, Mary, Rick, Katie, Joe, Pam, Cristian, Johnnie, Richard, Christy, Penny, and Captain Peter.

I am indebted to you, yacht crew, for endless adventures at sea and in port. What a life-changing experience it has been for me. And it is with great humility that I share with the world what you mean to me, Bruno and Maritza, as I continue to grow in wisdom as your chef. You place complete trust in me and allow me to be my best self while we are on board together. And to Captain Mark and Jena, I will never take for granted what I am continually learning from you on the deck, in the engine room, around the marina, and everywhere else. Here's to many years ahead, both working and playing on the open seas together—with our fearless mascot, Thurston, at the helm, of course!

Gratitude galore to the team at HMY Yachts. Your vast inventory of yachts and admirable professionalism in yacht sales made our photo shoot not only possible but perfect. Thank you for the out-of-this-world photos taken in your beautiful yacht galleys, now available for all of us to see (and purchase too).

A special shout-out to the local and not-so-local farmers and suppliers whose fresh ingredients inspire so many of my international recipes. Your commitment to quality shines through in every dish. All of us reading this cookbook owe our happy, healthy tummies to you working your magic in fields and farms around the globe.

To the talented chefs and professors who generously shared their techniques and wisdom with me during my culinary education and training (University of Central Florida Rosen College of Hospitality Management and Walt Disney World), I am indebted. Through your example, I learned how to hone my passion for creating beautiful meals and serving others with a personalized touch. I am so proud to say I learned from the best: Dr. Mejia, Dr. Lavendol, Chef Judy, Chef Kate, Chef Michael, and Chef Sergio. Because of your selfless investment of time in me, I am now able to use my talents to make a difference in the world of culinary arts.

And to my amazing team at Harper Celebrate, you have my heartfelt gratitude. Michael, Kara, Sabryna, Bonnie, Danielle, Robin, Emily, Lori, Carole, and Robert: Thank you, thank you, thank you for your guidance and expertise in bringing this project to life. I am especially proud of how we worked together so seamlessly. There has been such joy and celebration every step of the way! This adventure is one that I will never forget, and I owe so much to you and the entire HarperCollins family.

Finally, to my readers of this cookbook and to my followers on TikTok, Facebook, YouTube, Instagram, and other social media platforms, *you* are the reason I do what I do. Cheers to *you* as you relish these recipes. Be sure to celebrate all the richness in your life with family and friends gathered around your table. And pull up a chair for me, please! I want to be there with you. You see, at heart, this Galley Girl Gone Global is really your next-door neighbor. I'll show up in my shorts and flip-flops, throw on my apron and ball cap, and cook with you anytime. I hope we are cooking together for years to come, Little Chef.

And I hope this book brings you as much joy in the kitchen as it has brought me. Until we meet again for a meal together, bye, Little Chef!

Love,
Abby

Even a chef needs a break from the galley!

Take time to celebrate, Little Chef!

PROVISION POINTERS

Provisioning takes time. Perishable items perish due to time. Here is a list of all of the perishable items with pointers so that your provisioning will be timed perfectly.

*Store these ethylene-sensitive vegetables away from peppers, potatoes, tomatoes, and fruits.

**Store these fruits and vegetables away from other produce since they are ethylene producers, as well as vulnerable to ethylene exposure themselves.

VEGETABLE PROVISION POINTERS

Asparagus: Look for firm, closed tips, substantial stalks, and a rich green (or sometimes purple) color that fades to white at the bottom of the stalk. Asparagus will last for up to five days if stored properly in the refrigerator in a jar of water after cutting off 1 inch from the bottom of the stems and covering the tops with a loose resealable plastic bag left open. Check the water daily to keep it from getting cloudy.

Beets: Look for beets that are small, firm, a rich maroon, and unblemished, with leaves that are bright and strong. The taproot (thin and pointy tip) should be attached but not super "hairy." Beets will last for up to three weeks if stored properly in the refrigerator crisper.

***Broccoli:** Look for firm, crisp, fresh stalks and leaves. Place in the refrigerator in a resealable plastic bag left open. Broccoli will last for up to five days if stored properly.

***Cabbage:** Look for a head that is heavy, firm, and compact. Place the whole head in the refrigerator in a resealable plastic bag left partially open. Cabbage will last for up to two months if stored properly.

***Carrots:** Look for carrots that are firm, smooth, and vibrant in color. Carrots will last for up to a month if stored properly in the refrigerator crisper.

Celery: Look for stalks that are firm and crisp. Celery will last for up to two weeks if stored properly in the refrigerator crisper with aluminum foil wrapped around it. Celery can be chopped and frozen for a soup later on.

Corn: Look for bright-green husks that tightly hug the cob. Peel back the husk to look for moist and sticky silks. Press on a kernel to look for a milky liquid, indicating freshness. Corn will last for up to three days if stored properly in the refrigerator crisper in a resealable plastic bag left partially open.

***Cucumbers:** Look for cucumbers that are firm with a vibrant color. Farm-fresh cucumbers can be kept in a paper bag on the counter in a cool, dry place with no direct sunlight for a couple of days. Store-bought cucumbers should be refrigerated for up to seven days in the warmest part of the refrigerator, toward the front and away from the cooling element, wrapped in a paper towel and sealed in a resealable plastic bag.

***Eggplant:** Look for an eggplant with a shiny, firm, unblemished skin. Eggplant will last for up to seven days if stored properly in the refrigerator crisper in a resealable plastic bag left partially open.

Fennel: Look for bulbs that are firm and white with green fronds. Fennel will last for up to seven days if stored properly in the refrigerator crisper in a resealable plastic bag left partially open.

***Green Beans:** Look for crisp but tender beans that snap when broken. Green beans will last for up to seven days if stored properly in the refrigerator crisper by lining a resealable plastic bag with a paper towel (to absorb extra moisture) and sealing.

***Green Onions (scallions):** Look for bright-green tops, firm stems, and crisp white roots. Green onions will last for up to seven days if stored properly in a jar of water, root side down, and kept on the counter at room temperature or in the refrigerator with a resealable plastic bag, left open, over it. Check the water daily to keep it from getting cloudy. Bonus: After using the green onions, keep the roots. Plant the last 2 inches of the stalk (including the root) in your garden, or in a planter that you set on your kitchen (or galley, in my case) window. The green onions will yield two to three more harvests.

***Greens (collards and kale):** Look for bright, crisp leaves. Greens will last for up to seven days if stored properly by rolling the bunch in paper towels, then placing in an open, resealable plastic bag in the refrigerator crisper.

***Leeks:** Look for firm leeks with no blemishes. Leeks will last for up to two weeks if stored properly in the refrigerator crisper.

***Lettuce:** Look for leaves that are vibrant and crisp. Lettuce will last for up to ten days if wrapped whole in paper towels and placed in a resealable plastic bag left open. Even if the lettuce wilts slightly, do not fret, as you can soak it in ice water to crisp it up again.

Mushrooms: Look for firm, dry mushrooms with no slime. Place the fresh mushrooms (except morels) in the refrigerator for up to five days, unwashed, in a dry paper bag rather than any plastic wrap. Cook excess mushrooms and freeze for later on.

***Onions:** Look for dry, firm bulbs with no sprouts or soft spots. Never refrigerate onions. Instead, store in a dark, cool, ventilated place. To avoid crying when cutting an onion, stay clear of the root, the most tear-inducing part. Chop extra onions and freeze for later on.

****Peppers:** Look for peppers that are firm and vibrant in color. Peppers will last for up to two weeks if stored properly in the refrigerator crisper, separate from other produce.

****Potatoes:** Look for firm potatoes without sprouts. Never refrigerate potatoes since their starch turns to sugar. Instead, store in a cool, dark place, away from other produce.

***Shallots:** Look for shallots with a firm, smooth skin without blemishes. Never refrigerate shallots. Instead, store in a dark, cool, ventilated place.

***Spinach:** Look for leaves that are vibrant and crisp. Place in the refrigerator in an airtight container lined with paper towels. Spinach will last for up to seven days if stored properly in the refrigerator crisper.

***Squash (summer: yellow and zucchini):** Look for squash that are firm and smooth. Summer squash will last for up to four days if stored properly in the refrigerator crisper.

***Squash (winter: acorn and butternut):** Look for squash that are heavy, hard, and unblemished. Never refrigerate your winter squash. Instead, store in a dry, cool place for up to two months.

****Tomatoes:** Look for a rich color and a firm texture that has some "give" when pressed. Never refrigerate your tomatoes. Place them on your counter or in your pantry, separate from other produce. And if time gets away from you, cook your tomatoes and make a tomato sauce for later.

FRUIT PROVISION POINTERS

****Apples:** Look for apples that are firm with no bruises. Reduce the rate of decline by not leaving apples in a bowl on the counter since they overripen very quickly, even at 70°F. Apples can last for up to two months if you place them in the refrigerator crisper with a damp paper towel keeping them wrapped in comfort and away from other produce since they are an ethylene producer.

****Bananas:** Look for bright-yellow bunches without green around the ends, and with a bit of light-brown speckling (which indicates sweetness) if you are ready to use immediately. Bananas with more green at the ends still need a couple of days to ripen (and are actually ethylene sensitive); place them alone on the counter (not in the refrigerator) to do so. Once ripe, bananas then become ethylene producers and should be kept away from other produce to prevent overripening of the other produce. And if time gets away from you, freeze your almost-too-ripe bananas for banana bread or a smoothie later on.

****Berries:** Look for berries that are plump, firm, and free of mold. Wash, dry, and place them in a ventilated container lined with paper towels to reduce the rate of decline. Berries will last for up to three days if stored properly and are best when separated from other produce. And if time gets away from you, freeze your berries for a smoothie later on.

Citrus Fruits: Select your fresh citrus fruits, such as grapefruit, lemons, limes, and oranges, carefully. Look for firm, heavy fruit with a smooth skin. Reduce the chance of dried-out fruit by placing in an open container in the crisper drawer of the refrigerator for up to three weeks (twice as long as when left on the counter). Before eating or squeezing, set out for a couple of hours to restore their greatest juiciness. And if time gets away from you, squeeze your citrus and freeze the juice in small containers to have a source of citrus juice for whenever you need it.

****Fresh Fruits:** Select your fresh fruits, such as apricots, avocados, star fruits, cantaloupes, honeydew melons, kiwis, mangoes, papayas, peaches, nectarines, pineapples, plums, and pears, carefully. Look for fresh fruits that are unblemished, slightly soft to the touch, and fragrant to the nose. Often, fruit still needs to ripen (is still slightly firm to the touch) and will do so on the counter away from other produce. Once ripe, place the fruit in the refrigerator to hinder the ripening process, but use within one to two days.

****Plantains:** Look for plantains that are almost all black with a bit of yellow indicating ripeness. Give the plantain a little squeeze to make sure that it is slightly soft. If the plantains are still green, no worries, as time on the counter on their own will do the trick. Hasten the ripening process by placing in a paper bag to trap the ethylene gas. Set the bag in a warm, dry place, and the plantains will ripen within a few days. Be sure to use before they are completely black, which is an indication that they are too ripe.

HERB AND AROMATICS PROVISION POINTERS

Fresh Herbs: Look for leaves that are fragrant, crisp, and without brown spots. If you can secure an entire plant, plant it in your garden or leave it in its original planter to set on your kitchen counter. The herbs will stay alive for months. I keep all of my fresh herbs alive in my galley for the entire journey since sunshine and water are all that is required.

- **For basil:** If purchasing just the leaves of a basil plant, look for leaves that are fragrant, crisp, and without brown spots. Reduce the rate of decline by placing in the refrigerator in a ventilated container lined with paper towels. Basil will last for up to seven days if stored properly in the refrigerator crisper. And if time gets away from you, make pesto to salvage your basil.
- **For cilantro, parsley, dill, chives, mint, and tarragon:** If purchasing just the leaves of the

herb, reduce the rate of decline by placing in the refrigerator in a container lined with paper towels. Herbs will last for up to five days if stored properly in the refrigerator crisper.

- **For oregano, rosemary, sage, and thyme:** If purchasing just the leaves rather than a live plant, wrap the herbs loosely in a damp paper towel. Seal in a resealable plastic bag or container and place in the refrigerator, adding water to the paper towel every couple of days to remoisten. Lasting for up to three weeks, these herbs make all the difference in a freshly prepared meal.

***Garlic:** Look for dry, firm bulbs with no sprouts or soft spots. Never refrigerate your garlic. Instead, store in a dark, cool, ventilated place. With extra garlic, make garlic cubes for future soups and meals. Mince 1 part garlic and saturate with 3 parts olive oil to freeze in ice trays, ready to pop out when needed.

Ginger: Look for knobs that are smooth, firm, and unblemished. If planning to use your ginger within seven days, leave on the counter in a cool, dry spot, whole and unpeeled. To prolong ginger's life to one month, place it in the refrigerator in a dry sealed bag, unpeeled. Once peeled, it will last for up to two weeks.

DAIRY AND EGG PROVISION POINTERS

Cheese: Store in a designated cheese or produce drawer in a breathable cheese wrapping paper bag or parchment paper instead of plastic wrap. Fresh and soft cheeses such as brie, cottage cheese, cream cheese, goat, mascarpone, mozzarella, and ricotta can be refrigerated for up to two weeks. Hard cheeses such as cheddar, Gorgonzola, Gouda, Gruyère, Parmesan, Romano, and Swiss can last for up to six months if unopened and four weeks if opened. While freezing does affect the texture, cheese can be frozen for up to six months.

Cream-Based Products: Store cream on a shelf toward the back of the refrigerator (instead of in the refrigerator door) to ensure temperature control. Heavy whipping cream can last for up to a month in the refrigerator. Sour cream can last for up to two weeks after opening, whereas crème fraîche can keep for eight weeks if unopened and three days if opened. Do not leave any of the creams on the counter for more than an hour, and note that freezing changes the consistency and taste.

Eggs: If you are lucky enough to have access to farm eggs, good for you. Your farm eggs are fine on the counter for two weeks. If store-bought, choose refrigerated Grade A or AA eggs with shells that are uncracked, unblemished, clean, and strong. Store eggs with the large end up in their original carton on an inside shelf (instead of in the refrigerator door), away from pungent foods. In the refrigerator, eggs can be kept for up to six weeks, hard-cooked eggs for up to a week, and leftover yolks and whites for up to four days.

Milk: Select your milk based on preferred milk-fat content: whole milk (3.25%), reduced-fat milk (2%), low-fat milk (1%), and fat-free milk (0%). Whole milk creates the richest dishes. Store milk on a shelf toward the back of the refrigerator (instead of in the refrigerator door) to ensure temperature control. Consider freezing it for up to three months if not consumed within a week (or two with buttermilk). Consider nondairy options for allergies and intolerances: soy, oat, rice, coconut, cashew, and almond milk.

Yogurt: Select your yogurt based on the preferred style: Greek, regular, soy, skyr, kefir, coconut, or French yogurt. Plain Greek yogurt works best for recipes. It is protein packed, probiotic and prebiotic rich, sugarless, tangy, thick, and creamy. Store yogurt on a shelf toward the back of the refrigerator (instead of in the refrigerator door) to ensure temperature control.

PROTEIN PROVISION POINTERS

Beef: Keep beef separate from other foods to avoid cross contamination. Use your sense of touch (firm but tender to the touch without the imprint staying depressed and instead returning to its original shape), smell (no odor), and sight (no tears in the packaging or any excessive liquid). Look for a bright-red color for freshness (unless in a sealed bag, which is a darker purplish red since without air). In steaks, intramuscular fat, known as marbling, adds flavor and juiciness. Consume within the sell-by date. Or, freeze raw hamburger and stew meat for three to four months, chops for four to six months, roasts for four to twelve months, and steaks for six to twelve months.

Fish: Keep fish separate from other foods to avoid cross contamination. Use your sense of touch (firm but tender to the touch, without the imprint staying depressed and instead returning to its original shape), smell (like the ocean or no odor at all), and sight (no tears in the packaging or any excessive liquid and unclouded eyes if fish is whole). Consume within the sell-by date. Or, freeze raw oily fish (herring, mackerel, salmon, trout) for two to three months, raw shellfish (crabs, lobsters, mussels, oysters, scallops, shrimp) for three to six months, and raw lean fish (cod, flounder, grouper, halibut, mahi-mahi, perch, red snapper, whitefish) for six to eight months.

Pork: Keep pork separate from other foods to avoid cross contamination. Use your sense of touch (firm but tender to the touch, without the imprint staying depressed and instead returning to its original shape), smell (no odor), and sight (no tears in the packaging or any excessive liquid). Look for a pinkish-red color. Avoid pork that is pale in color. Fat should be white in color, with no dark spots. Small flecks of fat, called marbling, add flavor and tenderness. Consume within the sell-by date. Or, freeze bacon for one month, raw ground pork for three to four months, chops for four to six months, roasts for four to twelve months, and steaks for six to twelve months.

Poultry: Keep poultry separate from other foods to avoid cross contamination. Use your sense of touch (firm, but tender to the touch without the imprint staying depressed and instead returning to its original shape), smell (no odor), and sight (no tears in the packaging, no excessive liquid, and no sitting in its own juices and getting slimy). Look for a pink color. Avoid chicken, turkey, or duck that is gray in color, or with purple or green discoloration around the neck. Red wing tips are fine. Consume within the sell-by date. Or, freeze raw ground poultry for three to four months, raw poultry parts for nine months, or raw whole poultry for one year.

BREAD PROVISION POINTERS

Bread: Make homemade bread (I keep a sourdough starter in the refrigerator for almost all of my bread preparation). Or, choose bread with high fiber (minimum of two grams per slice), low salt and saturated fat, and no added sugar. Fresh bread should be enjoyed within two to three days. Store it on the counter or in a cabinet where conditions are cool and dry (not in the refrigerator), in a paper bag (not plastic). If the bread is not used within two to three days, consider freezing it in a freezer bag. If you will be using small portions over time, slice the bread, placing parchment or wax paper between each slice for easy access. When needed, remove from the freezer bag and defrost in the refrigerator overnight. Or pop a piece in the toaster or the whole loaf in a 325°F oven until warm, approximately twenty minutes. Finally, if time gets away from you, make croutons out of your stale bread by seasoning and drying out in a hot oven.

INDEX

ABOUT CHEF ABBY

Chef Abby Cheshire is a private yacht chef, culinary arts teacher, and social media influencer. When she's not teaching her high school students during the school year, Abby spends her summers traveling around the world and cooking global cuisine on a yacht. Her popular social media accounts, @abbyinthegalley, share videos of her unique cooking experience and ability to create fabulous meals in small spaces, on the high seas or anywhere with local and fresh ingredients. Abby has been featured in the *New York Times*, *Newsweek*, and other media, and she has worked with Food Network stars at the Super Bowl. Her social media platforms now have over 2.5 million followers and continue to grow. When she's not traveling the world by boat, she lives in Central Florida.

Follow Chef Abby's culinary adventures at

AbbyintheGalley

IRELAND
CANADA
UNITED STATES
MEXICO
THE BAHAMAS
HAWAII
N
NE
E
SE
S
SW
W
NW